UNIVERSITY LIBRARY
UW-STEVENS POINT

D0652558

The Language
of Argument

"This is not a stickup."

Reprinted from *The New Yorker,* March 25, 1974, p. 31. Cartoon by C. Barsotti.

The Language of Argument

Second Edition

DANIEL McDONALD

University of South Alabama

THOMAS Y. CROWELL COMPANY
New York   Established 1834

U-W-RK

Copyright © 1975 by Thomas Y. Crowell Company, Inc.
Copyright © 1966, 1971 by Chandler Publishing Company.
All Rights Reserved
Except for use in a review, the reproduction or utilization of this work
in any form or by any electronic, mechanical, or other means,
now known or hereafter invented, including photocopying and recording,
and in any information storage and retrieval system is forbidden
without the written permission of the publisher.
Published simultaneously in Canada by Fitzhenry & Whiteside, Ltd.,
Toronto.

Library of Congress Cataloging in Publication Data

McDONALD, DANIEL LAMONT, comp.
  The language of argument.

  Includes bibliographical references.
  1. College readers. 2. English language—Rhetoric.
I. Title.
PE1122.M263   1975   808'.04275   75-2290
ISBN 0-690-00806-6

Thomas Y. Crowell Company
666 Fifth Avenue
New York, New York 10019

Manufactured in the United States of America

    Previously published and copyrighted materials are reprinted with permission as
listed below:
Cartoon "This is not a stickup" by C. Barsotti, copyright © 1974 by The New Yorker
    Magazine, Inc. Reprinted by permission of *The New Yorker.*
Cartoon "I switched the plates . . ." by Sidney Harris, reprinted by permission of
    the artist.
Stanley Milgram, "A Behavioral Study of Obedience," copyright © 1963 by the
    American Psychological Association. Reprinted by permission of the APA and the
    author.
Susy Smith, "Why Does ESP Happen?" from *ESP for the Millions,* reprinted by per-
    mission of Sherbourne Press.
Ralph R. Greenson, "A Psychoanalyst's Indictment of *The Exorcist,*" reprinted by
    permission of Saturday Review/World.
Photograph "Big Mama" reprinted by permission of Wide World Photos.
Edward U. Condon, "Intelligent Life Elsewhere" from *The Scientific Study of Un-
    identified Flying Objects,* conducted by the University of Colorado under con-
    tract to the United States Air Force. Copyright © 1968 by the Board of Regents
    of the University of Colorado. All rights reserved. Reprinted by permission of
    Bantam Books, Inc.
Erich von Däniken, "Easter Island—Land of the Bird Men" from *Chariots of the
    Gods?.* English translation copyright © 1969 by Michael Heron and Souvenir
    Press. Reprinted by permission of G. P. Putnam's Sons.
Alan F. Guttmacher, "Why I Favor Liberalized Abortion," copyright © 1973 by The
    Reader's Digest Assn., Inc. Reprinted by permission of *Reader's Digest.*

iv

Photographs "Aborted Children" reprinted by permission of Religious News Service.

Jeannine Gramick, "The Myths of Homosexuality," reprinted by permission of *Intellect.*

David A. Noebel, "Heroin, Marijuana, and LSD" from *The Beatles: A Study in Drugs, Sex, and Revolution,* reprinted by permission of Christian Crusade Publications.

Ruth Adams and Frank Murray, "Vitamin E in the Hands of Creative Physicians" from *Vitamin E: Wonder Worker of the 70's?,* reprinted by permission of Larchmont Books.

Paperback cover of *Joshua Son of None* reprinted by permission of Dell Publishing Co., Inc.

M. J. Sobran, Jr., "Of Ms. and Men," reprinted by permission of *Natural Review.*

Douglas MacArthur, "Duty, Honor, Country," copyright © 1962 by Dow Jones & Company, Inc. Reprinted by permission of *The National Observer.*

"Michigan Trial Reveals FBI Plot to Frame Klansmen," reprinted by permission of *The Thunderbolt.*

Lawrence Casler, "This Thing Called Love is Pathological," copyright © 1974 by Ziff-Davis Publishing Company. Reprinted by permission of *Psychology Today.*

Neil Postman and Charles Weingartner, "Teaching as a Subversive Activity" from *Teaching as a Subversive Activity,* copyright © 1969 by Neil Postman and Charles Weingartner. Reprinted by permission of Delacorte Press.

Cartoon "There Is No Middle Ground," reprinted by permission of *The Thunderbolt.*

William L. Laurence, "Report by Cancer Society Finds Higher Death Rate for Smokers," copyright © 1963 by The New York Times Company. Reprinted by permission of *The New York Times.*

Ashley Halsey, Jr., "Crime Higher in Gun Control Cities"; this material is reprinted by permission from *The American Rifleman,* a fully copyrighted publication of The National Rifle Association of America. Further reproduction without permission is forbidden.

Wayne H. Davis, "Overpopulated America," copyright © 1970 by The New Republic, Inc. Reprinted by permission of *The New Republic.*

Advertisement "We're a big company," reprinted by permission of Mobil Oil Corporation.

Advertisement for *Jane,* reprinted by permission of Waterman Getz Niedelman and Viking Press.

Clayton Thomas, "The Welfare Dollar Goes 'Round and 'Round," reprinted by permission of *National Review.*

Stephen Jay Gould, "The Nonscience of Human Nature," copyright © 1974 by The American Museum of Natural History. Reprinted by permission of *Natural History.*

Advertisement for Excedrin, reprinted by permission of Bristol-Myers Company.

Cartoon "How about Him?" by E. H. 'olf, reprinted by permission of National Catholic News Service.

Sara Sanborn, "Nizer: *The Implosion Conspiracy,*" reprinted by permission of *Nation.*

John S. Banahan, "What a Catholic Wishes to Avoid in Marriage" from *Instructions for Mixed Marriages,* copyright © 1957 by Bruce Publishing Co., reprinted by permission of Macmillan Publishing Co., Inc.

Photograph "Smoking is very glamorous," reprinted by permission of American Cancer Society.

Cartoon "They'll go away if you put the light out"; this material is reprinted by permission from *The American Rifleman,* a fully copyrighted publication of the National Rifle Association of America. Further reproduction without permission is forbidden.

W. H. Auden, "O What is that Sound," copyright © 1937 and renewed 1965 by W. H. Auden. Reprinted from *Collected Shorter Poems* 1927–1957 by permission of Random House, Inc.

282500

Laurence Perrine and Jane Johnston, "Auden's 'O What is that Sound,' " copyright © 1972 by The Explicator Literary Foundation, Inc. Reprinted by permission of *The Explicator* and the authors.

Advertisement "Five Pounds Overweight," reprinted by permission of Liberty National Life Insurance Company.

Cartoon "Too bad he can't be released on a technicality" by Don Hesse, copyright © 1974 by St. Louis Globe Democrat. Reprinted by permission of Los Angeles Times Syndicate.

S. L. Varnardo, "Some Thoughts on Professor Shockley," reprinted by permission of *National Review* and the author.

Joel Fort, "Pot: A Rational Approach," originally appeared in *Playboy* magazine: copyright © 1969 by Joel Fort. Reprinted by permission of *Playboy* and the author.

Advertisement "Are we blind to the real energy crisis?," reprinted by permission of American Electric Power Service Corporation.

Photograph "And Senator McGovern wants . . ." reprinted by permission of Liberty Lobby.

James V. McConnell, "Criminals Can Be Brainwashed—Now" reprinted by permission of the author.

Max A. Coots, "Amnesty: Transcending the Debate," copyright © 1974 by America Press, Inc., 106 W. 56 St., N.Y., N.Y. 10019. Reprinted by permission of *America*. All rights reserved.

Advertisement for *Hitler's Daughter,* reprinted by permission of Lyle Stuart, Inc.

Photograph "100,000 doctors have quit smoking cigarettes," reprinted by permission of American Cancer Society.

For *BECKY*

Contents

Subjects Discussed
in this Book

II PSYCHOLOGICAL HEALTH

Dangers and Possible Dangers

Proposed Solutions

III SOCIAL PROBLEMS

Problem Areas

Proposed Solutions: Legislation

IV RELIGION

V AREAS OF SPECULATION

Preface

The purpose of this text is to teach students how to read argument and to provide materials around which they can write argumentative essays of their own.

As in the preceding edition, the selections cover a range of provocative issues. Some are intended to be persuasive; some are not.

Besides offering more current articles, the new edition contains more pictorial argument—photographs, advertisements, and cartoons which seek to make a case. These should be useful in the classroom.

Further, this edition has a special section on "How to Write Argument."

I must record my indebtedness to Mrs. June Williams and to Andy Dees for their assistance in shaping this book. As always, my wife Irene made a significant contribution.

The editor who selects and annotates controversial articles must work to keep his own opinions out of his textbook. I *have* tried.

DMc

The Language
of Argument

Part I

THE FORMS
OF ARGUMENT

JACK: Well, I won't argue about the matter. You always want to argue about things.

ALGERNON: That is what things were originally made for.

Oscar Wilde, *The Importance of Being Earnest* (1895)

"Truth" and Argument

Ted Kennedy is handsome.
Capital punishment is wrong.
Pontiac is America's No. 1 Road Car.
Icksnak brack a brack disnold fleb.
Lyndon Johnson was president of the U. S.
I like pizza.

Which of these statements are true? On what evidence do you base your judgment? Are you prepared to defend it?

Before you begin to discuss the assertions, you should recognize two things: (1) Such statements cannot meaningfully be argued without a careful definition of terms, which in itself may be difficult to achieve. And (2) "truth," whatever it may denote in a philosophical realm, usually means "a statement for which the evidence offers a high degree of probability."

Some arguments rely more on definition of terms than on evidence. When two people argue whether Senator Ted Kennedy is handsome, they are not disagreeing about his hair, teeth, or clothes, but about the definition of "handsomeness." If they agree on a definition, they will probably agree about Ted Kennedy as well. Similarly, the question of whether capital punishment is wrong hinges not so much on the character of the act (the pain, the possibility of error, the protection afforded society) as on the definition of "wrongness."

Aesthetic and moral questions are often not susceptible to evidence because disputants cannot agree on the terms of argument. The meaning of any word is what people agree that it is (e.g., a telephone is called a "telephone" because people regularly use that word to denote it), but in more abstract areas people do not agree. What is "handsomeness"? What is "beauty"? Theoreticians have sought objective standards, but the quest seems fruitless. Is a

3

Greek temple more beautiful than a Gothic cathedral? Is Whistler's Mother handsomer than da Vinci's Mona Lisa, than Andy Warhol's Marilyn Monroe? Who can say? The decision rests on a subjective judgment, which does not lend itself to argument.

Like "beauty," the idea of "goodness" is not subject to easy definition. Seeking an objective basis for moral judgments, authorities have cited scriptural precedents; they have based systems on the inalienable rights of each human being; they have insisted that nature provides a moral example. But such definitions have won no universal acceptance. If two disputants agree that morality resides, say, in a "natural law," they might then *begin* to argue about capital punishment. But in general usage, moral terms remain so ill-defined that such issues sometimes cannot be argued meaningfully at all.

Moral and aesthetic questions are removed further from argument by the fact that they often elicit emotional responses. For example, two individuals who agree in defining "handsomeness" may still disagree about Ted Kennedy because one objects to his history or his political opinions. It is, of course, unreasonable to let emotions color such a judgment, but the attitude is not uncommon. Regarding capital punishment, one might be completely persuaded that the practice is cruel and barbaric—yet, at a given moment, argue that hanging is too good for a child murderer or a political assassin.

Vagueness of definition precludes argument in other areas as well. Pontiac has been advertised as "America's *No. 1 Road Car*"; Kent as America's "largest-selling *premium* cigarette"; and Shenley Reserve as "the whiskey *of elegance.*" Are these claims true? Until the key words are defined, the statements are no more subject to evidence than is "Icksnak brack a brack disnold fleb."

It is only when terms are defined and mutually accepted that one can begin marshaling evidence to prove the truth of an assertion. One can, for example, argue whether Jim Brown or Bronko Nagurski was the better football player, because their records, the merits of their supporting and opposing terms, and the qualities of a good running back are generally enough agreed on. Is it true that cigarette smoking causes lung cancer, that Spiro Agnew took bribes, that Volkswagen is an economical car to own? The questions can at least be argued.

One must be careful, however, about using the word "truth" in any argument. In theory, a statement is true if it conforms to reality; in practice, it is called "true" if available evidence gives it a high degree of probability. With minor exceptions, one can never be sure that any conclusion is absolutely true. Except in statements that repeat themselves ("Business is business" or "Either it is raining or it is not raining") or in statements which express one's own immediate feelings ("I like pizza"), there always exists an element of doubt.

It is a routine exercise for Socratic teachers to call all their students' certainties into doubt, to demonstrate that what is called "truth" is, in fact, a high degree of probability. Can one be sure that Lyndon Johnson was president of the United States? Newspapers said he was, but newspapers frequently print error. In 1948, the *Chicago Tribune* announced that Thomas Dewey had been elected president. Johnson might simply have been a created image. In George Orwell's *Nineteen Eighty-four,* the real rulers of Oceania used a fictitious Big Brother to control the citizenry. The world agrees that Johnson was president, but there is some dissent. Inmates in mental hospitals who think they are Jesus or Napoleon deny the existence of both Johnson and the twentieth century.

Despite such doubts, most people agree that Johnson was president. *And it is exactly this agreement which creates the "truth" of the statement.* Just as the words "telephone," "beauty," and "goodness" come to mean what a majority of people think they mean, so "truth" is whatever most people agree is true. Truth, as we know it, is statistically derived.

A reasonable man can insist that fire engines are red because he is expressing a general opinion. Though a "Napoleon" might call them a mass hallucination, he is sure that fire engines exist. Though the color-blind might cavil, he knows they are colored red. And though foreigners or semanticists might do otherwise, he uses the word "red." The reason he speaks the truth and the dissenters do not is that he is in the majority. If the majority did not perceive the engines, or saw them as green, or described them as "depar," he would be locked up as a babbling, color-blind visionary. "Truth" is what people agree to call true.

To assert that moral, aesthetic, and factual arguments are statistically derived, is not to argue that there is no such thing as absolute goodness, beauty, or truth. It is to declare that these ultimate values have little relevance in practical argument. They have little relation to this book. Much is expressed about the base of real-world argument in the story of two men in conversation: One muses, "I wonder if Rex Harrison is his real name." The other responds, "You wonder if Rex Harrison is whose real name?"

In argument, it is preferable to think in terms of probabilities and of the evidence which shapes probabilities. The following pages discuss kinds of evidence and ways of arranging evidence which give a conclusion a high or low degree of probability.

CAN ONE ARGUE THE TRUTH OF THESE STATEMENTS?

1. All men are created equal.
2. A valuable treasure chest is buried 306 feet below my chair.
3. Nothing does it like 7-Up!
4. Springfield is the capitol of Illinois.
5. "The purest and most thoughtful minds are those which love color the most."—John Ruskin
6. Babe Ruth was a better baseball player than Sandy Koufax.
7. "The word *cohort* is always misused."—Jerome Beatty, Jr.
8. Not all cigarettes are True.
9. Abortion is a sin.
10. "Criminologists believe that only a stiffening of the moral fabric of the nation and a spiritual renaissance can halt the steady increase of crime."—*Newsweek*

"I switched the plates. . . ."

"I switched the plates. We'll be printing the real thing, and the Treasury Department will be turning out counterfeits."

Reprinted from *Saturday Review*, August 16, 1969. Cartoon by Sidney Harris.

2

Induction

Polar bears are white.
The FBI is controlled by Jews.
Ban is preferred by 7 out of 10 American women.
Most labor leaders are crooks.
Women are better drivers than men.

Induction is the process of arriving at a general conclusion on the basis of incomplete evidence. Almost everything a person knows, he knows by induction.

One believes, for example, that polar bears are white. But because he has not seen all polar bears, his judgment is based on limited evidence. The two or three polar bears he has seen were white. Those shown in *National Geographic* magazine and in nature movies were white. Everyone he knows agrees they are white. From this information, he reasonably concludes that *all* polar bears are white. This process is induction. One considers evidence he has seen or heard to draw a conclusion about things he has not seen or heard. The intellectual movement from limited facts—called a *sample*—to a general conviction is called an inductive leap.

Most conclusions regarding past, present, and future events are based on this kind of leap. One believes that Balboa discovered the Pacific Ocean, that taking aspirin eases a headache, that the Democrats will win the next presidential election. Because he can never secure all the evidence relating to these questions, he reasonably makes judgments from the facts he has.

It is equally reasonable, on hearing induced conclusions, to inquire about the number and kinds of facts which went into them. For a statement to be creditable, its sample must be (1) known, (2) sufficient, and (3) representative. If one is told simply that the FBI is directed by Jewish conspirators, he can dismiss the charge on the ground that the sample is not *known*. No evidence is given to support the accusation. If he hears a famous athlete's low IQ cited to demonstrate that all athletes (or all members of the athlete's race or nationality) are intellectually inferior, he can respond that the sample is not *sufficient*. One example proves nothing about a whole group. And if he hears the cruelties of the Spanish Inquisition used to evidence the repressive views of Catholics in general, he can insist that the sample is not *representative*. Spanish practice in the fifteenth century is hardly typical of worldwide Catholicism today.

One frequently hears statements which simply lack evidence. Advertisements announce that "Ban is preferred by 7 out of 10 American women," that "4 out of 5 top movie stars use Lustre-Creme Shampoo." Rumor whispers that Viceroy filters are made of harmful fiberglass and that flouridated drinking water can cause brain damage. Such claims can safely be ignored until evidence is offered to support them.

A variation popular with sensational writers is to make an extravagant claim and point to concrete evidence—which happens to be unavailable. They charge that Warren Harding was murdered by his wife and that Franklin Roosevelt was poisoned by the Russians at Teheran—then regret that evidence is lost in the past. They affirm the existence of abominable snowmen, Atlantis, and the Loch Ness monster—then lament that proof remains out of reach. They know that UFO's are extraterrestrial spaceships and that a massive conspiracy led to the assassinations of John and Robert Kennedy—then insist that the U. S. Air Force, the FBI, and the CIA are withholding crucial evidence. These too are inductions with an absent sample.

Induction with an insufficient sample is common. One regularly hears charges like these:

> Most labor leaders are crooks. Look at Tony Boyle, Frank Brewster, and Jimmy Hoffa.
> The Social Security system is unfair. Let me tell you what happened to my father-in-law.
> Don't talk to me about Puerto Ricans. I lived next to a Puerto Rican family for two years.

Clearly the indicated samples—*three* labor leaders, *one* relative, *one* family—are inadequate evidence on which to base any broad conclusion.

Spokesmen commonly try to broaden the effect of limited examples by declaring them "typical" or "average." They remain limited examples. *In argument, the words "typical" and "average" deserve immediate suspicion.*

A sample is said to be unrepresentative when it is not typical of the whole class of things being studied. It is easy to see that one cannot gauge his town's attitude toward a proposed liquor tax by polling only the citizens at the corner bar or only members of the local WCTU chapter.

Nevertheless, conclusions based on an unrepresentative sample can be quite deceptive on first hearing: e.g., "Women are better drivers than men; they have fewer accidents." Here the sample is large enough—a substantial body of accident statistics—but it is not broad enough to be meaningful. The conclusion concerns *all* drivers, but the sample group includes only drivers who have had accidents. To be representative (i.e., typical of the whole area under discussion), the sample must include all four groups involved:

1. Men
2. Women
3. Drivers who had accidents
4. Drivers who had no accidents

With this broad sample one can see that there are fewer women in automobile accidents because there are fewer women driving. The isolated accident statistics are meaningless if not compared to those for all drivers.

Similarly, if one hears that 60 percent of all lung cancer victims are moderate-to-heavy smokers, or that 80 percent of all San Quentin convicts come from homes which served liquor, he can draw no significant conclusion. The sample includes only cancer victims and convicts; there is no general data with which to make comparisons. Perhaps 60 percent of *all* adults are moderate smokers and 80 percent of *all* homes serve liquor; then, of course, the statistics would be completely meaningless.

Any induced conclusion is open to question, then, if its sample is too small or is unduly weighted in some way. The Nielsen rating service claims to know the audience size for American television programs. But because its data comes from 1100 audiometers (one for every 50,000 homes), the sufficiency of the sample is doubtful. The Kinsey report was said to reveal the sexual habits of American women. But because the information came from 5940 women— most of whom were well-educated, white, non-Catholic, and Gentile, and all of whom were willing to describe their sex lives to interviewers—the representativeness of the sample is open to question. *Any poll with a selective sample—i.e., where some individuals choose to respond to it and others do not—is unrepresentative.*

A person can misuse a poll to make it substantiate a desired opinion. He can announce the results of surveys which were probably never taken. (Politicians have for years made good use of "private polls" to enhance the prestige of a lagging candidate.) He can phrase a poll question to draw the response he seeks. [In 1967, all Alabama parents were asked to respond to a questionnaire: "I (We) prefer that my (our) child shall be taught by a teacher of the following race: White. Negro. Other."] Or he can inflate someone else's poll. (In 1972, Washington television station WTTG asked viewers to write in their opinion of President Nixon's decision to mine North Vietnamese harbors; the final count showed 5157 supporting the president and a much smaller number opposing him. Later investigation showed that some 4000 of the votes favorable to the president came directly from the Committee to Reelect the President.)

What is an adequate sample on which to base a reliable judgment? There is no easy answer. Size varies with the character of the question and with the degree of probability one seeks. It should be remembered, however, that a small sample—if genuinely representative—can sustain a broad conclusion. George Gallup assesses the opinions of the American public by polling 1500 individuals. But because his sample is chosen so that every adult American has an equal chance of being interviewed, the Gallup Poll (like similar polls) is a reliable source of information. The mathematical probability is that, 95 times out of 100, a selection of 1500 anonymous people will give results no more than 3 percentage points off the figures which would be obtained by interviewing the whole population. (Modern polling can be disturbingly accurate. Just before the 1972 presidential election, the Gallup Poll reported that Nixon would receive 62 percent of the vote, and McGovern 38 percent; the Harris Poll predicted 61 percent and 39 percent. And after 77,734,195 individual citizens made their personal choice, the count showed 1 percent for minor candidates, 61 percent for Nixon, and 38 percent for McGovern.)

Even in everyday experience, one commonly uses very limited information to draw a tentative conclusion. This is not unreasonable. If one sees an acquaintance not wearing her engagement ring and behaving despondently, he may speculate that she has broken her engagement. The evidence is not sufficient for him to offer condolences, but it is enough to keep him from making jokes about marriage. If one hears from a friend that a newly opened restaurant is disappointing, he will probably choose not to eat there—

at least until he hears a contrary report. His conclusion is based on a minute sample, but it is all the sample he has. As his sample grows, so will his degree of conviction.

A final point: With induction, one should remember *Occam's razor*, the maxim that when a body of evidence exists, the simplest conclusion that expresses all of it is probably the best. A perfect illustration occurred in 1967 when New Orleans district attorney James Garrison sought to prove that Clay Shaw, a local businessman, was involved in the assassination of President Kennedy. He submitted that Shaw's address book carried the entry "Lee Odom, P. O. Box 19106, Dallas, Texas"; and that the number "PO 19106," when properly decoded, became "WH 15601," the unlisted phone number of Jack Ruby, slayer of Kennedy's assassin Lee Oswald. (The process involved "unscrambling" the numerals and—since P and O equal 7 and 6 on a telephone dial—subtracting 1300.) Thus Garrison used the entry in Shaw's address book as inductive evidence leading to a sensational conclusion. But Occam's razor suggests a simpler explanation, one which proved to be a fact: Shaw was acquainted with a businessman named Lee Odom, whose Dallas address was P. O. Box 19106.

HOW VALID ARE THESE EXAMPLES OF INDUCTION?

1. In a study of possible relationship between pornography and antisocial behavior, questionnaires went to 7500 psychiatrists and psychoanalysts, whose listing in the directory of the American Psychological Association indicated clinical experience. Over 3400 of these professionals responded. The result: 7.4 percent of the psychiatrists and psychologists had cases in which they were convinced that pornography was a causal factor in antisocial behavior; an additional 9.4 percent were suspicious; 3.2 percent did not commit themselves; and 80 percent stated they had no cases in which a causal connection was suspected.

2. "Proven most effective against colds"—Listerine Antiseptic advertisement

3. I'm not going to sign up for Professor Dendinger's class. Several of my friends had the course and disliked it.

4. When a rating service indicated that "The Walter Winchell File" ranked low in television popularity, Mr. Winchell, tak-

ing a letter poll of the readers of his newspaper column, declared that his was the most popular of all Friday productions.

5. Arguing that eighteenth-century English poetry was essentially prosaic, Matthew Arnold offered a passage from "Pope's verse, take it almost where you will":

   To Hounslow Heath I point and Banstead Down;
   Thence comes your mutton, and these chicks my own.

6. A study of 3400 New York citizens who had had recent heart attacks showed that 70 percent of them were 10–50 pounds overweight. Clearly, obesity is a cause of heart disease.

7. "I wouldn't marry a railroad man.
   I'll tell you the reason why.
   I never knew a railroad man
   Who wouldn't tell his wife a lie."
   —Lyric from "I Am a Rovin' Gambler"

A Behavioral Study of Obedience[1]

STANLEY MILGRAM

Obedience is as basic an element in the structure of social life as one can point to. Some system of authority is a requirement of all communal living, and it is only the man dwelling in isolation who is not forced to respond, through defiance or submission, to the commands of others. Obedience, as a determinant of behavior, is of particular relevance to our time. It has been reliably established that from 1933–45 millions of innocent persons were systematically slaughtered on command. Gas chambers were built, death camps were guarded, daily quotas of corpses were produced with the same efficiency as the manufacture of appliances. These inhumane policies may have originated in the mind of a single person, but they could only be carried out on a massive scale if a very large number of persons obeyed orders.

Obedience is the psychological mechanism that links individual action to political purpose. It is the dispositional cement that binds men to systems of authority. Facts of recent history and observation in daily life suggest that for many persons obedience may be a deeply ingrained behavior tendency, indeed, a prepotent impulse overriding training in ethics, sympathy, and moral conduct. C. P. Snow (1961) points to its importance when he writes:

> When you think of the long and gloomy history of man, you will find more hideous crimes have been committed in the name of obedience than have ever been committed in the name of rebellion. If you doubt that, read William Shirer's *Rise and Fall of the Third Reich*. The German Officer Corps were brought up in the most rigorous code of obedience . . . in the name of obedience they were party to, and assisted in, the most wicked large scale actions in the history of the world [p. 24].

While the particular form of obedience dealt with in the present study has its antecedents in these episodes, it must not be thought all obedience entails acts of aggression against others. Obedience serves numerous productive functions. Indeed, the very life of so-

Reprinted from the *Journal of Abnormal and Social Psychology,* October 1963, pp. 371 – 378.

[1] This research was supported by a grant (MSFG-17916) from the National Science Foundation. Exploratory studies conducted in 1960 were supported by a grant from the Higgins Fund at Yale University. The research assistance of Alan C. Elms and Jon Wayland is gratefully acknowledged.

14

ciety is predicated on its existence. Obedience may be ennobling and educative and refer to acts of charity and kindness, as well as to destruction.

GENERAL PROCEDURE

A procedure was devised which seems useful as a tool for studying obedience (Milgram, 1961). It consists of ordering a naive subject to administer electric shock to a victim. A simulated shock generator is used, with 30 clearly marked voltage levels that range from 15 to 450 volts. The instrument bears verbal designations that range from Slight Shock to Danger: Severe Shock. The responses of the victim, who is a trained confederate of the experimenter, are standardized. The orders to administer shocks are given to the naive subject in the context of a "learning experiment" ostensibly set up to study the effects of punishment on memory. As the experiment proceeds the naive subject is commanded to administer increasingly more intense shocks to the victim, even to the point of reaching the level marked Danger: Severe Shock. Internal resistances become stronger, and at a certain point the subject refuses to go on with the experiment. Behavior prior to this rupture is considered "obedience," in that the subject complies with the commands of the experimenter. The point of rupture is the act of disobedience. A quantitative value is assigned to the subject's performance based on the maximum intensity shock he is willing to administer before he refuses to participate further. Thus for any particular subject and for any particular experimental condition the degree of obedience may be specified with a numerical value. The crux of the study is to systematically vary the factors believed to alter the degree of obedience to the experimental commands.

The technique allows important variables to be manipulated at several points in the experiment. One may vary aspects of the source of command, content and form of command, instrumentalities for its execution, target object, general social setting, etc. The problem, therefore, is not one of designing increasingly more numerous experimental conditions, but of selecting those that best illuminate the process of obedience from the sociopsychological standpoint.

Related Studies

The inquiry bears an important relation to philosophic analyses of obedience and authority (Arendt, 1958; Friedrich, 1958; Weber, 1947), an early experimental study of obedience by Frank (1944), studies in "authoritarianism" (Adorno, Frenkel-Brunswik, Levinson, & Sanford, 1950; Rokeach, 1961), and a recent series of analytic and empirical studies in social power (Cartwright, 1959). It owes much to the long concern with *suggestion* in social psychology, both in its normal forms (e.g., Binet, 1900) and in its clinical manifestations (Charcot, 1881). But it derives, in the first instance, from direct observation of a social fact; the individual who is commanded by a legitimate authority ordinarily obeys. Obedience comes easily and often. It is a ubiquitous and indispensable feature of social life.

METHOD

Subjects

The subjects were 40 males between the ages of 20 and 50, drawn from New Haven and the surrounding communities. Subjects were obtained by a newspaper advertisement and direct mail solicitation. Those who responded to the appeal believed they were to participate in a study of memory and learning at Yale University. A wide range of occupations is represented in the sample. Typical subjects were postal clerks, high school teachers, salesmen, engineers, and laborers. Subjects ranged in educational level from one who had not finished elementary school, to those who had doctorate and other professional degrees. They were paid $4.50 for their participation in the experiment. However, subjects were told that payment was simply for coming to the laboratory and that the money was theirs no matter what happened after they arrived. Table 1 shows the proportion of age and occupational types assigned to the experimental conditon.

Personnel and Locale

The experiment was conducted on the grounds of Yale University in the elegant interaction laboratory. (This detail is relevant to the perceived legitimacy of the experiment. In further variations, the experiment was dissociated from the university, with conse-

TABLE 1
DISTRIBUTION OF AGE AND OCCUPATIONAL TYPES
IN THE EXPERIMENT

Occupations	20–29 years n	30–39 years n	40–50 years n	Percentage of total (Occupations)
Workers, skilled and unskilled	4	5	6	37.5
Sales, business, and white-collar	3	6	7	40.0
Professional	1	5	3	22.5
Percentage of total (Age)	20	40	40	

Note.—Total $N = 40$.

quences for performance.) The role of experimenter was played by a 31-year-old high school teacher of biology. His manner was impassive, and his appearance somewhat stern throughout the experiment. He was dressed in a gray technician's coat. The victim was played by a 47-year-old accountant, trained for the role; he was of Irish-American stock, whom most observers found mild-mannered and likable.

Procedure

One naive subject and one victim (an accomplice) performed in each experiment. A pretext had to be devised that would justify the administration of electric shock by the naive subject. This was effectively accomplished by the cover story. After a general introduction on the presumed relation between punishment and learning, subjects were told:

But actually, we know *very little* about the effect of punishment on learning, because almost no truly scientific studies have been made of it in human beings.

For instance, we don't know how *much* punishment is best for learning—and we don't know how much difference it makes as to who is giving the punishment, whether an adult learns best from a younger or an older person than himself—or many things of that sort.

So in this study we are bringing together a number of adults of different occupations and ages. And we're asking some of them to be teachers and some of them to be learners.

We want to find out just what effect different people have on each other as teachers and learners, and also what effect *punishment* will have on learning in this situation.

Therefore, I'm going to ask one of you to be the teacher here tonight and the other one to be the learner.

Does either of you have a preference?

Subjects then drew slips of paper from a hat to determine who would be the teacher and who would be the learner in the experiment. The drawing was rigged so that the naive subject was always the teacher and the accomplice always the learner. (Both slips contained the word "Teacher.") Immediately after the drawing, the teacher and learner were taken to an adjacent room and the learner was strapped into an "electric chair" apparatus.

The experimenter explained that the straps were to prevent excessive movement while the learner was being shocked. The effect was to make it impossible for him to escape from the situation. An electrode was attached to the learner's wrist, and electrode paste was applied "to avoid blisters and burns." Subjects were told that the electrode was attached to the shock generator in the adjoining room.

In order to improve credibility the experimenter declared, in response to a question by the learner: "Although the shocks can be extremely painful, they cause no permanent tissue damage."

Learning task. The lesson administered by the subject was a paired-associate learning task. The subject read a series of word pairs to the learner, and then read the first word of the pair along with four terms. The learner was to indicate which of the four terms had originally been paired with the first word. He communicated his answer by pressing one of four switches in front of him, which in turn lit up one of four numbered quadrants in an answer box located atop the shock generator.

Shock generator. The instrument panel consists of 30 lever switches set in a horizontal line. Each switch is clearly labeled with a voltage designation that ranges from 15 to 450 volts. There is a 15-volt increment from one switch to the next going from left to right. In addition, the following verbal designations are clearly indicated for groups of four switches going from left to right: Slight Shock, Moderate Shock, Strong Shock, Very Strong Shock, Intense Shock, Extreme Intensity Shock, Danger: Severe Shock.

(Two switches after this last designation are simply marked XXX.)

Upon depressing a switch: a pilot light corresponding to each switch is illuminated in bright red; an electric buzzing is heard; an electric blue light, labeled "voltage energizer," flashes; the dial on the voltage meter swings to the right; various relay clicks are sounded.

The upper left-hand corner of the generator is labeled Shock Generator, Type ZLB, Dyson Instrument Company, Waltham, Mass. Output 15 Volts–450 Volts.

Details of the instrument were carefully handled to insure an appearance of authenticity. The panel was engraved by precision industrial engravers, and all components were of high quality. No subject in the experiment suspected that the instrument was merely a simulated shock generator.[2]

Sample shock. Each naive subject is given a sample shock on the shock generator, prior to beginning his run as teacher. This shock is always 45 volts, and is applied by pressing the third switch of the generator. The shock is applied to the wrist of the naive subject, and has its source in a 45-volt battery wired into the generator. This further convinces the subject of the authenticity of the generator.

Shock instructions. The subject is told to administer a shock to the learner each time he gives a wrong response. Moreover—and this is the key command—the subject is instructed to "move one level higher on the shock generator each time the learner flashes a wrong answer." He is also instructed to announce the voltage level before administering a shock. This serves to continually remind subjects of the increasing intensity of shocks administered to the learner.

Preliminary and regular run. Pretests revealed that the procedure of reading words and administering shocks requires some practice before it can be handled smoothly. Therefore, immediately preceding the regular run, the teacher is given a preliminary series of 10 words to read to the learner. There are 3 neutral words in the

[2] A related technique, making use of a shock generator, was reported by Buss (1961) for the study of aggression in the laboratory. Despite the considerable similarity of technical detail in the experimental procedures, both investigators proceeded in ignorance of the other's work. Milgram provided plans and photographs of his shock generator, experimental procedure, and first results in a report to the National Science Foundation in January 1961. This report received only limited circulation. Buss reported his procedure 6 months later, but to a wider audience. Subsequently, technical information and reports were exchanged. The present article was first received in the Editor's office on December 27, 1961; it was resubmitted with deletions on July 27, 1962.

practice series (i.e., words that the learner answers correctly), so that shocks are administered for 7 of the words, with the maximum shock at 105 volts (moderate shock). Almost all subjects master the procedure by the time the preliminary run is over.

Subjects are then presented with a second list, and are told that the procedure is the same as for the first list; the experimenter adds, however:

> When you get to the bottom of the list, repeat it over again, and continue giving shocks, until the learner has learned all the pairs correctly.

The experimenter instructs the subject to

> start from 15 volts and increase the shock level one step each time the learner gives a wrong answer.

Feedback from the victim. In all conditions the learner gives a predetermined set of responses to the word pair test, based on a schedule of approximately three wrong answers to one correct answer. In the present experimental condition no vocal response or other sign of protest is heard from the learner until Shock Level 300 is reached. When the 300-volt shock is administered, the learner pounds on the wall of the room in which he is bound to the electric chair. The pounding can be heard by the subject. From this point on, the learner's answers no longer appear on the four-way panel.

At this juncture, subjects ordinarily turn to the experimenter for guidance. The experimenter instructs the subject to treat the absence of a response as a wrong answer, and to shock the subject according to the usual schedule. He advises the subjects to allow 5 – 10 seconds before considering no response as a wrong answer, and to increase the shock level one step each time the learner fails to respond correctly. The learner's pounding is repeated after the 315-volt shock is administered; afterwards he is not heard from, nor do his answers reappear on the four-way signal box.

Experimenter feedback. At various points in the experiment the subject may turn to the experimenter for advice on whether he should continue to administer shocks. Or he may indicate that he does not wish to go on. It was important to standardize the experimenter's responses to these inquiries and reactions.

If the subject indicated his unwillingness to go on, the experimenter responded with a sequence of "prods," using as many as necessary to bring the subject into line.

Prod 1: Please continue, *or* Please go on.
Prod 2: The experiment requires that you continue.
Prod 3: It is absolutely essential that you continue.
Prod 4: You have no other choice, you *must* go on.

The prods were always made in sequence: Only if Prod 1 had been unsuccessful, could Prod 2 be used. If the subject refused to obey the experimenter after Prod 4, the experiment was terminated. The experimenter's tone of voice was at all times firm, but not impolite. The sequence was begun anew on each occasion that the subject balked or showed reluctance to follow orders.

Special prods. If the subject asked if the learner was liable to suffer permanent physical injury, the experimenter said:

Although the shocks may be painful, there is no permanent tissue damage, so please go on. [Followed by Prods 2, 3, and 4 if necessary.]

If the subject said that the learner did not want to go on, the experimenter replied:

Whether the learner likes it or not, you must go on until he has learned all the word pairs correctly. So please go on. [Followed by Prods 2, 3, and 4 if necessary.]

Dependent Measures

The primary dependent measure for any subject is the maximum shock he administers before he refuses to go any further. In principle this may vary from 0 (for a subject who refused to administer even the first shock) to 30 (for a subject who administers the highest shock on the generator). A subject who breaks off the experiment at any point prior to administering the thirtieth shock level is termed a *defiant* subject. One who complies with experimental commands fully, and proceeds to administer all shock levels commanded, is termed an *obedient* subject.

Further records. With few exceptions, experimental sessions were recorded on magnetic tape. Occasional photographs were taken through one-way mirrors. Notes were kept on any unusual behavior occurring during the course of the experiments. On occasion, additional observers were directed to write objective descriptions of the subjects' behavior. The latency and duration of shocks were measured by accurate timing devices.

Interview and dehoax. Following the experiment subjects were interviewed; open-ended questions, projective measures, and attitude scales were employed. After the interview, procedures were undertaken to assure that the subject would leave the laboratory in a state of well being. A friendly reconciliation was arranged between the subject and the victim, and an effort was made to reduce any tensions that arose as a result of the experiment.

RESULTS

Preliminary Notions

Before giving an account of the experimental results, it is instructive to consider how persons predict others will perform when commanded to administer powerful shocks to another person. Fourteen Yale seniors, all psychology majors, were provided with a detailed description of the experimental situation. They were asked to reflect carefully on it, and to predict the behavior of 100 hypothetical subjects. More specifically, they were instructed to plot the distribution of obedience of "100 Americans of diverse occupations, and ranging in age from 20 to 50 years," who were placed in the experimental situation.

There was considerable agreement among the respondents on the expected behavior of hypothetical subjects. All respondents predicted that only an insignificant minority would go through to the end of the shock series. (The estimates ranged from 0 to 3%; i.e., the most "pessimistic" member of the class predicted that of 100 persons, 3 would continue through to the most potent shock available on the shock generator—450 volts.) The class mean was 1.2%. The question was also posed informally to colleagues of the author, and the most general feeling was that few if any subjects would go beyond the designation Very Strong Shock.

Result of Experiment I

Subjects accept situation. With few exceptions subjects were convinced of the reality of the experimental situation, that they were administering shocks to another person, and the most potent shocks were extremely painful. In the post-experimental interview subjects were asked: "How painful to the learner were the last few shocks that you administered to him?" Subjects were instructed to indicate their answers on a printed 14-point scale ranging from "Not at all painful" to "Extremely painful." The modal response was 14 (Extremely painful) with the mean at 13.42.

Signs of extreme tension. Many subjects showed signs of nervousness in the experimental situation, and especially upon administering the more powerful shocks. In a large number of cases the degree of tension reached extremes that are rarely seen in sociopsychological laboratory studies. Subjects were observed to sweat, tremble, stutter, bite their lips, groan, and dig their fingernails into their flesh. These were characteristic rather than exceptional responses to the experiment.

One sign of tension was the regular occurrence of nervous laughing fits. Fourteen of the 40 subjects showed definite signs of nervous laughter and smiling. The laughter seemed entirely out of place, even bizarre. Full-blown, uncontrollable seizures were observed for 3 subjects. On one occasion we observed a seizure so violently convulsive that it was necessary to call a halt to the experiment. The subject, a 46-year-old encyclopedia salesman, was seriously embarrassed by his untoward and uncontrollable behavior. In the post-experimental interviews subjects took pains to point out that they were not sadistic types, and that the laughter did not mean they enjoyed shocking the victim.

Distribution of scores. It has been conjectured that persons would not, in general, agree to administer shocks beyond the level designated as Very Strong Shock. The distribution of maximum shocks for this experiment is shown in Table 2. The obtained distribution of scores deviates radically from the prediction.

Upon command of the experimenter, each of the 40 subjects went beyond the expected breakoff point. No subject stopped prior to administering Shock Level 20. (At this level—300 volts—the victim kicks on the wall and no longer provides answers to the teacher's multiple-choice questions.)

Of the 40 subjects, 5 refused to obey the experimental commands beyond the 300-volt level. Four more subjects administered one further shock, and then refused to go on. Two broke off at the 330-volt level, and 1 each at 345, 360, and 375 volts. Thus a total of 14 subjects defied the experimenter. It is instructive to reprint their remarks at the point of defiance, as transcribed from the tape recordings:

[0124] I think he's trying to communicate, he's knocking. . . . Well it's not fair to shock the guy . . . these are terrific volts. I don't think this is very humane. . . . Oh, I can't go on with this, no, this isn't right. It's a hell of an experiment. The guy is suffering in there. No, I don't want to go on. This is crazy. [Subject refused to administer more shocks.]

[0123] He's banging in there. I'm gonna chicken out. I'd like to con-

TABLE 2
DISTRIBUTION OF BREAKOFF POINTS

Verbal designation voltage indication	Number of subjects for whom this was maximum shock
Slight Shock	
15	0
30	0
45	0
60	0
Moderate Shock	
75	0
90	0
105	0
120	0
Strong Shock	
135	0
150	0
165	0
180	0
Very Strong Shock	
195	0
210	0
225	0
240	0
Intense Shock	
255	0
270	0
285	0
300	5
Extreme Intensity Shock	
315	4
330	2
345	1
360	1
Danger: Severe Shock	
375	1
390	0
405	0
420	0
XXX	
435	0
450	26

tinue, but I can't do that to a man. . . . I'm sorry I can't do that to a man. I'll hurt his heart. You take your check. . . . No really, I couldn't do it.

These subjects were frequently in a highly agitated and even angered state. Sometimes, verbal protest was at a minimum, and the subject simply got up from his chair in front of the shock generator, and indicated that he wished to leave the laboratory.

Of the 40 subjects, 26 obeyed the orders of the experimenter to the end, proceeding to punish the victim until they reached the most potent shock available on the shock generator. At that point, the experimenter called a halt to the session. (The maximum shock is labeled 450 volts, and is two steps beyond the designation: Danger: Severe Shock.) Although obedient subjects continued to administer shocks, they often did so under extreme stress. Some expressed reluctance to administer shocks beyond the 300-volt level, and displayed fears similar to those who defied the experimenter; yet they obeyed.

After the maximum shocks had been delivered, and the experimenter called a halt to the proceedings, many obedient subjects heaved sighs of relief, mopped their brows, rubbed their fingers over their eyes, or nervously fumbled cigarettes. Some shook their heads, apparently in regret. Some subjects had remained calm throughout the experiment, and displayed only minimal signs of tension from beginning to end.

DISCUSSION

The experiment yielded two findings that were surprising. The first finding concerns the sheer strength of obedient tendencies manifested in this situation. Subjects have learned from childhood that it is a fundamental breach of moral conduct to hurt another person against his will. Yet, 26 subjects abandon this tenet in following the instructions of an authority who has no special powers to enforce his commands. To disobey would bring no material loss to the subject; no punishment would ensue. It is clear from the remarks and outward behavior of many participants that in punishing the victim they are often acting against their own values. Subjects often expressed deep disapproval of shocking a man in the face of his objections, and others denounced it as stupid and senseless. Yet the majority complied with the experimental commands. This outcome was surprising from two perspectives: first, from the standpoint of predictions made in the questionnaire described earlier. (Here, however, it is possible that the remoteness of the respondents from the actual situation, and the difficulty of conveying to them the concrete details of the experiment, could account for the serious underestimation of obedience.)

But the results were also unexpected to persons who observed the experiment in progress, through one-way mirrors. Observers often uttered expressions of disbelief upon seeing a subject administer more powerful shocks to the victim. These persons had a full acquaintance with the details of the situation, and yet systematically underestimated the amount of obedience that subjects would display.

The second unanticipated effect was the extraordinary tension generated by the procedures. One might suppose that a subject would simply break off or continue as his conscience dictated. Yet, this is very far from what happened. There were striking reactions of tension and emotional strain. One observer related:

> I observed a mature and initially poised businessman enter the laboratory smiling and confident. Within 20 minutes he was reduced to a twitching, stuttering wreck, who was rapidly approaching a point of nervous collapse. He constantly pulled on his earlobe, and twisted his hands. At one point he pushed his fist into his forehead and muttered: "Oh, God, let's stop it." And yet he continued to respond to every word of the experimenter, and obeyed to the end.

Any understanding of the phenomenon of obedience must rest on an analysis of the particular conditions in which it occurs. The following features of the experiment go some distance in explaining the high amount of obedience observed in the situation.

1. The experiment is sponsored by and takes place on the grounds of an institution of unimpeachable reputation, Yale University. It may be reasonably presumed that the personnel are competent and reputable. The importance of this background authority is now being studied by conducting a series of experiments outside of New Haven, and without any visible ties to the university.

2. The experiment is, on the face of it, designed to attain a worthy purpose—advancement of knowledge about learning and memory. Obedience occurs not as an end in itself, but as an instrumental element in a situation that the subject construes as significant, and meaningful. He may not be able to see its full significance, but he may properly assume that the experimenter does.

3. The subject perceives that the victim has voluntarily submitted to the authority system of the experimenter. He is not (at first)

an unwilling captive impressed for involuntary service. He has taken the trouble to come to the laboratory presumably to aid the experimental research. That he later becomes an involuntary subject does not alter the fact that, initially, he consented to participate without qualification. Thus he has in some degree incurred an obligation toward the experimenter.

4. The subject, too, has entered the experiment voluntarily, and perceives himself under obligation to aid the experimenter. He has made a commitment, and to disrupt the experiment is a repudiation of his initial promise of aid.

5. Certain features of the procedure strengthen the subject's sense of obligation to the experimenter. For one, he has been paid for coming to the laboratory. In part this is canceled out by the experimenter's statement that:

> Of course, as in all experiments, the money is yours simply for coming to the laboratory. From this point on, no matter what happens, the money is yours.[3]

6. From the subject's standpoint, the fact that he is the teacher and the other man the learner is purely a chance consequence (it is determined by drawing lots) and he, the subject, ran the same risk as the other man in being assigned the role of learner. Since the assignment of positions in the experiment was achieved by fair means, the learner is deprived of any basis of complaint on this count. (A similar situation obtains in Army units, in which—in the absence of volunteers—a particularly dangerous mission may be assigned by drawing lots, and the unlucky soldier is expected to bear his misfortune with sportsmanship.)

7. There is, at best, ambiguity with regard to the prerogatives of a psychologist and the corresponding rights of his subject. There is a vagueness of expectation concerning what a psychologist may require of his subject, and when he is overstepping acceptable limits. Moreover, the experiment occurs in a closed setting, and thus provides no opportunity for the subject to remove these ambiguities by discussion with others. There are few standards that seem directly applicable to the situation, which is a novel one for most subjects.

8. The subjects are assured that the shocks administered to the subject are "painful but not dangerous." Thus they assume that

---

[3] Forty-three subjects, undergraduates at Yale University, were run in the experiment without payment. The results are very similar to those obtained with paid subjects.

the discomfort caused the victim is momentary, while the scientific gains resulting from the experiment are enduring.

9. Through Shock Level 20 the victim continues to provide answers on the signal box. The subject may construe this as a sign that the victim is still willing to "play the game." It is only after Shock Level 20 that the victim repudiates the rules completely, refusing to answer further.

These features help to explain the high amount of obedience obtained in this experiment. Many of the arguments raised need not remain matters of speculation, but can be reduced to testable propositions to be confirmed or disproved by further experiments.[4]

The following features of the experiment concern the nature of the conflict which the subject faces.

10. The subject is placed in a position in which he must respond to the competing demands of two persons: the experimenter and the victim. The conflict must be resolved by meeting the demands of one or the other; satisfaction of the victim and the experimenter are mutually exclusive. Moreover, the resolution must take the form of a highly visible action, that of continuing to shock the victim or breaking off the experiment. Thus the subject is forced into a public conflict that does not permit any completely satisfactory solution.

11. While the demands of the experimenter carry the weight of scientific authority, the demands of the victim spring from his personal experience of pain and suffering. The two claims need not be regarded as equally pressing and legitimate. The experimenter seeks an abstract scientific datum; the victim cries out for relief from physical suffering caused by the subject's actions.

12. The experiment gives the subject little time for reflection. The conflict comes on rapidly. It is only minutes after the subject has been seated before the shock generator that the victim begins his protests. Moreover, the subject perceives that he has gone through but two-thirds of the shock levels at the time the subject's first protests are heard. Thus he understands that the conflict will have a persistent aspect to it and may well become more intense as increasingly more powerful shocks are required. The rapidity with which the conflict descends on the subject, and his realization that it is predictably recurrent may well be sources of tension to him.

---

[4] A series of recently completed experiments employing the obedience paradigm is reported in Milgram (1964).

13. At a more general level, the conflict stems from the opposition of two deeply ingrained behavior dispositions: first, the disposition not to harm other people, and second, the tendency to obey those whom we perceive to be legitimate authorities.

REFERENCES

Adorno, T., Frenkel-Brunswik, Else, Levinson, D. J., & Sanford, R. N. *The authoritarian personality*. New York: Harper, 1950.
Arendt, H. What was authority? In C. J. Friedrich (Ed.), *Authority*. Cambridge: Harvard Univer. Press, 1958. Pp. 81–112.
Binet, A. *La suggestibilité*. Paris: Schleicher, 1900.
Buss, A. H. *The psychology of aggression*. New York: Wiley, 1961.
Cartwright, S. (Ed.) *Studies in social power*. Ann Arbor: University of Michigan Institute for Social Research,1959.
Charcot, J. M. *Oeuvres completes*. Paris: Bureaux du Progres Medical, 1881.
Frank, J. D. Experimental studies of personal pressure and resistance. *J. gen. Psychol.*, 1944. 30, 23–64.
Friedrich, C. J. (Ed.) *Authority*. Cambridge: Harvard Univer. Press, 1958.
Milgram, S. Dynamics of obedience. Washington: National Science Foundation, 25 January 1961. (Mimeo).
Milgram, S. Some conditions of obedience and disobedience to authority. *Hum. Relat.*, 1964.
Rokeach, M. Authority, authoritarianism, and conformity. In I. A. Berg & B. M. Bass (Eds.) *Conformity and deviation*. New York: Harper, 1961. Pp. 230–257.
Snow, C. P. Either-or. *Progressive,* 1961 (Feb.) 24.
Weber, M. *The theory of social and economic organization*. Oxford: Oxford Univer. Press, 1947.

The description of a range of experiments in this area appears in Stanley Milgram's *Obedience to Authority* (New York: Harper, 1974).

DISCUSSION QUESTIONS

1. What is the implicit conclusion of the study? To whom does it apply?

2. Why does the author contrast the results of this experiment with the result anticipated by 14 psychology majors at Yale?

3. Can a brief experiment testing 40 persons "from New Haven and surrounding communities" lead to any reasonable conclusions about American citizens, about German history, about human nature?

4. What is the point of Table 1 [Distribution of Age and Occupational Types in the Experiment]?

5. Assuming the reader tends to relate this experiment to certain atrocity situations in recent history, comment on the purpose of notations 1–13 in the "Discussion" which concludes the article. Considering this purpose, can you mention any facts the author might have added?

6. Why does the essay relate the results of this experiment (i.e., the "cruel" actions of most of the members of the sample) to C. P. Snow's statement that "The German Officer Corps were brought up in the most rigorous code of obedience"?

7. Why does the author spell out the appearance (dress, manner, etc.) of the experimenter and of the victim? Is this different from his description of the electrical equipment?

Why Does ESP Happen?

SUSY SMITH

Ever since the earliest days of psychical investigation, re-searchers have been trying to find out why ESP happens, and hoping to understand all of its characteristics. Yet through all experimentation, then and subsequently, *psi* (as the psychic power is often called) has remained so elusive and unfathomable that no exact explanation of it has ever been formulated.

Because of this, research has tended to take the direction of trying primarily to indicate ESP's existence and to prove that it is repeatable. Tests have been made over and over again for almost a century with the object of identifying various forms of extrasensory perception and very little more. One wonders why it seems necessary for researchers to repeat this so endlessly, until it is realized that because of psi's very intangibility, proving its existence on acceptable scientific grounds becomes an enormous challenge.

The importance of tests which would utilize chance probabilities was remarked by Gurney: "Of course the first question for science is not whether the phenomena can be produced to order, but whether in a sufficient number of series the proportion of successes to failure is markedly above the probable result of chance." This basic statement has been repeated incessantly by others.

Although Gurney spoke so wisely of chance, it is Professor Charles Richet of France who gets credit for the initial use of the mathematics of chance in evaluating results of telepathy tests. And in 1885, Sir Oliver Lodge, another great physicist who interested himself in psychical research, proposed that conclusive evidence for telepathy might be produced by card-guessing in quantities. He worked out a mathematical formula for estimating the number of hits above those to be expected by chance. When the probability of naming the right card on the basis of chance was known it was easier to compute how much evidence of telepathy the results showed. While an experimenter in chemistry might be content to achieve a result in which the odds were 20-to-1 against chance, in a subject as offbeat as psychical research it seemed imperative to devise a system in which results could be estimated which were

Reprinted from *ESP For the Millions* (Los Angeles: Sherbourne Press, Inc., 1965), pp. 46–61.

200-, 2,000- or 20,000-to-1 against chance. With card tests repeated endlessly (known as quantitative testing) such results could be achieved.

Although some of these first tests were surprisingly well done, they are not now considered to have been as carefully executed as are those which have been conducted in recent years. With the new techniques he devised, Dr. J. B. Rhine can take the credit for having made quantitative testing for ESP acceptable and successful. Before he started in this field, Dr. Rhine had previously worked for many years with plant physiology and botany, in which he took three degrees at the University of Chicago. His wife, Louisa, was also a graduate in that field. When they encountered some impressive reports of paranormal events, the Rhines became interested in psychical research. After a year in which they both studied psychology at Harvard under Professor William McDougall, they were more than ever taken with parapsychology, in which McDougall had a keen interest.

When McDougall was called to the chair of psychology at Duke University he soon made a professional opportunity in parapsychology available to the Rhines. From 1930 to 1934 they carried forward pioneer experimental investigations in telepathy and clairvoyance, using students as laboratory subjects.

Dr. Rhine knew that in order to break down the persistent opposition to paranormal phenomena it would be necessary to find a method of examination which paralleled the laboratory techniques of other scientific research. He also knew that in order to rule out the argument that ESP was nothing but pure chance or coincidence, he would have to repeat his experiments in even greater numbers, and that he would have to perform each test under such rigid control that there could be no question of sensory cues. Helped by advances in the science of statistics, Rhine was able to devise techniques which made a very large number of experiments possible. First acting as agent (or conductor of the test) himself, Dr. Rhine found the students responding to his stimulating personality with cooperative enthusiasm. He soon had a few star performers who were able to produce outstanding ESP.

The tests were made with what were at first called the Zener cards (now usually referred to as ESP cards). In a pack of twenty-five playing-size cards there are five each of five different symbols: circle, square, cross, star, and wave. When the cards are run face down, by the mathematics of probability the subject would expect to guess one symbol correctly out of five trials. Running the entire twenty-five cards, the subject may be expected to average five chance hits. Repeatedly getting more than five hits is an indication of extrasensory perception, but it is only when hundreds of runs have been made and the score is still higher than chance that the test can be considered significant.

Since the time that these cards were first used at Duke there have been millions of runs made, under conditions varying to indicate whether the ESP is to be identified as telepathy, clairvoyance, general ESP, or precognition.

In 1934 a book entitled *Extrasensory Perception* by Dr. Rhine appeared. In it were accounts of the tests which had been run at Duke; and with its publication a new era in psychical research began. The Pearce-Pratt experiment, the book's most startling feature, introduced Dr. Rhine's research assistant, J. Gaither Pratt, and Hubert E. Pearce Jr., a ministerial student since deceased. Pearce was such an outstanding subject that he would average from six to eleven hits per run at any experimental session. Once, in an informal but nonetheless impressive set of circumstances, he scored a perfect run of 25 hits.

In this experiment which Rhine and Pratt carried out with Pearce in August and September, 1933, the aim was to set up conditions which would exclude all the factors that could reproduce extrachance scores except ESP. Dr. Pratt handled the pack of cards (known as the target pack) whose symbols were to be guessed by Pearce. He was in the Social Science Building at Duke. Pearce was seated 100 yards away in a reading cubicle in the stacks at the back of the Duke Library.

At the start of each session the two men synchronized their watches. After Pearce left for his cubicle, Pratt shuffled the cards and placed the pack at a left-hand corner of his table. At the agreed-upon starting time Pratt removed the top card and, without looking at it, placed it face down on a book in the middle of the table and left it there for a minute. He then removed the card, still face down, to the right-hand corner of the table and immediately picked up the next card and put it on the book. This routine was continued until all the cards were transferred, one at a time, to the other corner. Thus twenty-five minutes were taken for each run of twenty-five trials. Pratt then looked at the faces of the cards and recorded in duplicate the order in which they had fallen and, as a safeguard, before he met with Pearce, sealed one copy in an envelope for delivery to Dr. Rhine.

In the meantime, Pearce had put down on his record sheet dur-

ing each minute the symbol which he thought was on the card
Pratt had in position at the time. At the end of the run he, too,
made a duplicate of his record of the twenty-five calls and sealed
one copy in an envelope for Rhine's records before checking his
duplicate with Pratt. Thus each one of the men had individual
records which they could check independently of the others. In
this way, also, any question of the individual good faith of any one
of the three was disposed of.

Two runs through the pack were made per day and the total
series consisted of 12 runs of 300 trials. The number of hits expected on a theory of pure chance was 20 percent of 300 or 60
hits. Pearce obtained a total of 119 hits or just one short of double
the number expected from chance. His average run score was 9.9
hits per 25 or 39.7 percent of the total trials made. A score as large
as 119 hits in 300 trials would be expected to occur by chance only
once in approximately a quadrillion (1,000,000,000,000,000) of
such experiments. The experimenters were sure, therefore, that
every reasonable man would, without further argument, join them
in dismissing the chance explanation. Their optimism was magnif-
icent!

There are no known sensory processes that could be supposed to
operate under these conditions. No type of rational inference could
apply to a case of this kind. They, therefore, could hardly help but
decide that, whatever clairvoyance or the extrasensory perception
of objects *is,* this was a case of it. It was a case in which results
were obtained under the strictest control ever until that time observed.

The report of this Pearce-Pratt experiment initiated what Dr.
Rhine calls "what was doubtless the most heated controversy
American psychology has ever experienced." The results of the experiment were attacked on the grounds of poor observation, mathematical inadequacy, and even fraud.

But some of the criticism, or hypercriticism, while it might not
have applied directly to the Pearce-Pratt experiments, could still be
helpful in a general way to all ESP testing. So it was taken very
seriously by Drs. Rhine and Pratt and their associates. They made
efforts to correct anything to which these complaints might intelligently apply.

For instance, it was pointed out that if the Zener cards were too
thin, some persons might be able to read through their backs the
symbols on their faces. Against the contingency that this might

possibly have been the case, Dr. Rhine immediately saw to it that new decks were made of thicker material.

Another criticism: there was always a possibility that the sender, unknown to himself, might give certain unconscious cues which made the receiver's accurate guessing possible. Involuntary whispering might occur, or the sender's facial muscles might contract with the potential that anyone familiar with muscle reading could know which was the key symbol. Though certain sounds emitted by the agent might be far too faint for a guesser in the next room to be consciously aware of, yet they might be of sufficient intensity to register at a subconscious level, it was suggested. It was also insisted that checks be made to see if the sender was unconsciously reacting to a particular symbol by coughing, or tapping his feet.

The problem of inadequate shuffling of the cards was a more intelligent point. It was suggested that during repeated shufflings by hand it might be possible for several cards to stick together. So hand shuffling was discontinued altogether and shuffling machines were substituted. Special cuts were also concocted to eliminate any possibility of interference from the mind of the subject, in case such might be occurring. In many tests now performed a table of random numbers is used to prepare the deck so that each symbol is bound to be in a scientifically haphazard position.

There were also accusations that errors in recording must have been made in order to account for the greater-than-chance results. To check this, numerous re-evaluations were made of a great many previously scored tests. In one exhaustive recheck of 500,000 card matchings, only 90 mistakes were found. Seventy-six of those turned out to be hits which had not been recorded! It is now accepted from many rechecks of both successful and unsuccessful data, that no errors in checking were sufficient to affect results significantly.

To counteract the assumption that his mathematics might be wrong, Dr. Rhine called in the American Institute of Mathematical Statistics for an appraisal of his conclusions. Their reply, after a thorough checking of the procedures used at Duke, was: "On the statistical side recent mathematical work has established the fact that, assuming that the experiments have been properly performed, the statistical analysis is essentially valid. If the Rhine investigation is to be fairly attacked, it must be on other than mathematical grounds."

While spending years giving careful consideration to all the criticism of their previous work, Drs. Rhine and Pratt were at the same time conducting numerous experiments to see if results above chance could still be obtained when safeguards were set up against all counter-hypotheses that had been suggested. They could.

One of the most striking of these new tests was the Pratt-Woodruff series carried out in 1939. This experiment was designed to meet all the criticisms that had flourished during the years of controversy. It was carried out with more controls against all possible error than any other experiment which had ever been devised. I won't go into detail about how this was conducted, but the results were that in 2,400 runs through the pack of cards there were 489 hits above the number to be expected by chance. The likelihood that this could occur by chance is around one in a million.

Right after the publication of Rhine's book in 1934, psychical researchers had all been exuberant. But it was then found that others could not duplicate the amazing achievements of Rhine and Pratt. The English parapsychologists, particularly, became very discouraged after running numerous series of tests and always coming out with chance results. Eventually however, G. N. M. Tyrrell, a former radio engineer who had deserted electronics for the challenge of this new field of interest, was able to produce the same kind of well-founded results that distinguished Rhine's work. And his personality and techniques threw light on Rhine's accomplishments as well as his own, for Tyrrell had the same rare combination of qualities needed for dealing with so elusive a trait as ESP, hidden as it is in the subconscious. Tyrrell possessed not only scientific training but also a sympathetic approach which never impeded a subject who might be hesitant and doubtful of his extrasensory powers. In addition he had the ability to make a general conception from apparently unrelated particulars. After the report of Tyrrell's test was published, parapsychologists realized that it was also these qualities in Rhine that were largely responsible for his achievements.

Tyrrell was keenly aware of a fact that most researchers, intent on making their experimental conditions as like as possible to those of the physical sciences, had tended to forget; physical conditions are not the only ones operative in ESP. Psychological conditions, he told his fellow experimenters with some emphasis, were equally important. The reason they were surprised at being unable to duplicate Rhine's successes was their own *a priori* conception of ESP. They assumed it to be a fixed characteristic possessed by A, but not by B, and one which could always be revealed by a simple test with a pack of cards. But they were wrong. That so many percent of Dr. Rhine's subjects scored high did not imply that the same percentage would do so anywhere, in any conditions. The experimenter's task, said Tyrrell, is to remove the subject's inhibitions—to induce the faculty to work—to get the extrasensory material externalized. This needs personal influence.

Tyrrell's first successor to achieve fruitful results was W. Whately Carington, who devised a system of testing for ESP which used statistical methods of assessment with pictures of objects instead of the monotonous ESP cards.

His procedure was simple enough. At 7:00 on ten successive evenings, he would hang up one of a series of ten drawings in his study. Each drawing depicted a single target object which had been chosen at random. They remained there with the door locked until 9:30 the next morning. Between those hours his subjects—he had 251 of them, all living at a distance—were asked to draw what they imagined the target object to be. This series of ten constituted one experiment. After a gap in time the procedure was repeated. When a group of experiments was over, the shuffled drawings from the whole group were sent to an outside judge for matching up with the shuffled originals.

These experiments with drawings were a marked success, for the hits were significantly more than one would expect from chance. But in addition the experiments gave some clues about ESP which had not previously been suspected. Carington found, for instance, that percipients seemed to pick up ideas more often than visual forms, also that it did not seem to matter whether the target was actually drawn, so long as the agent had thought of it. But the most unexpected revelation was of the existence of "displacement."

Hits on a particular target were naturally most frequent on the night it was drawn. If the target on Monday was a pyramid, most percipients who drew pyramids drew them on Monday. But some people also drew pyramids on Sunday or Tuesday, even sometimes two days before or two days after Monday. This really started Carington to thinking. If hits on a target drawing could occur both before and after that drawing was made, what about card-naming experiments? Maybe similar displacement had occurred in them.

At Carington's urging, Dr. S. G. Soal, who had previously done many unsuccessful tests with the Zener cards, now re-evaluated his results with respect to displacement. He discovered that two of his subjects, Basil Shackleton and Gloria Stewart, had been scoring hits on either the card before or the card following the target. This seemed to have occurred with such regularity that Dr. Soal was encouraged to attempt new tests with these subjects. He took even more extreme precautions than before, but he had remarkable success this time.

In a grand total of 37,100 trials for telepathy, Miss Stewart hit the target card 9,410 times. Chance expectance for this number of trials was 7,420 hits. Her results showed odds against chance in the neighborhood of 10^{70}-to-1.

Basil Shackleton was also successful in telepathy tests, especially when checked for displacement. He struck the plus-1 card (the one immediately following the target card) 1,101 times in 3,789 trials, which represents odds against chance of 10^{35}-to-1.

Dr. Soal, like Carington, became bored to death with ESP cards. Abandoning the impassive Zener symbols, he substituted cards on which were vividly colored pictures of an elephant, a giraffe, a lion, a pelican, and a zebra. The more photogenic fauna were gratefully received by his subjects. For, in a long series of tests, the subject's interest declines and ESP declines with it. Then what is known as "psi missing" occurs. At some point along the seemingly interminable runs, the percipient will suddenly start hitting consistently lower than chance expectancy because he is utterly fatigued and bored. This is another indication that ESP exists, and is an unconscious power; for if he consciously tried to miss he couldn't succeed at it any better than he could make successful *hits* by consciously trying to do so.

Other characteristics of ESP have been established by laboratory experiments, such as the fact that time and space have been found to affect psi not at all. In the Pearce-Pratt tests, the two protagonists were 100 yards apart. Further tests were performed in England with subjects as distant as Scotland, Holland, and the United States, and in the United States with subjects in India. The far-away guessers did just as well as those close at hand. Illness was no obstacle to extrasensory perception, and although mental state affected it, physical conditions apparently did not.

Despite all the brilliant, if sporadic, achievements of the laboratory in demonstrating ESP by quantitative experiments, in spite of exhaustive and successful efforts by dedicated workers, the returns have been all too meager. Nevertheless, it can be truthfully said that for all its shortcomings, quantitative testing served its purpose well and thoroughly in establishing investigation of the paranormal as a legitimate scientific pursuit.

However, as has been noted, testing endlessly with cards is a highly boring procedure, because conclusions can be reached only by the assembling of overwhelmingly repetitious numerical data. There are, fortunately, other means which can be used for testing. These are called "Qualitative," and involve the drawing of pictures and other more spontaneous and interesting techniques. As Whately Carington showed in the tests he devised, they can also be controlled and evaluated statistically. And so at the present time the trend in formal experimentation is away from quantitative testing and toward the qualitative.

A simple example of a qualitative test is for me to think very firmly of a picture—say of a hat. You, in another room, trying to capture my thoughts, draw a picture of a hat and so identify it. If we could do anything so successful as this repeatedly, it would seem fairly evident to anyone, wouldn't it, that telepathy on your part is indicated?

A series of tests which gave this kind of interesting evidence was undertaken by the well-known American author, Upton Sinclair, and his wife, Mary Craig Sinclair. After watching a young man's feats of apparent telepathy, Sinclair and his wife had become curious, although they were doubtful of the genuineness of the performance. Mrs. Sinclair decided to resolve her doubts by learning "to do these things myself." In the experiments she attempted, Mrs. Sinclair was the percipient and her husband the agent. On a few occasions her brother-in-law, R. L. Irwin, who lived forty miles away, acted as agent.

The experiments usually followed this uninvolved procedure: The agent would make a set of drawings of fairly simple things—a bird's nest with eggs, a helmet, a tree, a flower—and enclose each one in its own opaque envelope. Then, or later, Mrs. Sinclair would relax on a couch, take the envelopes in hand one at a time, and after she believed that she knew its contents, she would draw them. She spent three years at this kind of testing. Out of 290 drawings, 65 were hits, 155 partial hits, and 70 failures. This is an extremely good rate of success. Upton Sinclair was convinced by it of the existence of telepathy. In his book, *Mental Radio,* he wrote:

> For the past three years I have been watching this work, day by day and night by night, in our home. So at last I can say that I am no longer guessing . . . Regardless of what anybody can say, there will never again be a doubt in my mind. I KNOW!

DISCUSSION QUESTIONS

1. The author describes the educational background and experience of Dr. and Mrs. Rhine, as well as their relationship to Professor McDougall. Is this a preface to her argument or part of it?

2. Why is the author not more enthusiastic about Hubert Pearce's making a perfect run of 25 hits?

3. One aim of the Pearce-Pratt experiment was "to set up conditions which would exclude all the factors that could reproduce extrachance scores except ESP." Were all such factors excluded? Can anything other than ESP explain the 1 in 1,000,000,000,000,000 results?

4. What is implicit in the criticism that some of the ESP results could have derived from see-through cards or from muscular cues?

5. The Pratt-Woodruff experiments were designed to answer all earlier test-criticisms, and it produced a 1 in 1,000,000 result. Is this not impressive evidence of ESP?

6. What advantages do these features give to individuals seeking to prove the existence of ESP?
    psychological conditions
    displacement
    psi missing
    qualitative experiments

7. The Upton Sinclair experiments produced 65 hits, 155 partial hits, and 70 failures. How reliable is this as evidence of ESP?

A Psychoanalyst's Indictment of *The Exorcist*

RALPH R. GREENSON, M.D.

The Exorcist is a menace, the most shocking major movie I have ever seen. Never before have I witnessed such a flagrant combination of perverse sex, brutal violence, and abused religion. In addition, the film degrades the medical profession and psychiatry. At the showing I went to, the unruly audience giggled, talked, and yelled throughout. As well they might: Although the picture is not X-rated, it is so pornographic that it makes *Last Tango in Paris* seem like a Strauss waltz.

Above all, I resent the way in which the movie depicts a twelve-year-old child who causes three deaths, inflicts untold suffering on everyone near and dear to her, and who, during seizures, shamelessly goes in for bloody masturbation with a crucifix—this, among other sexual perversities. Throughout, Regan, the afflicted child, is represented as being merely a poor innocent victim of demonic possession. The devil made me do it—that is the total explanation the film offers. Regan is not only quite innocent, says the movie, but also is burdened by no consequences of the experience—no memories, no scars, no inner conflict. It is significant that you never see or hear Regan struggle against the devil who possesses her.

The Exorcist is supposed to be based on a true instance of modern-day possession, but I wonder about that. Like most psychiatrists, I have seen patients with one or another of the hair-raising symptoms that plague Regan, but I have never encountered, or even heard of, any single patient bristling with all the bizarre, morbid symptoms the girl in the movie exhibits. It is my conviction that *The Exorcist* was contrived to appeal to a wide audience, to attract and scare the wits out of troubled and disoriented people—by appealing to their voyeuristic impulses, their sadism, and their masochism. It also tries to titillate these unfortunates by making their panic-fears sexually exciting. Those in the audience who do *not* quake and shiver may well be experiencing a "counterphobic reaction"—a kind of chest-pounding pride in their ability to absorb all this shocking stuff without blinking an eye or turning a hair.

Reprinted from *Saturday Review/World*, June 15, 1974, pp. 41–43.

And the women-haters among them will certainly applaud the film's shameless degradation of women's sexuality.

Am I putting the case too strongly? I think not. Just consider the movie's plot: Regan, a cheerful, healthy twelve-year-old girl, the only child of a divorced actress, gradually develops bizarre symptoms during sleep-symptoms alien to her character when she is awake. Strange knocking sounds fill her bedroom, her bed rises into the air, and she shouts profanities and blasphemies in a heavy masculine voice. As the illness progresses Regan develops coarse, masculine, waxy facial features, a black hairy tongue, and physical strength so prodigious that she has to be tied down in bed. All medical and psychiatric attempts at diagnosis and treatment fail pitifully, and the frantic mother finally persuades a priest with psychiatric training to call in an old priest experienced in exorcism. The old man dies of a heart attack during the exorcism rite. In desperation, the younger priest takes over the exorcist's role, takes Regan's demon into himself, and kills both himself and the devil by plunging out the window of the girl's upper-story bedroom.

Now, all these improbable, hyperthyroid goings-on are dynamite at the box office, but I soon learned that the film's effect on some people is devastating. Several months ago I received a hysterical phone call from an intelligent, stable, young social worker whom I had known professionally for six years. She was in a state of utter panic and begged me to see her immediately. I saw her at my home, where she told me, shivering with fright, that her husband had persuaded her to see *The Exorcist* the evening before. Almost from the moment she left the theater, she had experienced a return of intense fears and phobias she could only dimly recall from her early childhood. She was afraid to be alone in a room even if her husband was elsewhere in the house, afraid to be in the dark, afraid to leave the house, and so on. It was easy for me to show her that the movie had remobilized her fears of God's punishment carried out by the Devil, with which her parents had threatened her in her early childhood. This insight was partially helpful, and after a few visits I arranged to send her to a colleague for further psychotherapy.

A week later, I received another emergency call, this one from a brilliant young university professor who had to see me "in order to let the devils inside me come out." He chose me because he felt I would not be killed by his devils. I had to see him three times in one day to allow him to rave, rant, cry, stamp his feet, bang his fists, until he became exhausted. At the end of the third visit, when he was relatively coherent, he told me that he had long felt he had an evil, psychotic core but that *The Exorcist* had convinced him that this core was the Devil himself. I also arranged for him to have further therapy. Both he and the young social worker, seemingly much improved, are still undergoing treatment.

Naturally, these closely related emergency cases caused alarm bells to ring in my mind. Asking around among colleagues of mine—men with impeccable institutional bona fides—I found that all of them had also recently treated patients who had suffered disruption, "freaking out," or other psychotic episodes after seeing *The Exorcist*.

Inquiring further, I learned that acute neurotic and psychotic reactions to this picture were common right across the country. One survey reported an average of six men fainting and six women vomiting at every showing. An editorial in the *Journal of the American Medical Association* said, "The Exorcist is heady stuff. Men and women, having seen it or part of it, leave because they cannot tolerate it; they faint, they vomit, they are consulting physicians in the belief that they or their children are 'possessed.'"

This is not to say, of course, that *everyone* who sees the film will be harmed. People who are psychologically healthy will be untouched, disgusted, or even slightly amused by the lurid plot. But for people whose emotional equilibrium is unstable, the story may be quite different. The young social worker mentioned above had, on seeing the picture, regressed back to childhood and was reliving fears she had experienced when she was four or five years old. In all, it is safe to say that the picture may well prove harmful to anyone whose emotional and mental balance is precarious.

What is "demonic possession," and why should a fictional movie on the subject cause grown men and women to quake and shiver? I believe that Freud has given us the basic psychological understanding of the phenomenon and the key to its treatment. Freud thought that the old belief in witchcraft and the Devil, angels and gods, never died out but merely went underground, repressed in the unconscious mind while being repudiated by man's rational mind. In all of us, therefore, the spirit of heavenly goodness or hellish evil persists. We see this overtly in psychotics and covertly in neurotics and other emotionally infantile characters. We also find it in the dreams of normal persons, especially in nightmares and in "daymares," frightening conscious fantasies. Although we feel relatively helpless temporarily, with the return of consciousness, the mature self restores our adult identity. To Freud, the

Devil represented the patient's bad and reprehensible wishes, de-
rivatives of instinctual impulses that had been repressed. Today,
said Freud, we recognize such fantasies as having their abode in
our mental and emotional life. Freud believed that the feeling of
being possessed by the Devil stems from the fact that the Devil is a
substitute for the father. In *The Exorcist,* please note, young
Regan had lost her father by divorce—a disruptive, often shatter-
ing, experience for a child.

The Devil and God, said Freud, are both derived from the father.
God, as he is perceived by children, is an exalted father figure.
Religious people call God "our Father" and call themselves "His
children." This primal image of father survives in all of mankind.
It is ambivalent: It contains love and hate simultaneously, a longing to please and submit along with spite and defiance. Some part
of it may be conscious, but in most rational people it is predomi-
nantly repressed and unconscious.

Hence, the good, loving father is God, and Satan is created out
of the hateful impulses the child feels toward the terrible, wrath-
ful, and punitive father. The father is thus the prototype of both
God and the Devil. Religions teach that God created man in his
image. Psychoanalysis, on the other hand, teaches that the child
created God out of his primitive perceptions of his father and projects his own feelings and impulses onto his ambivalently loved
God. This father-God-Devil relationship is, then, the backdrop
against which we can make sense of the panic and hysteria induced by *The Exorcist* and can comprehend the larger, even more
frightening, current drift toward superstition and irrational fear.

Mysticism, supernaturalism, occultism, are flourishing today because many people are disillusioned by the deterioration of our
moral standards, the social and economic inequities, the excessive
permissiveness and punishments, the hypocrisy and the corruption of people in high places. This makes people feel disoriented,
powerless, and tempts them to regress into mysticism, to gain a
sense of belonging and of bliss. We see it in the emotionally sick,
the dropouts, the disenfranchised, and the hard-drug users, among
others.

Being possessed is not only a negative force, however; sometimes people are possessed by feeling-states that give them great
power and enormous creativity. Think of how hypnosis can give a
frail woman strength enough to carry three grown men. Think of
Beethoven's frenzied periods of creativity. Also, do not forget that

one of the most powerful sensations of being possessed is the feeling of righteous indignation, which endows one with great strength. We would attack a giant to protect a child of ours who was being mistreated. Many of us have discovered endurance we never knew we had when fighting injustice or illness.

What can we do about the perils of demonology in our time? I have only few and inadequate answers.

Above all, we must not absolve people of responsibility for their actions: If you kill or maim or steal, no matter what the psychological explanation, that is wrong and calls for punishment of some kind. We can blame Watergate, Vietnam, and the atom bomb for our moral shortcomings, but these external considerations, as horrendous as they may be, are no excuse for our own self-centeredness, greed, and immorality.

If there are devils outside us, they cannot be used to explain away our wrongdoings. We must come to realize that the fault is with our own *inner* devils: our passion for money and possessions, our frantic search for easy solutions, instant bliss, or oblivion, which pass for peace of mind. Add to this list our general apathy, which we disguise by giving out tokens of charity and kindness so long as they don't make us uncomfortable. These are some of the personal sources of our inner unease and discontent.

What all this means in practical terms is that we must set limits to permissiveness and to "social" explanations of personal misconduct. Further, we must all assume some responsibility for the horrors of our world today, from Bangladesh, Vietnam, Watergate, to the famine in India. We have to accept the fact that we are all part of the brotherhood of man, whether we like it or not. We can and must do more to help our fellow man. Otherwise, we will become not just a sick society, but worse—a morally corrupt one.

It is against this background that *The Exorcist* is a menace to the mental health of our community. It should be X-rated. (I have seen parents taking four- and five-year-old children to showings of the picture!) In these unstable times, when the President of the United States shows more concern for Lt. Calley than for the students murdered at Kent State, when we have peace with dishonor in Vietnam, and also Watergate, *The Exorcist* pours acid on our already corroded values and ideals. In the days when we all had more trust in our government, our friends, and ourselves, *The Exorcist* would have been a bad joke. Today it is a danger.

DISCUSSION QUESTIONS

1. The author begins with a declaration that *"The Exorcist* is a menace." Considering the entire essay, try to establish who is menaced by the movie.

2. It is asserted that many viewers will suffer severe psychological reactions from seeing the picture. On what evidence does the author base this induced conclusion? How large and how representative is his sample?

3. What evidence supports the claim that "the film degrades the medical profession and psychiatry."

4. In three separate places, the author describes types of people who saw the film and their reactions. What are his conclusions? How do they accord?

5. What is the author's objection to the idea of demonic possession? Trace the line of argument which allows him to relate *The Exorcist* to Kent State, Vietnam, Watergate, etc.

6. How reasonable is Freud's explanation of the psychological basis of possession and exorcism? How helpful is the author's analysis of *The Exorcist* aiming to support that explanation?

7. Has the author any recommendation other than that the film "should be X-rated"? How would an X-rating help?

Big Mama!

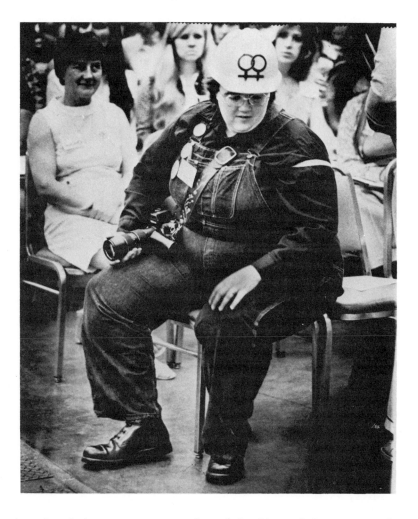

Armed with her camera, a member of the National Organization for Women appears at their seventh annual convention, Houston, Texas. (AP Wirephoto)

Reprinted from the Mobile *Press-Register*, May 26, 1974. *Wide World Photos*

DISCUSSION QUESTIONS

1. In what way can this photograph be considered an example of inductive argument?

2. What is the implicit conclusion?

3. Discuss the sample as known, sufficient, and representative.

4. What inferences might be drawn from the picture of the women in the background? Would any conclusion be justified?

5. Would the photograph be equally credible if the central figure appeared at a National Education Association convention? At a DAR convention?

3

Deduction

Socrates is mortal.
You haven't registered; so you can't vote.
Gerald Ford prefers blondes.
Scott Daniel will make a fine husband.
Socrates is a cat.

Deduction is the opposite of induction. Whereas induction moves from specific facts to a general conclusion, deduction moves from a general statement to a specific application. Because there are many kinds of deduction—some quite complicated—this discussion aims to be no more than a useful oversimplification.

The vehicle of deduction is the *syllogism*. This is an argument that takes two existing truths and puts them together to produce a new truth. Here is the classical example:

MAJOR PREMISE: All men are mortal.
MINOR PREMISE: Socrates is a man.
CONCLUSION: Socrates is mortal.

In everyday affairs, one meets many examples of deductive thinking. Often, however, the syllogism is abbreviated, with one of the parts implied rather than stated:

You haven't registered; so you can't vote.
(IMPLICIT MAJOR PREMISE: Anyone who does not register cannot vote.)

No man lives forever. Even old Bob Richards will die someday. (IMPLICIT MINOR PREMISE: Bob Richards is a man.)

Anyone can make a mistake. After all, Nick is only human. (IMPLICIT CONCLUSION: Nick can make a mistake.)

Many informal arguments can easily be resolved into syllogistic form. One does this to more systematically judge their reliability.

A deductive argument is considered reliable if it fulfills three

49

conditions: (1) Its premises must be true. (2) Its terms must be unambiguous. (3) Its syllogistic form must be valid. These requirements will be considered in turn.

First, the premises must be true. Because the major premise of a syllogism is derived by induction (i.e., it is a general statement drawn from specific facts), one can judge its reliability by asking if the facts which produced it are known to be sufficient and representative. Here is a vulnerable example:

> Gentlemen prefer blondes.
> Gerald Ford is a gentleman.
> Gerald Ford prefers blondes.

The syllogism reaches an unreliable conclusion because the major premise is doubtful. The generalization exists only as a clichéd platitude (and as a title by Anita Loos); it is induced from no known sample. Political spokesmen regularly use dubious major premises (e.g., a war hero would make a good president; a divorced man would make a poor one; etc.) to produce a desired conclusion.

Second, the terms of the argument must be unambiguous. If definitions change within a syllogism, arguments can be amusingly fallacious (e.g., all cats chase mice; my wife is a cat . . .); but some can be misleading. The advertisement "See *Travels with My Aunt*—the Academy Award winning movie" is based on this syllogism:

> The Academy Award winning movie is worth seeing.
> *Travels with My Aunt* is this year's Academy Award winning movie.
> *Travels with My Aunt* is worth seeing.

Here the term "Academy Award winning movie" is ambiguous. In the major premise, it refers to the movie chosen the best of the year; in the minor premise, to a movie winning one of the many minor awards given annually. *Travels with My Aunt* won the award for "costume design."

Third, a reliable syllogism must have a valid form. This requirement introduces a complex area because there are many types of syllogisms, each with its own test for validity. Commonly, "valid form" means that the general subject or condition of the major premise must appear in the minor premise as well. It is easy to see how this argument is false:

All thieves have ears.
All Presbyterians have ears.
All Presbyterians are thieves.

But what makes the argument unreliable syllogistically is that the major term "thieves" does not appear in the minor premise. A major premise about "all thieves" can only lead to a conclusion about thieves. Similarly, the premises, "If Carter loses his job, his wife will leave him" and "Carter does not lose his job," produce no necessary conclusion; the major condition "lose his job" does not occur in the minor premise.

When an invalid syllogism appears as argument, it usually maintains that features with one quality in common have a kind of identity. Such argument is not uncommon:

The father of Miss Wells's baby has blood type O.
Charles Harwell has blood type O.
Therefore . . .

The American Communist party opposes loyalty oaths.
Gene Knepprath opposes loyalty oaths.
Therefore . . .

Abraham Lincoln was a much-attacked president.
Richard Nixon was a much-attacked president.
Therefore . . .

Because the major term does not occur in both premises, the conclusions are no more valid than the argument that all Presbyterians are thieves.

These three tests, then, permit one to judge the reliability of a deductive argument.

It should be added that because any syllogism begins with an induced major premise, certain arguments can be analyzed as either induction or deduction. Here is an example: "Scott Daniel doesn't drink or smoke; he'll make some girl a fine husband." One can read this as a syllogism and attack the implicit major premise "Anyone who does not drink or smoke will make a fine husband." Or he can treat it as induction and argue that the sample (the fact that Scott Daniel does not drink or smoke) is insufficient to sustain a conclusion about his prospects as a husband. With such arguments, it is best not to quibble over terms; either approach is satisfactory.

And, having weighed a syllogism, it is best to judge it, not as true or false, but as reliable or unreliable. An unreliable conclusion, it must be remembered, may nevertheless be true. From the doubtful major premise ("Anyone who does not drink or smoke . . ."), one cannot reasonably deduce that Scott Daniel will make a fine husband. But he might, in fact, make a very fine husband. In rejecting the syllogism as unreliable, one simply says that the fact is not proven by *this* argument.

One can recognize the distinction between truth and a reasonable conclusion by recalling a passage from Ionesco's *Rhinoceros*. The Logician argues, "All cats die. Socrates is dead. Therefore Socrates is a cat." And his student responds, "That's true. I've got a cat named Socrates."

HOW RELIABLE ARE THESE EXAMPLES OF DEDUCTION?

1. Of course Polly Patterson is a poor driver. She's a woman, isn't she?

2. Some years ago, *Human Events* attacked the physical fitness program proposed by President Kennedy by warning that both Hitler and Mussolini fostered comparable programs.

3. How can you say you don't believe in miracles? The sunrise that occurs every day is a miracle.

4. Professor Reston's new book on marriage should be pretty good. After all, he's been married four times.

5. All lemons are yellow. My girl friend's brother is a lemon. My girl friend's brother is yellow.

6. I'm from ~~Milwaukee~~ LA Crosse and I ought to know. Blatz is ~~Milwaukee~~'s LACrosse finest beer.

7. "Well I used to be bad when I was a kid, but ever since then I have gone straight, as I can prove by my record—thirty-three arrests and no convictions."—Big Jule, *Guys and Dolls*

8. Both Catholics and Protestants are Christians. No one can be both Catholic and Protestant. Therefore, no one can be a Christian.

9. I love you; therefore I am a lover. All the world loves a lover. You are all the world to me. Therefore, you love me.

Intelligent Life Elsewhere

EDWARD U. CONDON

Whether there is intelligent life elsewhere (ILE) in the Universe is a question that has received a great deal of serious speculative attention in recent years. A good popular review of thinking on the subject is *We Are Not Alone* by Walter Sullivan (1964). More advanced discussions are *Interstellar Communication,* a collection of papers edited by A. G. W. Cameron (1963), and *Intelligent Life in the Universe* (Shklovskii and Sagan, 1966). Thus far we have no observational evidence whatever on the question, so therefore it remains open. A early unpublished discussion is a letter of 13 December 1948 of J. E. Lipp to Gen. Donald Putt (Appendix D). This letter is Appendix D of the Project Sign report dated February 1949 from Air Materiel Command Headquarters No. F-TR-2274-IA.

The ILE question has some relation to the ETH [Extra-terrestrial Hypothesis] or ETA [Extra-terrestrial Actuality] for UFOs as discussed in the preceding section. Clearly, if ETH is true, then ILE must also be true because some UFOs have then to come from some unearthly civilization. Conversely, if we could know conclusively that ILE does not exist, then ETH could not be true. But even if ILE exists, it does not follow that the ETH is true.

For it could be that the ILE, though existent, might not have reached a stage of development in which the beings have the technical capacity or the desire to visit the Earth's surface. Much speculative writing assumes implicitly that intelligent life progresses steadily both in intellectual and in its technological development. Life began on Earth more than a billion years ago, whereas the known geological age of the Earth is some five billion years, so that life in any form has only existed for the most recent one-fifth of the Earth's life as a solid ball orbiting the Sun. Man as an intelligent being has only lived on Earth for some 5000 years, or about one-millionth of the Earth's age. Technological development is even more recent. Moreover the greater part of what we think of as advanced technology has only been developed in the last 100 years. Even today we do not yet have a technology capable of putting

Reprinted from *Scientific Study of Unidentified Flying Objects* (New York: Bantam Books, 1968), pp. 26–33.

men on other planets of the solar system. Travel of men over interstellar distances in the foreseeable future seems now to be quite
out of the question. (Purcell, 1960; Markowitz, 1967.)

The dimensions of the universe are hard for the mind of man to
conceive. A light-year is the distance light travels in one year of
31.56 million seconds, at the rate of 186,000 miles per second, that
is, a distance of 5.88 million million miles. The nearest known star
is at a distance of 4.2 light-years.

Fifteen stars are known to be within 11.5 light-years of the Sun.
Our own galaxy, the Milky Way, is a vast flattened distribution of
some 10^{11} stars about 80,000 light-years in diameter, with the Sun
located about 26,000 light-years from the center. To gain a little
perspective on the meaning of such distances relative to human affairs, we may observe that the news of Christ's life on Earth could
not yet have reached as much as a tenth of the distance from the
Earth to the center of our galaxy.

Other galaxies are inconceivably remote. The faintest observable
galaxies are at a distance of some two billion light-years. There are
some 100 million such galaxies within that distance, the average
distance between galaxies being some eight million light-years.

Authors of UFO fantasy literature casually set all of the laws of
physics aside in order to try to evade this conclusion, but serious
consideration of their ideas hardly belongs in a report on the scientific study of UFOs.

Even assuming that difficulties of this sort could be overcome,
we have no right to assume that in life communities everywhere
there is a steady evolution in the directions of both greater intelligence and greater technological competence. Human beings
now know enough to destroy all life on Earth, and they may lack
the intelligence to work out social controls to keep themselves
from doing so. If other civilizations have the same limitation then
it might be that they develop to the point where they destroy themselves utterly before they have developed the technology needed to
enable them to make long space voyages.

Another possibility is that the growth of intelligence precedes
the growth of technology in such a way that by the time a society
would be technically capable of interstellar space travel, it would
have reached a level of intelligence at which it had not the slightest interest in interstellar travel. We must not assume that we are
capable of imagining now the scope and extent of future technological development of our own or any other civilization, and so we
must guard against assuming that we have any capacity to imag-

ine what a more advanced society would regard as intelligent conduct.

In addition to the great distances involved, and the difficulties which they present to interstellar space travel, there is still another problem: If we assume that civilizations annihilate themselves in such a way that their effective intelligent life span is less than, say, 100,000 years, then such a short time span also works against the likelihood of successful interstellar communication. The different civilizations would probably reach the culmination of their development at different epochs in cosmic history. Moreover, according to present views, stars are being formed constantly by the condensation of interstellar dust and gases. They exist for perhaps 10 billion years, of which a civilization lasting 100,000 years is only 1/100,000 of the life span of the star. It follows that there is an extremely small likelihood that two nearby civilizations would be in a state of high development at the same epoch.

Astronomers now generally agree that a fairly large number of all main-sequence stars are probably accompanied by planets at the right distance from their Sun to provide for habitable conditions for life as we know it. That is, where stars are, there are probably habitable planets. This belief favors the possibility of interstellar communication, but it must be remembered that even this view is entirely speculation: we are quite unable directly to observe any planets associated with stars other than the Sun.

In view of the foregoing, we consider that it is safe to assume that no ILE outside of our solar system has any possibility of visiting Earth in the next 10,000 years.

This conclusion does not rule out the possibility of the existence of ILE, as contrasted with the ability of such civilizations to visit Earth. It is estimated that 10^{21} stars can be seen using the 200-inch Hale telescope on Mount Palomar. Astronomers surmise that possibly as few as one in a million or as many as one in ten of these have a planet in which physical and chemical conditions are such as to make them habitable by life based on the same kind of biochemistry as the life we know on Earth. Even if the lower figure is taken, this would mean there are 10^{15} stars in the visible universe which have planets suitable for an abode of life. In our own galaxy there are 10^{11} stars, so perhaps as many as 10^8 have habitable planets in orbit around them.

Biologists feel confident that wherever physical and chemical conditions are right, life will actually emerge. In short, astronomers tell us that there are a vast number of stars in the universe accompanied by planets where the physical and chemical conditions are suitable, and biologists tell us that habitable places are sure to become inhabited. (Rush, 1957.)

An important advance was made when Stanley L. Miller (1955) showed experimentally that electrical discharges such as those in natural lightning when passed through a mixture of methane and ammonia, such as may have been present in the Earth's primitive atmosphere, will initiate chemical reactions which yield various amino acids. These are the raw materials from which are constructed the proteins that are essential to life. Miller's work has been followed up and extended by many others, particularly P. H. Abelson of the Carnegie Institution of Washington.

The story is by no means fully worked out. The evidence in hand seems to convince biochemists that natural processes, such as lightning, or the absorption of solar ultraviolet light, could generate the necessary starting materials from which life could evolve. On this basis they generally hold the belief that where conditions make it possible that life could appear, there life actually will appear.

It is regarded by scientists today as essentially certain that ILE exists, but with essentially no possibility of contact between the communities on planets associated with different stars. We therefore conclude that there is no relation between ILE at other solar systems and the UFO phenomenon as observed on Earth.

There remains the question of ILE within our solar system. Here only the planets Venus and Mars need be given consideration as possible abodes of life.

Mercury, the planet nearest the Sun, is certainly too hot to support life. The side of Mercury that is turned toward the Sun has an average temperature of 660° F. Since the orbit is rather eccentric this temperature becomes as high as 770° F, hot enough to melt lead, when Mercury is closest to the Sun. The opposite side is extremely cold, its temperature not being known.[1] Gravity on Mercury is about one-fourth that on Earth. This fact combined with the high temperature makes it certain that Mercury has no atmosphere, which is consistent with observational data on this point. It is quite impossible that life as found on Earth could exist on Mercury.

Jupiter, Saturn, Uranus, Neptune and Pluto are so far from the Sun that they are too cold for life to exist there.

Although it has long been thought that Venus might provide a

[1] Mercury rotates in 59 days and the orbital period is 88 days, so there is a slow relative rotation.

suitable abode for life, it is now known that the surface of Venus is also too hot for advanced forms of life, although it is possible that some primitive forms may exist. Some uncertainty and controversy exists about the interpretation of observations of Venus because the planet is always enveloped in dense clouds so that the solid surface is never seen. The absorption spectrum of sunlight coming from Venus indicates that the principal constituent of the atmosphere is carbon dioxide. There is no evidence of oxygen or water vapor. With so little oxygen in the atmosphere there could not be animal life there resembling that on Earth.

Although it is safe to conclude that there is no intelligent life on Venus, the contrary idea is held quite tenaciously by certain groups in America. There are small religious groups who maintain that Jesus Christ now sojourns on Venus, and that some of their members have travelled there by flying saucers supplied by the Venusians and have been greatly refreshed spiritually by visiting Him. There is no observational evidence in support of this teaching.

religious group says there is life on Venus

In the fantasy literature of believers in ETH, some attention is given to a purely hypothetical planet named Clarion. Not only is there no direct evidence for its existence, but there is conclusive indirect evidence for its nonexistence. Those UFO viewers who try not to be totally inconsistent with scientific findings, recognizing that Venus and Mars are unsuitable as abodes of life, have invented Clarion to meet the need for a home for the visitors who they believe come on some UFOs.

Clarion, made up planet

The postulate that Clarion moves in an orbit exactly like that of the Earth around the Sun, but with the orbit rotated through half a revolution in its plane so that the two orbits have the same line of apsides, but with Clarion's perihelion in the same direction from the Sun as the Earth's aphelion. The two planets, Earth and Clarion, are postulated to move in their orbits in such a way that they are always opposite each other, so that the line Earth-Sun-Clarion is a straight line. Thus persons on Earth would never see Clarion because it is permanently eclipsed by the Sun.

If the two orbits were exactly circular, the two planets would move along their common orbit at the same speed and so would remain exactly opposite each other. But even if the orbits are elliptical, so that the speed in the orbit is variable, the two planets would vary in speed during the year in just such a way as always to remain opposite each other and thus continue to be permanently eclipsed.

However, this tidy arrangement would not occur in actuality

because the motion of each of these two planets would be perturbed by the gravitational attractions between them and the other planets of the solar system, principally Venus and Mars. It is a quite complicated and difficult problem to calculate the way in which these perturbations would affect the motion of Earth and Clarion.

At the request of the Colorado project, Dr. R. L. Duncombe, director of the Nautical Almanac office at U.S. Naval Observatory in Washington, D. C., kindly arranged to calculate the effect of the introduction of the hypothetical planet Clarion into the solar system. The exact result depends to some extent on the location of the Earth-Sun-Clarion line relative to the line of apsides and the computations were carried out merely for one case.

These calculations show that the effect of the perturbations would be to make Clarion become visible from Earth beyond the Sun's limb after about thirty years. In other words, Clarion would long since have become visible from Earth if many years ago it were started out in such a special way as has been postulated.

The computations revealed further that if Clarion were there it would reveal its presence indirectly in a much shorter time. Its attraction on Venus would cause Venus to move in a different way than if Clarion were not there. Calculation shows that Venus would pull away from its otherwise correct motion by about 1″ of arc in about three months time. Venus is routinely kept under observation to this accuracy, and therefore if Clarion were there it would reveal its presence by its effect on the motion of Venus. No such effect is observed, that is, the motion of Venus as actually observed is accurately in accord with the absence of Clarion, so therefore we may safely conclude that Clarion is nonexistent.[2]

In his letter of transmittal Dr. Duncombe comments "I feel this is definite proof that the presence of such a body could not remain undetected for long. However, I am afraid it will not change the minds of those people who believe in the existence of Clarion."

We first heard about Clarion from a lady who is prominent in American political life who was intrigued with the idea that this is where UFOs come from. When the results of the Naval Observatory computations were told to her she exclaimed, "That's what I don't like about computers! They are always dealing death blows to our fondest notions!"

Mars has long been considered as a possible abode of life in the

[2] These calculations assume Clarion's mass roughly equal to that of the Earth.

solar system. There is still no direct evidence that life exists there, but the question is being actively studied in the space research programs of both the United States and Soviet Russia, so it may well be clarified within the coming decade.

At present all indications are that Mars could not be the habitation of an advanced civilization capable of sending spacecraft to visit the Earth. Conditions for life there are so harsh that it is generally believed that at best Mars could only support the simpler forms of plant life.

An excellent recent survey of the rapidly increasing knowledge of Mars is *Handbook of the Physical Properties of the Planet Mars* compiled by C. M. Michaux (NASA publication SP-3030, 1967). A brief discussion of American research programs for study of life on Mars is given in *Biology and Exploration of Mars,* a 19-page pamphlet prepared by the Space Science Board of the National Academy of Sciences, published in April 1965.

The orbit of Mars is considerably more eccentric than that of the Earth. Consequently the distance of Mars from the Sun varies from 128 to 155 million miles during the year of 687 days. The synodic period, or mean time between successive oppositions, is 800 days.

The most favorable time for observation of Mars is at opposition, when Mars is opposite the Sun from Earth. These distances of closest approach of Mars and Earth vary from 35 to 60 million miles. The most recent favorable time of closest approach was the opposition of 10 September 1956, and the next favorable opposition will be that of 10 August 1971. At that time undoubtedly great efforts will be made to study Mars in the space programs of the U.S.S.R. and the United States.

Some of the UFO literature has contended that a larger than usual number of UFO reports occur at the times of Martian oppositions. The contention is that this indicates that some UFOs come from Mars at these particularly favorable times. The claimed correlation is quite unfounded; the idea is not supported by observational data. (Vallee and Vallee, 1966, p. 138.)

Mars is much smaller than Earth, having a diameter of 4200 miles, in comparison with 8000 miles. Mars' mass is about one-tenth the Earth's, and gravity at Mars' surface is about 0.38 that of Earth. The Martian escape velocity is 3.1 mile/sec.

At the favorable opposition of 1877, G. V. Schiaparelli, an Italian astronomer, observed and mapped some surface marking on Mars which he called "canali," meaning "channels" in Italian. The word was mistranslated as "canals" in English and the idea was put forward, particularly vigorously by Percival Lowell, founder of the Lowell Observatory of Flagstaff, Arizona, that the canals on Mars were evidence of a gigantic planetary irrigation scheme, developed by the supposed inhabitants of Mars (Lowell, 1908). These markings have been the subject of a great deal of study since their discovery. Astronomers generally now reject the idea that they afford any kind of indication that Mars is inhabited by intelligent beings.

Mars has two moons named Phobos and Deimos. These are exceedingly small, Phobos being estimated at ten miles in diameter and Deimos at five miles, based on their brightness, assuming the reflecting power of their material to be the same as that of the planet. The periods are $7^h 39^m$ for Phobos and $30^h 18^m$ for Deimos. They were discovered in August 1877 by Asaph Hall using the then new 26-inch refractor of the U. S. Naval Observatory in Washington. An unsuccessful search for moons of Mars was made with a 48-inch mirror during the opposition of 1862.

I. S. Shklovskii (1959) published a sensational suggestion in a Moscow newspaper that these moons were really artificial satellites which had been put up by supposed inhabitants of Mars as a place of refuge when the supposed oceans of several million years ago began to dry up (Sullivan, 1966, p. 169). There is no observational evidence to support this idea. Continuing the same line of speculation Salisbury (1962), after pointing out that the satellites were looked for in 1862 but not found until 1877, then asks, "Should we attribute the failure of 1862 to imperfections in existing telescopes, or may we imagine that the satellites were launched between 1862 and 1877?" This is a slender reed indeed with which to prop up so sensational an inference, and we reject it.

DISCUSSION QUESTIONS

1. "Thus far we have no observational evidence whatever on the question [of ILE], so therefore it remains open." Is an open question one for which one answer is just as likely as another?

2. For ETH to be true, the author submits, there must be not only ILE, but ILE which has both "the technical capacity [and] the desire to visit the Earth's surface." Trace and evaluate the syllogism built on this major premise.

3. "In short, astronomers tell us that there are a vast number of stars in the universe accompanied by planets where physical and chemical conditions are suitable, and biologists tell us that habitable places are sure to become inhabited." Reconstruct this as a valid syllogism. Discuss the reliability of the inductive evidence supporting the major and minor premises.

4. The discussion of ILE within our solar system is based on the implicit major premise: Where physical and chemical conditions are right, advanced forms of life may have developed. Trace the deductive argument.

5. Arrange the argument affirming Clarion in syllogistic form. Evaluate the major premise.

6. Arrange the argument denying Clarion in syllogistic form. Evaluate the minor premise.

7. How does the author attack this deduction:
   If a larger than usual number of UFO reports occurs at the times of Martian oppositions, it is likely that UFO's come from Mars.
   A larger than usual number of UFO reports do occur at the times of Martian oppositions.
   Therefore, it is likely that UFO's come from Mars.

8. In an essay which is generally formal and scholarly in tone, why does the author mention the groups who believe that Christ now lives on Venus, the lady who introduced the subject of Clarion, and Shklovskii's and Salisbury's sensational thesis concerning the satellites of Mars?

Easter Island—
Land of the Bird Men

ERICH VON DÄNIKEN

The first European seafarers who landed on Easter Island at the beginning of the eighteenth century could scarcely believe their eyes. On this little plot of earth, 2350 miles from the coast of Chile, they saw hundreds of colossal statues lying scattered about all over the island. Whole mountain massifs had been transformed, steel-hard volcanic rock had been cut through like butter, and 10,000 tons of massive rocks lay in places where they could not have been dressed. Hundreds of gigantic statues, some of which are between 33 and 66 feet high and weigh as much as 50 tons, still stare challengingly at the visitor today—like robots which seem to be waiting solely to be set in motion again. Originally these colossuses also wore hats; but even the hats do not exactly help to explain the puzzling origin of the statues. The stone for the hats, which weighed more than ten tons apiece, was found at a different site from that used for the bodies, and in addition the hats had to be hoisted high in the air.

Wooden tablets, covered with strange hieroglyphs, were also found on some of the statues in those days. But today it is impossible to find more than ten fragments of those tablets in all the museums in the world, and none of the inscriptions on those still extant has yet been deciphered.

Thor Heyerdahl's investigations of these mysterious giants produced three clearly distinguishable cultural periods, and the oldest of the three seems to have been the most perfect. Heyerdahl dates some charcoal remains that he found to about A.D. 400. It has not been proved whether the fireplaces and remains of bones had any connection with the stone colossuses. Heyerdahl discovered hundreds of unfinished statues near rock faces and on the edges of craters; thousands of stone implements, simple stone axes, lay around as if the work had been abandoned quite suddenly.

Easter Island lies far away from any continent or civilization. The islanders are more familiar with the moon and the stars than any other country. No trees grow on the island, which is a tiny

Reprinted from *Chariot of the Gods?* (New York: Bantam Books, 1970), pp. 90–96.

speck of volcanic stone. The usual explanation, that the stone giants were moved to their present sites on wooden rollers, is not feasible in this case, either. In addition, the island can scarcely have provided food for more than 2000 inhabitants. (A few hundred natives live on Easter Island today.) A shipping trade, which brought food and clothing to the island for the stonemasons, is hardly credible in antiquity. Then who cut the statues out of the rock, who carved them and transported them to their sites? How were they moved across country for miles without rollers? How were they dressed, polished, and erected? How were the hats, the stone for which came from a different quarry from that of the statues, put in place?

Even if people with lively imaginations have tried to picture the Egyptian pyramids being built by a vast army of workers using the "heave-ho" method, a similar method would have been impossible on Easter Island for lack of manpower. Even 2000 men, working day and night, would not be nearly enough to carve these colossal figures out of the steel-hard volcanic stone with rudimentary tools—and at least a part of the population must have tilled the barren fields, gone fishing, woven cloth, and made ropes. No, 2000 men alone could not have made the gigantic statues. And a larger population is inconceivable on Easter Island. Then who did do the work? And how did they manage it? And why do the statues stand around the edge of the island and not in the interior? What cult did they serve?

Unfortunately, the first European missionaries on this tiny patch of earth helped to ensure that the island's dark ages stayed dark. They burned the tablets with hieroglyphic characters; they prohibited the ancient cults of the gods and did away with every kind of tradition. Yet thoroughly as the pious gentlemen went to work, they could not prevent the natives from calling their island the Land of the Bird Men, as they still do today. An orally transmitted legend tells us that flying men landed and lighted fires in ancient times. The legend is confirmed by sculptures of flying creatures with big, staring eyes.

Connections between Easter Island and Tiahuanaco automatically force themselves upon us. There as here, we find stone giants belonging to the same style. The haughty faces with their stoic expressions suit the statues—here as there. When Francisco Pizarro questioned the Incas about Tiahuanaco in 1532, they told him that no man had ever seen the city save in ruins, for Tiahuanaco had been built in the night of mankind. Traditions call Easter

Island the "navel of the world." It is more than 3125 miles from Tiahuanaco to Easter Island. How can one culture possibly have inspired the other?

Perhaps pre-Inca mythology can give us a hint here. In it the old god of creation, Viracocha, was an ancient and elemental divinity. According to tradition Viracocha created the world when it was still dark and had no sun; he sculpted a race of giants from stone, and when they displeased him, he sank them in a deep flood. Then he caused the sun and the moon to rise above Lake Titicaca, so that there was light on earth. Yes, and then—read this closely—he shaped clay figures of men and animals at Tiahuanaco and breathed life into them. Afterward, he instructed these living creatures of his own creation in language, customs, and arts, and finally flew some of them to different continents which they were supposed to inhabit thenceforth. After this task the god Viracocha and two assistants traveled to many countries to check how his instructions were being followed and what results they had had. Dressed as an old man, Viracocha wandered over the Andes and along the coast, and often he was given a poor reception. Once, at Cacha, he was so annoyed by his welcome that in a fury he set fire to a cliff which began to burn up the whole country. Then the ungrateful people asked his forgiveness, whereupon he extinguished the flames with a single gesture. Viracocha traveled on, giving instructions and advice, and many temples were erected to him as a result. Finally he said good-bye in the coastal province of Manta and disappeared over the ocean, riding on the waves, but he said he intended to come back.

The Spanish conquistadors who conquered South and Central America came up against the sagas of Viracocha everywhere. Never before had they heard of gigantic white men who came from somewhere in the sky. Full of astonishment, they learned about a race of sons of the sun who instructed mankind in all kinds of arts and disappeared again. And in all the legends that the Spaniards heard, there was an assurance that the sons of the sun would return.

Although the American continent is the home of ancient cultures, our accurate knowledge of America is barely 1000 years old. It is an absolute mystery to us why the Incas cultivated cotton in Peru in 3000 B.C., although they did not know or possess the loom. The Mayas built roads but did not use the wheel, although they knew about it. The fantastic five-strand necklace of green jade in the burial pyramid of Tikal in Guatemala is a miracle. A miracle because the jade comes from China. The sculptures of the Olmecs are incredible. With their beautifully helmeted giant skulls, they can be admired only on the sites where they were found, for they will never be on show in a museum. No bridge in the country could stand their weight. We can move smaller "monoliths" weighing up to fifty tons with our modern lifting appliances and loaders, but when it comes to hundred-tonners like these our technology breaks down. But our ancestors could transport and dress them. How?

It even seems as if the ancient peoples took a special pleasure in juggling with stone giants over hill and dale. The Egyptians fetched their obelisk from Aswan, the architects of Stonehenge brought their stone blocks from southwest Wales and Marlborough, the stonemasons of Easter Island took their ready-made monster statues from a distant quarry to their present sites, and no one can say where some of the monoliths at Tiahuanaco come from. Our remote ancestors must have been strange people; they liked making things difficult for themselves and always built their statues in the most impossible places. Was it just because they liked a hard life?

I refuse to think that the artists of our great past were as stupid as that. They could just as easily have erected their statues and temples in the immediate vicinity of the quarries if an old tradition had not laid down where their works ought to be sited. I am convinced that the Inca fortress of Sacsahuamán was not built above Cuzco by chance, but rather because a tradition indicated the place as a holy spot. I am also convinced that in all the places where the most ancient monumental buildings of mankind were found the most interesting and important relics of our past lie still untouched in the ground, relics, moreover, which could be of tremendous importance for the further development of present-day space travel.

The unknown space travelers who visited our planet many thousands of years ago can hardly have been less farsighted than we think we are today. They were convinced that one day man would make the move out into the universe on his own initiative, using his own skills.

It is a well-known historical fact that the intelligences of our planet have constantly sought for kindred spirits, for life, for corresponding intelligences in the cosmos.

Present-day antennae and transmitters have broadcast the first radio impulses to unknown intelligences. When we shall receive an answer—in ten, fifteen, or a hundred years—we do not know. We do not even know which star we should beam our message at, because we have no idea which planet should interest us most. Where do our signals reach unknown intelligences similar to human beings? We do not know. Yet there is much to support the belief that the information needed to reach our goal is deposited in our earth for us. We are trying hard to neutralize the force of gravity; we are experimenting with elementary particles and antimatter. Are we also doing enough to find the data which are hidden in our earth, so that we can at last ascertain our original home?

If we take things literally, much that was once fitted into the mosaic of our past with great difficulty becomes quite plausible: not only the relevant clues in ancient texts but also the "hard facts" which offer themselves to our critical gaze all over the globe. Lastly, we have our reason to think with.

So it will be man's ultimate insight to realize that his justification for existence to date and all his struggles to advance really consisted in learning from the past in order to make himself ready for contact with the existence in space. Once that happens, the shrewdest, most die-hard individualist must see that the whole human task consists in colonizing the universe and that man's whole spiritual duty lies in perpetuating all his efforts and practical experience. Then the promise of the "gods" that peace will come on earth and that the way to heaven is open can come true.

As soon as the available authorities, powers, and intellects are devoted to space research, the results will make the absurdity of terrestrial wars abundantly clear. When men of all races, peoples, and nations unite in the supranational task of making journeys to distant planets technically feasible, the earth with all its mini-problems will fall back into its right relation with the cosmic processes.

Occultists can put out their lamps, alchemists destroy their crucibles, secret brotherhoods take off their cowls. It will no longer be possible to offer man the nonsense that has been purveyed to him so brilliantly for thousands of years. Once the universe opens its doors, we shall attain a better future.

I base the reasons for my skepticism about the interpretation of our remote past on the knowledge that is available today. If I admit to being a skeptic, I mean the word in the sense in which Thomas Mann used it in a lecture in the twenties: "The positive thing about the skeptic is that he considers everything possible!"

DISCUSSION QUESTIONS

1. The central argument of this essay is deductive. Analyze these syllogisms:

   The Easter Island statues could not have been carved, moved, and erected by mere humans.
   The Easter Island statues were carved, moved, and erected.
   The Easter Island statues were carved, moved, and erected by superhuman agents.

   The Easter Island statues were carved, moved, and erected by superhuman agents.
   Space travelers who could visit Earth must be superhuman agents.
   The Easter Island statues were carved, moved, and erected by space travelers who visited Earth.

2. What implication does the author intend to convey with these lines:

   "None of the inscriptions on those[wooden tablets] still extant have yet been deciphered."

   "Thousands of stone implements, simple stone axes, lay around as if the work had been abandoned quite suddenly."

   "They could not prevent the natives from calling their island the Land of the Bird Men, as they still do today."

   "And why do the statues stand around the edge of the island and not in the interior? What cult did they serve?"

   What evidence supports these implications?

3. On what evidence does the author maintain that the island could not have more than 2000 inhabitants?

4. What is his purpose in telling the pre-Incan myth of Viracocha? Is that story significantly different from stories in the classical and Christian traditions?

5. Consider the transition leading to the author's first mention of "unknown space travelers." How does he approach the subject?

6. How does the essay relate to these statements taken from the *Encyclopaedia Britannica* and from Father Sebastian Englert's *Island at the Center of the World* (1970)?

"Easter Island . . . . is about 11 mi. long and 15 mi. wide."

"The writing engraved on wooden tablets . . . . takes the form of symbols, strongly stylized, representing human beings, birds, fish, crustaceans, plants, ceremonial articles, and designs of a purely geometrical character."

"The statues were cut from compressed volcanic ash, a soft and easily worked stone."

"The usual height of the images on the *ahu* was from 12 to 20 feet."

"A native account states that they were dragged into position (presumably with ropes, the native hemp and hibiscus fibre furnishing adequate materials) and that round pebbles were placed underneath to serve as rollers. Seaweed may also have been used to minimize friction with the ground."

"The statues probably were erected on the *ahu* by being hauled up an incline made of earth or stones and then gradually up-ended into position by the withdrawing of the supporting material from under their bases."—*Britannica*

"Judging by the many examples abandoned along roads, the statues appear to have been moved in a prone position and head first."

"The topknots were carved in much the same manner as the statues, by excavating a channel around them and breaking them loose. Being cylindrical they could be rolled relatively easily to their *ahu* locations."

"Its purpose [that of carving large statues] appears to have been to commemorate illustrious ancestors of the various kin-groups, whose mana was thought to bring benefit to the communities."

"[The population of Easter Island] could never have exceeded 3000 or 4000."—Englert

Neither source mentions the island as the "Land of the Bird Men."

Why I Favor Liberalized Abortion

ALAN F. GUTTMACHER, M.D.

A straggly line of young people bearing placards, some also with babies and children, partially blocked the entrance to the Peter Bent Brigham Hospital in Boston as I went there to speak not long ago. One youth wore a white surgeon's gown spattered with red paint, and carried a sign that cried "Murderer"; across his chest was the identification, "Dr. Guttmacher."

My reaction was one of sadness. For much of my life, I have been subjected to similar denunciation. Until recent years, its focus was my stand in favor of birth control. Now that contraception is applauded, and used by virtually all Americans, I am condemned for my liberal stand on abortion.

The ironic fact is that those who oppose and those who favor legalization of abortion share a common goal—the elimination of *all* abortions. The difference is that while anti-abortionists believe this can be accomplished by tough, punitive statutes, the abortion-law reformers point to evidence showing that these laws have never worked in the past and never will. In the years preceding liberalization of abortion laws in this country, for example, a conservative estimate is that at least one million illegal operations were being performed annually. Those who favor liberalization want to substitute safe abortion for the dangerous, clandestine variety, until contraception is so widely practiced that unwanted pregnancy—and therefore the need for abortion—disappears.

HISTORIC DECISION

The debate over abortion has been raging for years but, as the political reality of liberalization has come into sharper focus, the dispute has grown more intense. Whenever a bill is introduced to modify an abortion statute, state legislators are assaulted with arguments and pressures from each side. The basic anti-abortion argument is that respect for life demands protection of the fetus.[1]

Reprinted from *The Reader's Digest,* November 1973, pp. 143–147.

[1] My own speculations lead me to conclude that life begins only after the birth of a fetus sufficiently mature to survive outside its mother's body. Until then, there is only potential life—just as there is even before fertilization.

The basic pro-abortion argument is that the decision to remain pregnant is a highly personal one, to be made only by the woman involved and with full freedom of choice. The proabortionists respect life, too, but they argue that every child should be given the invaluable birthright of being born *wanted*.

Beginning in 1967, 12 states partially, and four almost fully, liberalized their abortion laws. Meanwhile, in order to decide the issue on a national level, the Supreme Court agreed to determine the constitutionality of the abortion laws of two states, Texas and Georgia. The Texas law permitted abortion only to preserve the life of the mother. The Georgia law was more liberal, but required that abortion be performed in an accredited hospital, that it be approved by a hospital committee and that the pregnant woman be a Georgia resident.

Last January, the Court declared—by identical 7-to-2 margins— that both statutes were unconstitutional on the ground of interference with the right of privacy guaranteed by the Constitution. They ruled that a fetus has no legal rights, since the Constitution makes it clear that a fetus is not a person until birth, and constitutional rights are guaranteed only to *persons*.

The Court further ruled that it was illegal for a state to place *any* restrictions on abortion, except that it be performed by a licensed doctor during the first three months of pregnancy. During the second three months, regulations could be imposed to protect the patient (for example, requiring that abortions be performed in a hospital only). But such regulations could not interfere with the ready availability of abortion to any woman desiring it.

The wide sweep of the Court's decisions surprised and pleased protagonists and agonized antagonists. Some states are accepting the inevitable, while others continue to interpose roadblocks which eventually will be crumbled by the courts. For now, it is clear that the only way to negate the Court's judgment is via a constitutional amendment—a tortuous process requiring approval by Congress and then by three quarters of the 50 state legislatures.

Toward Perspective

As must be clear from the foregoing, I am a long-time advocate of liberalized abortion and thus hardly qualify as a neutral discussant. I do believe, however, that my many years in private and hospital practice, and in the arena of public debate, give me a special vantage point to try to put this difficult subject in perspective.

To understand my thinking, one must first understand how and why I became convinced that abortion should be made legal. Justice Harry Blackmun, in his preface to the majority opinion of the Supreme Court, wrote: "One's philosophy, one's experiences, one's exposure to the raw edges of human existence . . . and the moral standards one establishes and seeks to observe, are all likely to influence and to color one's thinking and conclusions about abortion." His words concisely explain the basis for my own change in attitude, from one of firm opposition to abortion, except in cases of great medical need, to one which would allow a woman free choice.

When I was introduced to obstetrics in 1922 as a third-year medical student, there was general acceptance of the highly restrictive abortion laws then in force. None of my teachers at the Johns Hopkins Medical School in Baltimore appeared to question the propriety of the Maryland statute, which permitted abortion only when no other therapeutic measure would "secure the safety of the mother." Nor did I. Indeed, I graduated from medical school firm in the belief that abortion was a simple, straightforward matter: bad guys did it; good guys did not.

However, four years of hospital residency, and several experiences during my early years of practice, radically changed my attitude.

TRAGIC ROSTER

The second person I ever saw die was a Mrs. K, the mother of four children, who succumbed to the effects of an illegal, probably self-induced abortion. Unlike most who die, Mrs. K was not granted the blessing of coma, but remained conscious to the moment of death, screaming vainly for life.

Only a few months later, a mature-looking 15-year-old girl was brought to our surgical floor mortally ill from a bungled abortion. The senior staff was asked to consult to decide whether the child's slim chance for recovery would be helped by surgery, or by simply marking time. After a half-hour, it was decided to operate. The child died four hours later.

There are many other tragedies on the roster of illegal-abortion deaths I have witnessed. Many examples also cross my mind of the psychological destruction that enforced continuation of pregnancy sometimes causes. The common denominator in all these cases is that the victims came from "the wrong side of the railroad tracks." During my early years as a doctor in Baltimore, the city had two physician-abortionists, who practiced virtually unmolested. I knew them both. They did creditable work for a high fee—a fee unavailable to most who came from the wrong side of the tracks.

Lacking the fee, the poor could take their chances with Mary S, an ill-trained, granny-type midwife, or with Bill T, an operating-room orderly who had surreptitiously filched instruments from the hospital and set up an abortion shop. Or they could perform an abortion on themselves. All manner of articles were used for this: hatpins, clothes hangers, pencils, pens, slippery-elm bark—even, on one occasion, a goose quill. The sharp object was introduced through the cervix into the uterus, rupturing the fetal sac to bring on miscarriage—and often dangerous infection at the same time.

Extraordinary Results

All these exposures "to the raw edges of human existence" influenced and colored my "thinking and conclusions about abortion" in the early '30s. Today I believe that my long advocacy of liberalization has been fully justified by the extraordinary results achieved wherever liberalization has taken place—and especially in New York City during the first 24 months under New York State's recently changed law. Results from California, Hawaii and Washington State have been equally satisfactory, although not as fully recorded.

I believe that three criteria enable one to judge the success or failure of legal abortion. First: Does the law promote reduction in abortion deaths and abortion-connected illness? Second: Does it largely eliminate ethnic and economic discrimination? Third: Does it curtail the number of illegal abortions?

During the first two years (July 1, 1970, to June 30, 1972) under New York's liberal statute, deaths from illegal abortion in New York City declined from an average of 23 to an average of 7 per year, while admissions to ten city hospitals for infected abortions declined dramatically. At the same time, the number of pregnancy and delivery fatalities unassociated with abortion fell from 35 to 27 per 100,000 births. This was so probably because there were fewer high-risk mothers—mothers less than 17 and more than 35 years of age, and mothers coming from the most impoverished segment of the community—giving birth. For the first time, safe abortion was available to them, and they have used it.

CORRECTING THE MIX

Prior to 1970 the relatively few legal abortions performed in New York City were done primarily for affluent white women. The ratio of white to nonwhite was more than 5 to 1, and of white to Puerto Rican 26 to 1. Recent data on the city's residents reveal a striking change in this ethnic mix. Forty-seven percent of abortions during the second year of the liberalized law were performed on black women, 42 percent on whites, and 11 percent on Puerto Ricans.

It is difficult to assess the true impact on the prevalence of illegal abortion of the removal of abortion from the criminal code. Deaths and illness from illegal abortion in New York City have declined sharply, which is a pretty good index. In addition, it has been calculated that 70 percent of New York's legal abortions were substitutes for those which would have been done illegally under a restrictive statute. In other words, legalizing abortion does not increase the number of abortions so much as it provides a safe substitute for illegal procedures.

Indeed, the number of legal operations performed in New York City seems already to have leveled off. During the first year under the new law, 174,000 legal procedures took place. During the second year, the total climbed to 228,000. But during the last year (from July 1972 through June 1973), the total dropped to 197,000. According to Dr. Christopher Tietze, a leading statistician in the abortion field who works for the Population Council, that figure should continue to decline until it levels off, some years from now, at around 100,000. Similar stabilization has occurred in Eastern Europe and Japan, following liberalization.

THE SECOND LINE

At this point, a word of caution is in order: Abortion should never be used casually, or as a substitute for mass contraception. From observation as a physician, and as president of Planned Parenthood, I decry the necessity for so large a number of abortions, for each abortion bespeaks medical or social failure. If every act of intercourse in which pregnancy is not the desired result were protected by effective contraception, few abortions would be performed. The first line of defense against unwanted conception must be contraception, which is both medically safer and socially preferable. Legal abortion can only be justified as the second line.

I realize that the subject of abortion is deeply divisive, with reaction felt more in the emotions than in the mind. For this reason, dispassionate factual discussions are more beneficial than the tossing about of violent slogans. I also realize that legalized abortion is far from the ideal solution to unwanted conception. Yet a lifetime of work in the field has convinced me that liberalized abortion is an absolutely essential tool to ease the lot of many women and families in a tough, tough world.

DISCUSSION QUESTIONS

1. The author's argument can be put in syllogistic form:
   A medical procedure which preserves life and health is good.
   Legal abortion preserves life and health which would be lost in a dangerous clandestine operation.
   Legal abortion is good.
   How would an antiabortion spokesman challenge this deduction?

2. How effective as argument are the author's description of "the roster of illegal-abortion deaths I have witnessed"; his reference to Mary S. and Bill T., who performed illegal operations; and his discussion of attempts of self-induced abortion?

3. The author contends that keeping abortion illegal penalizes women who come from "the wrong side of the railroad tracks," that it constitutes "ethnic and economic discrimination." Is this a difficult argument for the antiabortion spokesman to answer?

4. "In addition, it has been calculated that 70 percent of New York's legal abortions were substitutes for those which would have been done illegally under a restrictive statute." How could such a calculation be made.

5. What kinds of argument can be made to establish when a fetus becomes a person?

Aborted Children

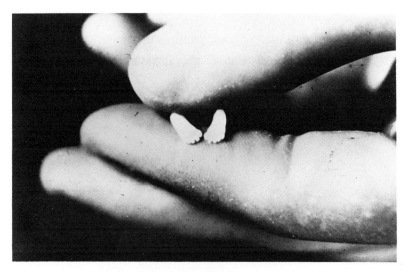

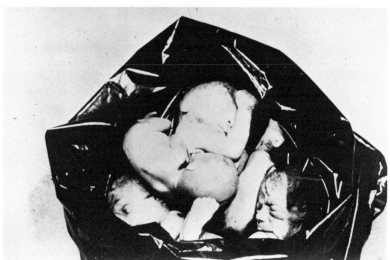

Reprinted from *Christian Crusade Weekly*, February 25, 1973, p. 2. *Religious News Service Photo*

DISCUSSION QUESTIONS

1. Put the argument of these pictures in the form of a syllogism.
2. How would an advocate of liberalized abortion attack the syllogism?
3. What other title might have been given the pictures?

4

Argument by Authority

Everyone knows Kennedy stole the 1960 election.
Trust John R. Brinkley, M. D., C. M., Dr. P. H.
Chicago Tribune asks Nixon's resignation.
"Musical is. . . . a delight"—*New Yorker*
Scientist offers new book affirming Atlantis.

Many of the things a person believes (or is asked to believe) must be accepted simply on the authority of an expert. His doctor says he has glaucoma. His mechanic says the car needs a valve job. His newspaper reviews a new book and calls it dreadful. Scientific authorities say his universe is expanding. In such instances, one is asked to accept a view on the basis of someone's testimony.

It is reasonable to credit such testimony if it fulfills two conditions: (1) The speaker must be a genuine expert in the subject at hand, and (2) there must exist no reasonable probability of his being biased. When Zsa Zsa Gabor, for example, turns from her acting career to praise the effects of acupuncture, one can justly question her expertness in the area. And when Walt Frazier appears proclaiming the excellence of Colgate toothpaste, one knows he is being paid for the advertisement and infers a degree of bias.

It must be remembered, of course, that these unreliable arguments are not necessarily false. Zsa Zsa Gabor may be expressing an important truth about acupuncture, and Walt Frazier may be giving his honest opinion of Colgate toothpaste. Nevertheless, it would be unreasonable to accept the arguments *solely* on the authority of these speakers. One should relate their views to other evidence and to the word of other authorities.

Many arguments raise the question of genuine expertness. The authority cited may be unnamed. (An advertisement for *The Illustrated Encyclopedia of Sex* includes glowing recommendations from "A Doctor," "A Teacher," "A Judge," and "A Minister.") He may be unfamiliar. (*"Future Profile* is an important book—readable, provocative, and profoundly informed"—Dr. Winston X. Reynolds.) He may be known largely by his degrees. (A Kansas medico, in recommending goat-gland surgery to restore virility, signed himself "John R. Brinkley, M. D., C. M., Dr. P. H., ScD. . . .") And he may appear with magnified credentials. (A temperance circular quoting William Gladstone on "the ravages of drink," describes him as "the greatest prime minister in English history.")

Sometimes speakers of unquestioned authority (like William Gladstone) express themselves in areas outside their competence. One hears physicists talking politics, evangelists discussing evolution, and movie stars recommending floor wax. An advertisement describes a star third baseman, then adds, "His good judgment on the ball field holds true with his selection of wearing apparel. That's why he picks Munsingwear all the way." A religious newspaper headlines an article by L. Nelson Bell, M. D., "A Physician Looks at the Virgin Birth," then prints his biblical argument based on a reading of Isaiah, Matthew, and Luke. Dr. Bell makes no medical references at all. Such spokesmen must be judged on the quality of their evidence, not on their word as experts.

Equally questionable as authorities are "God" and "everyone." Because the claim is not subject to hard evidence, one can maintain almost any conclusion by saying it conforms to the divine will. At a California Democratic rally in 1956, for example, a clergyman announced that Adlai Stevenson was God's choice for president of the United States. A correspondent to the *Mobile Press,* in 1969, expressed confidence that tragedies falling on the Kennedy family were divine justice answering their misdeeds. And a more recent correspondent declared it would violate "Christ's plan for the world" if the United States gave up its holdings in Panama.

Christian spokesmen often quote passages from the Bible to declare the will of God, and thus open up a rich area of argument. As mentioned earlier, religious questions often do not lend themselves to meaningful discussion because disputants cannot agree on necessary definitions. Clearly, an argument involving biblical authority can be persuasive only when addressed to someone who already accepts the validity of Scripture and interprets it in the same sense as the speaker. (Large differences exist, for example, between those who claim the Bible *is* the word of God, those who believe it *contains* the word of God, those who accept it as an anthology of great literature, and those who reject it altogether.) And even where preliminary accord exists, problems remain. Because the biblical texts were written over some 1300 years and represent a wide variety of authors, occasions, opinions, literary types, and translations, a spokesman can find a passage or two to support *any* argument he chooses to maintain. Bishop James Pike illustrated this by asking ironically: "How many persons have been reborn from meditating on the last line of Psalm 137: 'Blessed shall be he that taketh and dasheth the little ones against the stones'?" Consequently, the reader facing a scriptural argument should take time to trace the references. He will find that authors often quote passages out of context and, that, not uncommonly, they quote from an inaccurate memory and refer to lines scarcely related to the issue at hand.

The authority of "everyone" is cited in statements beginning "they say," "everyone knows," "all fair-minded people agree," and so on. Such argument can be convincing in instances where "they" (i.e., some notable majority) have demonstrably committed themselves in an area they are competent to judge. Arguments announcing "More women choose Simplicity than any other pattern" and "Budweiser—Largest Selling Beer in the World" tend to be impressive because, in these areas, a mass authority is superior to that of any particular expert. It is important to note that America's democratic procedures and its jury system both rely on the expertness of "everyone."

But mass authority can be distorted in a number of ways. It can be claimed arbitrarily. ("Everyone knows that John Kennedy stole the 1960 election.") It can be coupled with ambiguous language. ("More men get more pleasure out of Roi-Tan than any other cigar at its price.") And it can be invoked in areas which call for technical expertness. (A Gallup Poll reported that 48 percent of Americans believe that flying saucers are real.) In such instances, "everyone" is a dubious authority.

The word of a genuine expert will not, of course, settle all questions. Many issues are notably complex, and on these authorities differ. Legal authorities disagree whether particular eavesdropping measures violate constitutional safeguards. Scientists differ in arguing whether certain pesticides are dangerous. Sociologists cannot agree whether pornography contributes to criminal acts. Which opinions should the layman accept? In such cases, it is probably wise to credit the larger body of expert opinion or to withhold judgment and await further pronouncements in the area.

It should be recognized that some authorities have a more established reputation than others. Many periodicals carry reviews of books, plays, and movies, for example, but those of the major New York City newspapers, *The Christian Science Monitor,* and such national magazines as *Time, Harper's, Saturday Review/World,* and *The New Yorker* generally are deemed most critically reliable.

If a book, movie, or play wins praise from these critics, the reviews may be quoted in magazine advertisements and on book jackets. If an advertisement quotes reviews from other sources, it strongly suggests that the work was *not* praised by the major critics. The advertisement for Ian Fleming's *On Her Majesty's Secret Service,* for example, boasted these reviews:

"Packed with danger, mystery, crime and wild pursuit . . . I can recommend it with confidence to readers who sat up late nights to finish the preceding 10."—Vincent Starret, *Chicago Tribune*

"Hair raiser."—*Boston Herald*

"Astonishing . . . ingenious."—*Diner's Club Magazine*

"The hottest sleuth in the suspense field, James Bond, really tops himself in this new Ian Fleming thriller."—*St. Paul Dispatch*

"More fun than Tarzan and Superman combined."—*Denver Post*

"Taut, instructive and artfully told."—*Chicago Daily News*

"You can't argue with success."—Anthony Boucher, *New York Times Book Review*

"A fine surge of adrenalin in our veins."—*Columbus Dispatch*

"Solid Fleming."—*New York Herald Tribune Books*

Though it appears at first glance that authorities were unanimous in acclaiming this novel, such is scarcely the case. Only two of the quoted reviews were from major critics, and these were notably less enthusiastic than the others. *The New York Times* declared it would not argue with general taste. And the *New York Herald Tribune* said the novel is a good example of the kind Fleming writes.

This is not to suggest that a reader should not enjoy Ian Fleming's novels. He should, however, recognize the varying standards of critical authorities and not misread such advertisements as expressions of universal acclaim. He should be unimpressed, for example, when he sees the paperback edition of Harry Kressing's *The Cook* print a series of rave reviews under the heading, "A Selection of Quotes from the Nation's Press."

Even when a spokesman is an admitted expert in the field under discussion, his argument should be examined for the possibility of bias. An argument is said to have a probable bias if the authority profits from the view he expresses or if he reflects the predictable loyalty or routine antagonism of a group. To dismiss the testimony of such a person is not to call him a liar or even to say he is wrong; it means that a condition exists which makes it unreasonable to accept a conclusion solely on his authority.

An authority profits from making an argument when it enhances his financial position, his prestige, or both. The money factor is easy to recognize when Dennis Weaver recommends Bankamericard, when Sybil Leek makes lecture tours proclaiming she is a witch, and when spokesmen for outdoor movies protest the unnaturalness of daylight savings time. The effect of prestige is clear when men discuss their income, their reading habits, and their sex life. (In sensitive areas, individuals even lie to themselves. David Hendin—in *Death as a Fact of Life* (1970)—cites studies to show that "there is barely any relationship between what people think that they think about death and the way they actually feel about it when it must be faced.") However, the effect of money and prestige on an expert are sometimes difficult to establish. Few genuine scientific authorities have affirmed the existence of the Loch Ness monster or the abominable snowman, for example; but these few have won a level of recognition—along with television appearances, speaking engagements, and book contracts—which they could never gain voicing more orthodox opinions. These experts may be presenting their honest opinion; but the resultant acclaim must be taken into consideration when assessing their testimony.

Similarly, argument by authority is presumed biased if it is totally predictable—i.e., when it reflects the traditional loyalty or antagonism of a particular group. An example is this criticism of the movie *Martin Luther:*

Although technically well produced and acted, I detected in it the writing and directing techniques of "emphasis and omission" often employed by communist film propagandists.

The reviewer is William H. Mooring of *The Catholic Herald.* Equally predictable statements are pamphlets on smoking and health distributed by The Tobacco Institute, and the publicized study of pain relievers produced by The Bayer Company.

This presumption of bias appears most notably in political argument. When any Democrat is nominated for president, the man and his platform will be lauded in Democratic periodicals (*Washington Post, St. Louis Post-Dispatch, Commonweal*) and condemned by Republican publications (*Chicago Tribune, Los Angeles Times, National Review*). When any president finishes a State of the Union message, opposition spokesmen will call his program inadequate, wrong-headed, and potentially dangerous. These claims must be judged on specific evidence; such predictable views carry little authority.

Besides a doubtful expert and a biased opinion, other misleading features attend argument by authority. Statements are sometimes abridged. (The advertisement for Kyle Onstott's *Mandingo* offers the review: ". . . like no other book ever written about the South . . ."—*Dallas News.*) Assertions may be irrelevant to the present issue. (The paperback edition of *Nightmare in Pink* carries Richard Condon's opinion that "John D. MacDonald is the great American storyteller.") Quotations appear without source. (See *Hand in Hand*—"The Most Widely Praised Motion Picture of Them All!") Undated statements can be impressive. (Commonly, in political campaigns, opposition spokesmen will embarrass a candidate by citing statements he made a decade or two earlier.) And exact quotations can be presented in distorting context. (Under the heading "How L.B.J. Would Remake America," *Common Sense* printed a sentence from the president's 1964 State of the Union message: "We are going to try to take all the money that we think is unnecessarily being spent and take it from the 'haves' and give it to the 'have nots' that need it so much." As the context of his speech made clear, Johnson did not advocate taking from the rich to give to the poor; he proposed taking money from the more heavily funded federal programs and putting it in those with small appropriations.) And with the advent to the tape recorder, new techniques are possible. (In the 1972 campaign in Alabama, opponents spliced together separate parts of a taped interview and broadcast Senator John Sparkman's voice, saying ". . . will the cause of desegregation be served? If so, the busing is all right.")

Expert testimony can lend itself to bald misstatement of fact, either on the part of an authority or of those who quote him. A national columnist attacked Quentin Reynolds as a communist, a voluptuary, and a war profiteer. A U.S. senator called newsman Drew Pearson a child molester. Many have circulated the story that three Pennsylvania students on LSD became blind from staring at the sun for several hours, and that a Michigan teacher took off all of her clothes to demonstrate female anatomy to her coed sex-education class. These events never occurred.

Similarly, fictional quotations appear as evidence. For many years, the statement "We shall force the United States to spend itself to destruction" has been attributed to Nikolai Lenin and used to ground American political argument. More recently, spokesmen have circulated a statement protesting the communist threat and concluding, "We need law and order"; they ascribe this to Adolf Hitler. Both quotations are fictional. In the 1972 Florida primary, letters were mailed on Senator Edmund Muskie's stationery accusing his Democratic opponents, Senators Humphrey and Jackson, of sexual indiscretions; the letters were written by Republican partisans intending to discredit all three men. Not long ago, a news story arguing that marijuana may cure cancer quoted Dr. James H. Kostinger, director of research for the Pittsburgh Academy of Forensic Medicine, who had been conducting studies in this area for four years. Investigation revealed that the academy did not exist and that no medical school in Pittsburgh had ever heard of Dr. James H. Kostinger.

HOW RELIABLE ARE THESE ARGUMENTS FROM AUTHORITY?

1. "*Miracle of Saint Therese* is a film of unusual spiritual worth."—*Messenger of the Sacred Heart*

2. In the Song of Solomon 6:10, God describes a pure woman as being "fair as the moon, clear as the sun." I do not believe our Lord will permit the fairness and beauty of the moon to be corrupted by sinful men seeking to establish bases from which they can spread military death and destruction.

3. *Shakespeare of London* by Marchette Chute. "The best biography of Shakespeare."—Bernadine Kielty, *Book-of-the-Month Club News*

4. From 1958 to 1963, the rate of forcible rape in this country decreased by 1 percent. But from 1964 to 1969 it jumped 67 percent. A survey conducted by Hollywood Social Studies polled police chiefs, vice squad commanders, and juvenile division commanders from the nation's 56 largest cities, plus 72 others ranging down to 10,000 population. Over 91 percent of these authorities thought that revealingly short skirts were part of the cause of this rise in rape statistics. Only 5 percent said they were not.

5. Budweiser—"Somebody still cares about quality."

6. In 1968 Pope Paul VI said that bones found beneath St. Peter's Basilica 18 years earlier had been identified "in a manner we can think of as convincing" as those of the apostle St. Peter.

7. Winston is America's largest-selling cigarette.

8. CHRISTIANS AWAKE—The Communists are trying to disarm you. Jesus told His disciples to arm themselves. Read St. Luke 22:36 and 37.—Whitehouse Gun-shop, Merced, Calif.

9. Some 600 cities representing 40,000,000 people have either refused fluoridation or thrown it out after having tried it.

The Myths of Homosexuality

SISTER JEANNINE GRAMICK, SSND *

Along with the cries of liberation from women, blacks, Chicanos, Indians, and other oppressed groups come public declarations of independence from America's homosexual communities. The significant departure from the bondage of "straight" oppression can be traced back to June, 1969, when the gay patrons of the Stonewall Inn, a bar in Greenwich Village, became "militant." For the first time in their corporate history, American homosexuals took a public stand in defense of their human rights, and actively resisted harassment by the New York City Police Department. The violent resistance of the Stonewall was much more than the spontaneous outburst of a small group of angry people tired of being treated as third-class citizens. The action symbolized a much more universal feeling slowly, but steadily, growing in America's gay community. American homosexuals were no longer content in being forced to lead a dual life of straight by day and gay by night. The leaders of America's newest vocal minority—conservatively estimated at about 6,000,000 people—were chanting "Two, four, six, eight; gay is just as good as straight." No longer must gay people feel they should hide in the "closet," the leaders said. Society should accept openly the homosexual life-style. Merle Miller recently told what it is like to be a homosexual,[1] while a Los Angeles student, just out of his "closet," commented, "Now that everyone knows, I really feel at ease with myself for the first time in my life." [2] "Coming out" is bound to have a profound impact on a homosexual's life. No longer should the gay person live with the fear of discovery resulting in possible rejection by friends or the threat of the loss of a job. Society's attitudes are slowly, ever so slowly, changing.

To change social attitudes radically is a common goal of the multitudinous gay organizations which have been mushrooming

Reprinted from *Intellect,* November 1973, pp. 104–107.

* The author has been involved with the reconciliation of the Church and the homosexual since the spring of 1971.

[1] Merle Miller, "What It Means to Be a Homosexual," *New York Times Magazine,* January 17, 1971, pp. 9–11.
[2] Lynn Young, "Militant Homosexual; Gay Liberation Movement," *Newsweek,* 78:45–48, August 23, 1971.

steadily since 1950. While the number of homophile organizations soared to 40 in 1968, there are now related chapters or new independent gay groups on most campuses of the nation's leading universities.[3] A major thrust of homophile groups is attitudinal change; but attitudes can change only when people accept exposure to new ideas, accurate facts, and a willingness to investigate all sides of a question. Education as a conveyor of truth plays a large role in the reshaping of people's attitudes. Solid education about homosexuality and homosexuals must replace the stereotypes with the truth, the myths with the realities. What are the myths that hamper and limit persons who are homosexuals?

A common and long held myth in American society labels the male homosexual as an effeminate, limp-wristed individual. A revealing episode of the popular television show, "All in the Family," portrayed Archie Bunker meeting a noticeably effeminate friend of his son-in-law. Seeking more masculine companionship, Archie visits the local tavern and complains of this "queer" to a regular patron, who is decidedly masculine in appearance. The former football player, after patiently listening to Archie's tale, reveals that he himself is also homosexual. The stunned and incredulous look of Archie Bunker mirrors the surprise of most of the American public. The Institute for Sex Research at Indiana University,[4] however, estimated that only 15% of male homosexuals are easily recognizable, and only five per cent of lesbians are identifiable as "butch" or masculine in appearance. The homosexual doctor in the British film, *Sunday, Bloody Sunday,* and the divorced man and his lover in the recent television production, "That Certain Summer," were certainly not the lisping, mincing brand of homosexual that American society has grown accustomed to expect. There are, undoubtedly, effeminate male homosexuals and masculine-type lesbians, but these constitute only a small minority of the gay population. Unfortunately, these individuals, as well as transvestites, who frequently need professional psychiatric help, are the ones most likely to come into the public view, and consequently play a large part in forming public opinion about homosexuals. A prominent psychologist who chaired the Task Force on Homosexuality for the National Association for Mental Health has con-

[3] Foster Gunnison, Jr., "The Homophile Movement in America," in Ralph W. Weltge, ed., *The Same Sex* (Philadelphia: Pilgrim Press, 1969), pp. 113–128.
[4] M. Kimball Jones, *Toward a Christian Understanding of the Homosexual* (New York: Association Press, 1966), p. 28.

cluded that "there is no essential relation between effeminacy of body build, manner, or speech, and homosexuality." [5]

On Nov. 20, 1970, the National Association for Mental Health included the following observations in its statement on homosexuality: [6] "Throughout history, in all cultures, a certain number of persons have been drawn to deviational sexual behavior. Such behavior does not constitute a specific mental or emotional illness." Yet the professional world of psychiatry and psychology is not unanimous in categorizing homosexuality as non-pathological. On the contrary, psychiatry has been the traditional archenemy of the happy homosexual. Most psychiatrists view homosexuality as a neurotic disorder. The statements of one psychiatrist that "Homosexuality is . . . a neurotic distortion of the total personality. . . . There are no healthy homosexuals" are representative of the traditional approach taken by most psychiatrists even today. All psychoanalytic theories assume, not conclude, that adult homosexuality is psychopathologic. [7] Some psychiatrists, however, are beginning to doubt the validity of this assumption. Hoffman conducted a non-clinical study of homosexuality, and found that there were a significant number of homosexuals who, by reasonable clinical criteria, could not be considered mentally ill. [8] Pomeroy, a prominent New York psychologist and staff member of the Institute for Sex Research for 20 years, has written:

If my concept of homosexuality were developed from my practice, I would probably concur in thinking of it as an illness. I have seen no homosexual man or woman in that practice who was not troubled, emotionally upset, or neurotic. On the other hand, if my concept of marriage in the U. S. were based on my practice, I would have to conclude that marriages are all fraught with strife and conflict, and that heterosexuality is an illness. In my 20 years of research in the field of sex, I have seen many homosexuals who were happy, who were practicing and conscientious members of their community, and who were stable, productive, warm, relaxed, and efficient. Except for the fact that they were homosexual, they could be considered normal by any definition. [9]

To resist the pressures of a society in which the church calls one a sinner, the state brands one a criminal, and the medical profession

[5] Ibid., pp. 27–28.

[6] Edmund Bergler, *Homosexuality: Disease or Way of Life?* (New York: Hill and Wang, 1957), p. 9.

[7] Irving Bieber, *Homosexuality: A Psychoanalytical Study* (New York: Vintage Books, 1965), p. 18.

[8] Martin Hoffman, *The Gay World* (New York: Bantam Books, 1969), p. 13.

[9] Wardell B. Pomeroy, "Homosexuality," in Weltge, op. cit., p. 13.

labels one as sick, a homosexual must be a very strong personality indeed. A heterosexual person of average stamina would collapse emotionally in the face of such hostilities. Rather than point to homosexuals who are psychologically maladjusted as confirmation of the thesis that homosexuality is a disease, one should look with wonder upon those homosexuals who are psychologically sound, the obstacles of society notwithstanding.

In a classic study, Hooker found 30 homosexuals who, she felt, were reasonably well-adjusted and were not in treatment, and 30 heterosexuals who were matched for age, education, and I.Q. She gave all 60 males a battery of psychological tests, including the Rorschach and the Thematic Apperception Test. She submitted the results for analysis to three of her colleagues who did not know which of the tests had been given to the homosexuals and which to the heterosexuals. The clinicians who interpreted the tests were unable to distinguish any significant difference between the two groups tested. The general conclusion was that there is no inherent connection between homosexual orientation and clinical symptoms of mental illness.[10]

Thompson conducted a study on personal adjustment of male and female homosexuals. Groups of white, well-educated homosexuals were matched for age, sex, and education with heterosexual controls. The results indicated that the homosexual group did not differ in any way from heterosexuals in defensiveness, personal adjustment, self-confidence, or self-evaluation.[11] Similar results were reported by Chang and Block.[12] Much more research is certainly necessary but the question of homosexuality probably will remain moot in the medical profession for many decades.

There are many other myths about homosexuality that need to be eradicated by sound education. The general American public views all homosexuals as perverted pederasts who seduce unsuspecting young boys. Each year, a small number of male homosexuals, less than one per cent of the total homosexual population, are arrested for attacking youths. Each year, an even greater number of heterosexual males are arrested for attacking young girls. Yet, the public does not conclude that heterosexuality is a

[10] Evelyn Hooker, "The Adjustment of the Male Overt Homosexual," *Journal of Projective Techniques*, 21:18–31, February 1957.

[11] Norman L. Thompson, Jr., Boyd R. McCandless, and Bonnie R. Strickland, "Personal Adjustment of Male and Female Homosexuals and Heterosexuals," *Journal of Abnormal Psychology*, 78:237–240, October 1971.

[12] Judy Chang and Jack Block, "A Study of Identification in Male Homosexuals," *Journal of Consulting Psychology*, 24:307–310, August 1960.

perversion, but rather rightly concludes that some heterosexuals are perverts. Most homosexuals hold views similar to their heterosexual counterparts regarding child molesting. The only logical conclusion can be that some homosexuals are perverts.

In 1965, the Institute for Sex Research published a massive volume on sex offenders, which showed that those who were arrested for sex offenses with boys under 16 are generally bisexual.[13] Such male perverts are preoccupied with satisfying sexual urges with young boys or young girls. It is not fair to label all such youth-molesters as homosexual. It is a grosser error to judge all homosexuals as child seducers.

A third myth claims that all homosexuals are promiscuous. It is probably fair to assert that many, if not most, male homosexuals in the visible gay subculture are promiscuous. Can it then be logically concluded that homosexuality, *per se,* is an undesirable or warped form of sexuality? In present-day American culture, heterosexual relationships are undergoing deep stress regarding permanence. However, it is not logical to conclude from this phenomenon that heterosexuality, *per se,* is undesirable or warped. People, of whatever sexual orientation, generally are experiencing difficulty in maintaining their love relationships. The homosexual, unlike his or her heterosexual counterpart, lacks most of the social and cultural factors which tend to provide a supportive atmosphere of a stable relationship. A gay executive, for example, cannot bring a gay lover to a formal company dinner dance at the local country club, nor can a gay professor invite a lover to the school's Christmas party. Heterosexual marriages are sanctioned by churches, and even rewarded by the state. A homosexual couple receives no tax benefits or reduced family rates for excursions and sundry entertainment. The strong social components which reinforce heterosexual marriages are simply not available to the homosexual couple.

Despite the great social pressures they must endure, many homosexuals have been able to maintain a stable, permanent relationship. Housing and job discrimination is not infrequent. Many social and church facilities are barred from use by homosexuals because "respectable" people do not desire to associate with them. (Such reactions are reminiscent of the white middle-class citizen who passionately denied feelings of prejudice while keeping the black man far removed from his neighborhood and his church.)

[13] Jones, op. cit., p. 29.

Many "broad-minded" heterosexuals complain, "I don't mind fags as long as they keep quiet about it. They don't have to tell anyone." The experience of Jack Baker, a 29-year-old law student and president of the graduate student body at the University of Minnesota, who caused a stir by applying for a marriage license to J. Michael McConnell in May, 1970,[14] is not unique. Learning of Baker's homosexuality, his brother retorted, "Don't come around this house any more." [15] Still, Baker maintains, "All this hypocrisy and double life is a lot of nonsense and there just comes a time when you've had enough of it." [16]

The criminal status of homosexuality in most states of the U. S. likewise does not foster stable homosexual relationships. Using laws to persecute homosexuals goes back to the fourth century, when Christianity became the dominant religion of the Roman Empire. Most of the major Western countries, however, have discarded archaic laws, prohibiting homosexual acts between consenting adults, excepting most states of the U.S. In 1961, Illinois adopted the recommendation of the American Law Institute, and exempted homosexuals from its Model Penal Code. Connecticut, Oregon, Colorado, Alaska, and Idaho have followed suit in eliminating laws prohibiting private homosexual behavior between consenting adults. While the existing laws against sodomy and oral intercourse apply equally to heterosexual and homosexual acts, the laws have been enforced almost exclusively against homosexual behavior. Penalties range from one year to possible life imprisonment. Federal policy denies security clearances to homosexuals, and one-fifth of all jobs in private industry require security clearances. Legal reform is a major goal of the gay organizations. Gay crusaders maintain the major policy reason for abolishing existing laws against homosexual behavior is simply that private acts by consenting adults are matters of private morality, and are not properly the concern of the state.

Not all societies view homosexuality as a taboo. A study of 193 world cultures reported by Hock and Zubin [17] showed that male homosexuality was accepted by 28% of the cultures and rejected by 14%, while 58% showed partial acceptance or equivocation.

[14] Nick Coleman, "Two Homosexuals Plan to Wed," *Minnesota Daily*, May 19, 1970.

[15] Young, op. cit.

[16] Kay Tobin and Randy Wicker, *The Gay Crusaders* (New York: Paperback Library, 1972), p. 140.

[17] Paul Hoch and Joseph Zubin, *Psychosexual Development in Health and Disease* (New York: Grune and Stratton, 1949).

Pomeroy [18] reports that 53% of 225 American Indian cultures accepted male homosexuality, while only 24% of the cultures rejected it. Although the cowboys of the Wild West in the 19th century scorned effeminate men, they did not loathe homosexual behavior. Overt homosexuality was probably more common among this group than among any other group of males in the U. S.[19]

Still, 20th-century American society is less than tolerant of homosexuality. An anthropologist recounts: "Among the generality of Americans, homosexuality is regarded not with distaste, disgust, or abhorrence, but with panic; it is seen as an immediate and personal threat. . . . The lives of most American men are bounded, and their interests drastically curtailed, by this constant necessity to prove to their fellows, and to themselves, that they are not . . . homosexuals. It is difficult to exaggerate the prevalence of this unconscious fear." [20] After years of research in the field of sex, Kinsey concluded that human beings can not be classified simply as heterosexual or homosexual. Kinsey devised a seven-point scale, ranging from "exclusively heterosexual" to "exclusively homosexual." An individual may be located at different points on the scale at different periods of his or her life. Kinsey explained that human beings "do not represent two discrete populations, heterosexual and homosexual. The world is not to be divided into sheep and goats. . . . It is a fundamental of taxonomy that nature rarely deals with discrete categories. Only the human mind invents categories and tries to force facts into separate pigeon-holes. The living world is a continuum in each and every one of its aspects. The sooner we learn this concerning human sexual behavior, the sooner we shall reach a sound understanding of the realities of sex." [21]

Education must replace homosexual myths with homosexual realities: most homosexuals do not fit the stereotyped images; very few homosexuals are child-molesters; not all homosexuals are promiscuous. A gay person is more similar to a heterosexual of common educational and socioeconomic background than to another gay person of different educational and socioeconomic background. The only thing all homosexuals have in common is sexual, erotic orientation. Attitudinal change can occur only through ex-

[18] Pomeroy, op. cit., p. 4.
[19] Ibid., p. 11.
[20] Geoffrey Garer, *The American People*, revised edition (New York: Norton, 1964), pp. 128–129.
[21] Alfred Kinsey et al., *Sexual Behavior in the Human Male* (Philadelphia: Saunders, 1948), p. 639.

posure, contact, education, and confrontation with truth in the existential situation. Barbara Gittings, a leading gay activist for over 14 years, has observed very aptly: "The only way to break down misunderstanding and prejudice is by meeting and working with and learning to understand people." [22] But then, most people probably have met and worked with homosexuals without realizing it.

DISCUSSION QUESTIONS

1. In her opening sentence, the author identifies homosexuals with "women, blacks, Chicanos, Indians, and other oppressed groups." What does this imply about homosexuals?

2. America's homosexual population is "conservatively estimated at about 6,000,000 people." How reliable is this kind of estimate?

3. To counter the notion that the male homosexual is "an effeminate, limp-wristed individual," the author cites four authorities. Identify them and evaluate their relative value in argument.

4. To respond to the view of many psychiatrists that "adult homosexuality is psychopathologic," the author cites the work of Hoffman, Pomeroy, Hooker, Thompson, and Chang and Block. Do these studies do more than show that *some* homosexuals are well-adjusted, stable, and productive? To respond to the initial charge, do they need to do more than this?

5. To argue that homosexuals do not deserve the image of child seducers, the author argues that homosexual attacks on youth are less frequent than heterosexual attacks. Analyze this as induction with an unrepresentative sample.

6. Does the author deny that homosexuals are promiscuous? What is her response to this "myth"?

7. Comment on the effect of the footnotes in the essay.

[22] Barbara Gittings, "The Homosexual and the Church," in Weltge, op. cit., p. 151.

Heroin, Marijuana, and LSD

DAVID A. NOEBEL

Narcotics, of course, are dangerous even when administered under the care of a physician. Both heroin and marijuana are exceedingly dangerous. Heroin is the strongest and most addictive opium derivative and is either sniffed into the nasal passages through the nose or mixed in water and heated to form a solution and injected intravenously with a hypodermic directly into the bloodstream. Marijuana is a derivative from the hemp weed, which affects the nervous system and the brain of the user, causing mental unbalance for varying periods of time and in which a sufficient dose of the active substance—tetrahydrocannabianol—is capable of producing all the hallucinatory and psychotic effects relative to LSD (which is conceded to be one of the most powerful drugs known).

Repeated use of heroin produces psychological and physical dependence in which the user has an overwhelming compulsion to continue using the drug. Under heroin the body develops a tolerance for it in the bloodstream and virtually all bodily functions are attuned to that presence. Of course, once the victim has the habit, he stops at nothing to satisfy it, and since heroin is considered incurably addictive, when the narcotic is no longer in the body, death can result even during the withdrawal process.

Marijuana, on the other hand, is no less to be desired. In a timely article on narcotics, Dr. Susan Huck, in a personal interview with the noted geneticist, Dr. Louis Diaz de Souza (who has spent 18 years investigating the effects of marijuana on the human body) found that "even one smoke of marijuana does calamitous damage to the chromosomes." The doctor told her that damage to one chromosome, "may mean that the child will be hemophilian, or mongoloid, or afflicted with leukemia. The chromosome may pass from one generation to another. The child of the marijuana user may show this damage or his child may show it." [1]

Unfortunately, a semantic argument has developed over the usage of the word "addictive" and "dependent." Some argue the

---

Reprinted from *The Beatles: A Study in Drugs, Sex and Revolution* (Tulsa, Okla.: Christian Crusade Publications, 1969), pp. 13–17.

[1] *American Opinion*, May 1969, p. 58.

drug is not addictive, but rather the user only becomes dependent on it. Others, e.g., Dr. Hardin Jones, of the Donner Laboratory at the University of California (Berkeley), maintains that marijuana is habit-forming and with continued use it is addictive. Naturally, the argument makes little difference since (1) few are so sophisticated as to see any difference between "addictive" and "dependent" and (2) since it takes the user away from reality and removes his normal inhibitions, marijuana is harmful apart from either word. Smith, Kline & French Laboratories, in a special report prepared primarily for educators, found marijuana not only impairing the user's ability to drive an automobile, but producing such physical effects as dizziness, dry mouth, dilated pupils and burning eyes, urinary frequency, diarrhea, nausea and vomiting.[2]

Dr. Hardin Jones in his research found marijuana not only habit-forming and addictive with continued use, but also reported (1) that although it does not lead to the use of harder narcotics through chemical addiction, it promotes a curiosity about the harder drugs; (2) that its effect is cumulative, witness that a neophyte needs several joints to "turn on," whereas a professional can get high on one; (3) that it interferes with normal perceptions; (4) that its cumulative impact brings repeated hallucinations that disturb the reference memory, causing (5) wholesale abandonment of goals and ambitions.

Jones goes on to say that marijuana and other drugs are in a very real sense sexual stimulants. Marijuana is a mild aphrodisiac. "It enhances sensitivity and makes a person more receptive to sensual stimuli," he says, "but this condition only lasts a short period of time and chronic marijuana users find that sex activities without the drug are difficult and confusing." [3]

And the world-famous authority on marijuana, Dr. Constandinos J. Miras, of the University of Athens, who has been studying man and marijuana for over twenty-five years, found marijuana users to have abnormal brain wave readings and marked behavioral changes. Longtime users, for example, revealed chronic lethargy and loss of inhibitions for two years after their last usage. Many of his subjects were slipping into less demanding jobs as the habit got a firmer grip on them and were variously depressed and exalted, not always sure when they were having hallucinations. Others went through a rapid succession of physical changes—crying, laughing, sluggishness, hunger for sugar, hallucinating. The

[2] *Tulsa Daily World*, May 5, 1967, p. 8.
[3] *Tulsa Daily World*, September 25, 1969, p. 16A.

idea of the so-called harmless use of marijuana is either ignorance or deception. And one State official in Maryland remarked that marijuana not only induces a lethargy in most people, but a dangerous attitude toward the community.

The hallucinogens which are popularly known as psychedelics (since they produce sensations distorting time, space, sound and color) include LSD, STP and DMT. All hallucinogens create hallucinations which lessen the user's ability to discriminate between fact and fancy, and studies indicate that LSD may cause chromosome damage which could result in mental deficiencies and blood diseases in children born to users. One of the foremost authorities in the United States on LSD is Dr. J. Thomas Ungerleider. He states that, "LSD has been called a conscious-expanding drug. In fact, it is quite the reverse. It decreases one's ability to select and pay attention. Therefore, it decreases conscious functions. Sensations do become intensified. Perception, however, is not enhanced, and visual and auditory acuteness are not revolutionized, but rather are distorted." Since LSD dulls the user's objective judgment, which is replaced by purely subjective values, Dr. Ungerleider says, "LSD seems to affect a person's value system." [4]

Then, too, both the amphetamines and barbiturates are danger drugs. Amphetamines, often called pep pills, produce a feeling of excitation which usually manifests itself in appetite loss with an increasing ability to go without sleep for long periods of time. The most common amphetamines are Benzedrine (called Bennies), Dexedrine (called Dexies) and Methadrine (referred to as crystal or speed). The danger, of course, with amphetamines as well as barbiturates is the psychological desire to continue using the drugs. The most common barbiturates are Amytal (referred to as Blue Heavens), Nembutal (or Yellow Jackets) and Seconal (called Red Devils or Red Birds). In the jargon of drug addicts, barbiturates in general are referred to as "goofballs" and affect the central nervous system and the brain by slowly depressing the mental and physical functions of the body. A person under the influence of a barbiturate will be disoriented to time, place and person and may experience delusions and hallucinations.

Obviously, such drugs cannot be equated with apple pie and vanilla ice cream. And any drug—marijuana, for example, which at one moment makes a person feel so tiny he is not able to step off an eight-inch curb, and yet an hour later makes him feel so huge

[4] *Tulsa Tribune,* February 24, 1967, p. 14.

he could step off a ten-story building—is dangerous. Any individual, who under the influence of marijuana can barrel down the highway at 80 mph and assume he is only traveling 20 mph, or drive through a red light which appears to be green and smash into a row of cars which appeared to be a mile away, is dangerous. And, any drug—LSD, for example, which makes a person feel he can fly like a bird and so take off from a four-story building only to discover he is flying to his death—is not safe.

DISCUSSION QUESTIONS

1. Because no experimental studies are described in the essay, the reader must base his judgment on the testimony of a number of authorities. Compare and evaluate them:
   (a) David A. Noebel
   (b) Dr. Susan Huck
   (c) Dr. Louis Diaz de Souza
   (d) *American Opinion*
   (e) some [who] argue the drug is not addictive
   (f) others
   (g) Dr. Hardin Jones
   (h) the Donner Laboratory at the University of California (Berkeley)
   (i) Smith, Kline & French Laboratories
   (j) a special report prepared primarily for educators
   (k) *Tulsa Daily World*
   (l) Dr. Constandinos J. Miras
   (m) the University of Athens
   (n) one State official in Maryland
   (o) Dr. J. Thomas Ungerleider
   (p) *Tulsa Tribune*
   (q) Christian Crusade Publications

2. The author writes that "Narcotics, of course, are dangerous even when . . . ," that "The danger, of course, with amphetamines as well as barbiturates is . . . ," that LSD "is conceded to be one of the most powerful drugs known," that "heroin is considered incurably addictive," that "such drugs cannot be equated with apple pie," and so on. Comment on the value of this argumentative technique.

3. In the statements taken directly from *American Opinion*, who is being quoted?

4. Compare these statements about the effects of marijuana with those cited in Fort's "Pot: A Rational Approach," p. 235. Which seem more credible? How can one account for this wide range in opinion?

Vitamin E in the
Hands of Creative Physicians

RUTH ADAMS AND FRANK MURRAY

Of all of the substances in the medical researcher's pharmacopoeia, perhaps the most maligned, neglected and ignored is vitamin E. In spite of this apparent ostracism in the United States, however, some of the world's leading medical authorities are using alpha tocopherol—more commonly known as vitamin E—to successfully treat and cure a host of mankind's most notorious scourges.

For those medical researchers who are at work trying to treat and prevent heart attacks—our No. 1 killer—and to help many more thousands who are dying of related circulatory disorders, vitamin E is playing a major role. And for many athletes, vitamin E (in the form of wheat germ oil, specially formulated oils for stamina and endurance, vitamin E capsules and perles etc.) has long been as indispensable as calisthenics.

"There are over 570,000 deaths from heart attacks each year," says a publication of the American Heart Association, "many thousands of them among people in the prime of life—and growing indications that heart disease may be a disease of prosperity."

In scientific minds, vitamin E may be related to fertility and reproduction, said an article in *Medical World News* for April 18, 1969. But a famous ball player, Bobby Bolin of the San Francisco Giants, credits the vitamin with keeping his pitching arm in condition. He developed a sore shoulder in 1966, resulting in a poor pitching season for two years. He began to take vitamin E. The article said that he expected to be a "regular starter" at the beginning of the 1969 season, and that vitamin E was responsible for the good news.

It isn't surprising that many athletes have discovered the benefits of taking vitamin E regularly. The vitamin is in short supply in most of our diets. Vitamin E is an essential part of the whole circulatory mechanism of the body, since it affects our use of oxygen. When you have plenty of vitamin E on hand, your cells can get along on less oxygen. This is surely an advantage for an athlete,

Reprinted from *Vitamin E, Wonder Worker of the '70's?* (New York: Larchmont Books, 1972), pp. 17–26, 31–32.

who expends large quantities of oxygen. And, according to recent research at the Battelle Memorial Institute, which we will discuss in greater detail in a later section of this book, vitamin E, along with vitamin A, are important to anyone who lives in the midst of constant air pollution.

From *The Summary*, a scientific journal published by the Shute Institute in Canada, a publication we will frequently refer to . . . , we learn additional facts about vitamin E. Dr. Evan Shute, who heads the clinic, and Dr. Wilfrid E. Shute, his brother, have pioneered in work with vitamin E for more than 20 years. *The Summary* condenses and abstracts for doctors and medical researchers some of the material on relevant subjects that has appeared in medical journals throughout the world.

For instance, a Hungarian doctor reports on the encouraging effects of vitamin E in children born with certain defects. Of all vitamin deficiencies, she believes that vitamin E is the most important in preventing such occurrences. She has given the vitamin with good results in quite large doses to children who would otherwise be almost incapacitated. Mothers, too.

She tells the story of a woman who had three deficient children, two of them with Down's Syndrome or mongolism. When she was pregnant for the fourth time, the physician sent her away for a rest—"tired, aging, torpid" as she was, with "a diet rich in proteins, liver, vegetables and fruit with large doses of vitamins, especially vitamin E, and thyroid hormone." She returned in six weeks to give birth to a perfectly healthy baby!

As for another insidious disorder—chronic phlebitis—Dr. Evan Shute says that most doctors have no idea of how common this condition is. It should be looked for in everyone, he says, certainly every adult woman. After describing the symptoms—a warm swollen foot and an ache in the leg or foot which is relieved by raising the feet higher than the head—he tells his physician readers, "Look for chronic phlebitis and you will be astounded how common it is. Treat it with vitamin E and you will be deluged with grateful patients who never found help before."

Describing a symposium on the subject of vitamins E, A and K, Dr. Shute tells us that speakers presented evidence that vitamin E is valuable in doses of 400 milligrams daily for treating claudication—a circulatory condition of the feet and legs—and that a similar dosage helps one kind of ulcer.

High dosage of vitamin E improves survival time of persons with hardening of the arteries and should always be given to such patients, according to Dr. Shute. He adds that there are some 21 articles in medical literature, aside from the many he himself has written, showing that vitamin E dilates blood vessels and develops collateral vessels—thus permitting more blood to go through, even though the vessel is narrowed by deposits on its walls.

An article that appeared in *Postgraduate Medicine* in 1968 by Dr. Alton Ochsner, a world-famous lung surgeon, states that he has used vitamin E on every surgical patient over the past 15 years and none has developed damaging or fatal blood clots.

Dr. Shute goes on to say that at the Shute Clinic all surgery patients are routinely given vitamin E both as a preventive and as a curative measure.

He quotes an article in *Annals of Internal Medicine,* saying that thrombosis or clot formation "has become the prime health hazard of the adult population of the Western world." Dr. Shute adds these comments: "Here is a real tragedy. Twenty years after we introduced a simple and safe clotting agent, alpha tocopherol, to the medical world, everything else is tried, including (dangerous drugs) and the anti-coagulants, with all these the results are extremely unsatisfactory. When will the medical profession use vitamin E as it should be used for this condition?"

He quotes a statement from the *Journal of the American Medical Association* showing that the average teenage girl or housewife gets only about half the amount of iron she should have from her diet in the United States. Then Dr. Shute says, "Another nutritional defect in the best fed people on earth! In one issue the *JAMA* shows the average American is often deficient in iron and vitamin A. Now what about vitamin E?" He, of course, has pointed out many times that this vitamin is almost bound to be lacking in the average diet. As we mention elsewhere . . . up to 90% of the vitamin E content of various grains is lost during the flaking, shredding, puffing processes that are used to make breakfast cereals.

Dr. Shute then quotes a newsletter on the U. S. Department of Agriculture survey revealing that only half of all American diets could be called "good." He comments thusly, "One continually reads claptrap by nutritionists contending that the wealthiest country in the world feeds everybody well. This obviously isn't true. It is no wonder that deficiency of vitamin E is so common when even the diet recommended by the National Research Council of the U. S. A. contains something like 6 milligrams of vitamin E per day before it is cooked!"

In another issue of *The Summary,* we learn how two Brazilian researchers are working on heart studies done on rats that were made deficient in vitamin E. Of 26 rats, only six normal ones were found. All the rest showed some heart damage when they were tested with electrocardiograms and other devices.

Two German researchers report on the action of an emulsified vitamin E solution on the heart tissues of guinea pigs. They found that the vitamin protects the heart from damage by medication, and helps to prevent heart insufficiency. Dr. Shute adds that this paper indicates that vitamin E should be investigated further in hospital clinics.

Animals deficient in vitamin E produced young with gross and microscopic defects of the skeleton, muscles and nervous system. They had harelips, abdominal hernias, badly curved backs and many more defects. This was reported in *The Journal of Animal Science,* Volume 22, page 848, 1963.

Two American obstetricians report in the *American Journal of Obstetrics and Gynecology* that they know of no way to prevent serious damage and death for many premature infants. Dr. Shute comments, "These authors apparently have not seen our reports on the use of vitamin E in the prevention of prematurity." He goes on to say, "No comparable results have ever been reported."

A report in the journal, *Fertility and Sterility,* indicates that in six percent of patients studied, the cause of abortion and miscarriage lay in the father's deficient sperm, not in any deficit of the mother's. The authors studied carefully the medical histories of many couples who had been married several times. Dr. Shute comments, "We have long advocated alpha tocopherol for poor sperm samples, especially in habitual abortion couples."

A Romanian farm journal reports that extremely large amounts of vitamin E, plus vitamin A, were given to 77 sterile cows. Within one to one and a half months, their sexual cycles were restored and 70 percent of them conceived.

A German veterinarian reports in a 1960 issue of *Teirarztliche Umschau* that he uses vitamin E for treating animals with heart conditions. A one-year-old poodle with heart trouble regained complete health after 14 days on vitamin E. A three-year-old thoroughbred horse with acute heart failure was treated with vitamin E for two weeks, after which time its electrocardiogram showed only trivial changes even after exercise. The vet uses, he says, large doses of the vitamin.

And an Argentinian physician reports in *Semana Med.* that vitamin C is helpful in administering vitamin E. It works with the vitamin to retain it in body tissues. Dr. A. Del Guidice uses the two vitamins together in cases of cataracts, strabismus and myopias. He also noted that patients with convulsive diseases are much helped by vitamin E—massive doses of it—so that their doses of tranquilizers and sedatives can be lessened.

A letter from Dr. Del Guidice to Dr. Shute tells of his success in treating mongolism in children with vitamin E. For good results, he says, it must be given in large doses from the age of one month on. He continues his treatment for years sometimes, and claims that spectacular results can be achieved in this tragic disease.

Two Japanese scientists report in the *Journal of Vitaminology* that hair grew back faster on the shaven backs of rabbits when they applied vitamin E locally for 10 to 13 weeks.

And again from Argentina comes word of vitamin E given to 20 mentally defective children in large doses. In 75 percent, the intelligence quota was raised from 12 to 25 points, "with improved conduct and scholarly ability. Less attention fatigue was noted in 80 percent, and 90 percent had improved memory." A short experience with neurotic adults· showed that vitamin E brought a definite reduction in phobias, tic, obsessions and other neurotic symptoms.

In one issue of *The Summary,* Dr. Shute prints a letter of his to the editor of the *British Medical Journal* (July 1966) urging this distinguished man to consider vitamin E as a treatment for pulmonary embolism. He says, "I have used nothing else for years and no longer even think of embolism (that is, blood clots) in my patients, even in those with records of previous phlebitis. Dosage is 800 International Units a day." He adds a PS to readers of *The Summary:* "The Editor could not find space for this letter unfortunately."

A *British Medical Journal* editorial comments on our present methods of treatment for blood clots in leg veins. Raising the foot of the bed, bandaging the legs and getting the patient on his feet doesn't seem to be very helpful, says the editor. Using anticoagulants seems to help some, but we should speedily develop some new methods of treatment. Dr. Shute comments that one would think that vitamin E has a clear field, since nothing else is very effective. It is easy to use, he goes on, safe and effective.

Each issue of *The Summary* contains many articles that have appeared in world medical literature on vitamin E and related subjects. In other countries, vitamin E is treated quite seriously in medical research, is routinely used in hospitals and clinics. In our country, such use is rare.

These are just a few of the case histories that Dr. Shute reports, at his own expense, in *The Summary*. The book is not available for nonmedical people, since it is written in highly technical terms. However, we suggest that you recommend these publications to your doctor, if you or someone you know is suffering from a disorder that might be treated successfully with vitamin E. The address is: Dr. Evan Shute, Shute Foundation for Medical Research, London, Ontario, Canada.

DISCUSSION QUESTIONS

1. The case for vitamin E is supported by reference to a range of authorities. These include the following:
   (a)   A publication of the American Heart Association
   (b)   An article in *Medical World News*
   (c)   Bobby Bolin of the San Francisco Giants
   (d)   Many athletes
   (e)   Recent research at the Battelle Memorial Institute
   (f)   *The Summary*
   (g)   The Shute Institute in Canada
   (h)   Dr. Evan Shute
   (i)   Dr. Wilfred E. Shute
   (j)   A Hungarian doctor
   (k)   Speakers at a symposium on the subject of vitamin E
   (l)   21 articles in medical literature
   (m)   An article in *Postgraduate Medicine*
   (n)   Dr. Alton Ochsner
   (o)   An article in *Annals of Internal Medicine*
   (p)   A statement from the *Journal of the American Medical Association*
   (q)   A newsletter on a U. S. Department of Agriculture survey
   (r)   The National Research Council of the United States
   (s)   Two Brazilian researchers
   (t)   Two German researchers
   (u)   *The Journal of Animal Science*
   (v)   Two American obstetricians
   (w)   *American Journal of Obstetrics and Gynecology*

(x)   A Romanian farm journal
(y)   A German veterinarian
(z)   *Teirarztliche Umschau*
(aa) An Argentinian physician
(bb) *Semana Med.*
(cc) Dr. Del Guidice
(dd) Two Japanese scientists
(ee) *The Journal of Vitaminology*
(ff) Editorial in the *British Medical Journal*
Evaluate the relative authority of these.

2. A number of consecutive paragraphs give quotations from respected medical journals along with Dr. Shute's commentary. Do these say the same thing?

3. The authors begin by noting that vitamin E has been "maligned, neglected, and ignored" by American doctors. How can this occur if the vitamin has been so successful in tests and studies?

4. Studies show that animals and humans deficient in vitamin E improve significantly when given the vitamin. Doesn't this *prove* that vitamin E should be added to most people's diets?

5. Who publishes *The Summary*?

6. How successful a pitcher was Bobby Bolin in 1969?

Paperback Cover of *Joshua Son of None* by Nancy Freedman

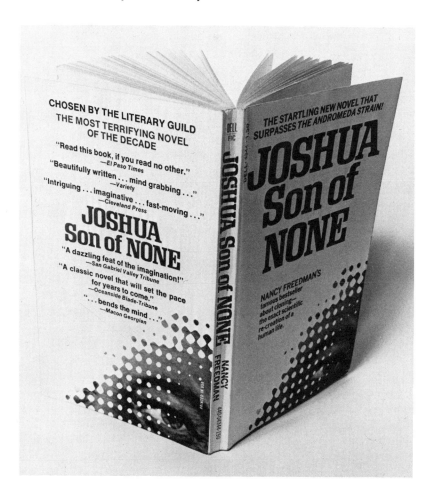

Dell paperback, 1974.

DISCUSSION QUESTIONS

1. Evaluate this argument by authority, paying special attention to the following:
   (a) The words of the journals that reviewed the book
   (b) The words of praise that do not come from these journals
   (c) The ellipsis marks

2. How substantial are these journals as critical authorities? What other sources might you want to check before buying the book?

3. What does "Chosen by the Literary Guild" tell you?

5

Semantic Argument

Federal spending is irresponsible and dangerous.
Drive a Buick Apollo.
Oil heat is SAFE.
Support right-to-work laws.
Arguments hypostatize the bigoted
renitency. . . .

The importance of individual words in argument has already been mentioned. Meaningful discussion is impossible unless disputants agree on the definition of key terms, and deductive argument is unreliable if it employs ambiguous words. Yet to be considered, however, is the kind of argument that makes its point, not by presenting or arranging evidence, but by using impressive language.

Semantic argument should convince no one. It is simply a conclusion offered without evidence. Its effectiveness derives from the nature of words. A word can have two levels of meaning. It has a denotative meaning—i.e., some specific thing or condition to which it refers (*mailman, swim, beige*). And it can have a connotative meaning—i.e., certain emotional responses which it arouses. Connotations can be negative (*politician, deal, filibuster*) or affirmative (*statesman, negotiation, right of unlimited debate*). Semantic argument consists in using connotative words to characterize an issue or to enhance the tone of a discussion.

Connotative words (sometimes called "purr words" and "snarl words") do not prove anything. Commonly they simply label a thing as good or bad. American politicians of both parties regularly run for office, for example, on a program of obedience to God, family, and country; adherence to law and order; separation of powers; and economic progress without inflation. They oppose absenteeism, wasteful spending, communism, flag-burning, anarchy, and stagnation. The essence of such persuasion is its vagueness. In the given list, only "flag-burning" has an unequivocally clear meaning.

107

Such argument can praise any entity (a party platform, a current novel, a union demand) as *authentic, just, reasonable, natural,* and *realistic* or condemn it as *irresponsible, asinine, phony, dangerous,* and *superficial.* It can laud any citizen as a *Samaritan,* a *patriot,* and an *independent* thinker or reject him as a *do-gooder,* a *reactionary,* and a *pseudointellectual.* (One man's *academic freedom* is another man's *brainwashing.*) These terms have little specific meaning. Their nature was illustrated some years ago when actress Jayne Mansfield told interviewer Mike Wallace that her career was "based on womanliness, not sex." Asked to spell out the difference, she responded, "One is a ruder word than the other."

Such language depends on its emotional associations. An automobile is more appealing when named *Thunderbird,* a bill when called a *right-to-work law,* and a military settlement when termed *peace with honor.* A hair preparation can be discredited as *greasy kid stuff,* a business practice as *payola,* and a senator as part of a *military-industrial complex.* Advertisers have called up an impressive range of associations to offer *Blue Cross, Right Guard, Cashmere Bouquet, Old Grand-Dad,* and *Lincoln Continental Mark IV*—plus *Lark, GL-70, Hai Karate,* and *Brut by Fabergé.* The contrasting technique is to qualify dramatic events by using language which avoids emotional connotations. Government spokesmen, for example, have been effectively bland in describing a lost H-bomb as a *military artifact,* massive bombing missions as *protective reaction strikes,* and false statements about political espionage as *inoperative.*

Even names of people carry meaningful associations. In comic fiction, for instance, one knows immediately that *Mary Worth* is good and that *Snidely Whiplash* is bad. And real-life examples demonstrate American rejection of vague or aristocratic names. Hollywood hired an actor named *Leroy Scherer* and starred him as *Rock Hudson.* Household Finance Corporation has loan officers across the country who are presented to the public as *friendly Bob Adams.* John Varick Tunney had always been called *Varick* until he chose to enter politics; after Opinion Research of California polled citizen response to the name *Varick,* he reverted to his unused first name and is now *Senator John Tunney.* A similar insight led the former postmaster-general seeking a U. S. Senate seat from Alabama to begin his campaign literature: "His name is Winton Malcolm Blount, but everyone calls him *Red.*"

Semantic argument can also work indirectly. That is, in particular contexts, a purr word expressed is also a snarl word implied—

and vice versa. To advertise that *Oil heat is SAFE,* for example, is to imply that gas and electric heat are dangerous. To describe a movie as *not recommended for immature audiences* is to boast it is impressively sexual or violent. When political advertisements emphasize that a candidate is *a devoted family man,* there is a strong probability his opponent is divorced. Senator Ted Kennedy's next opponent will probably be too civilized to mention Chappaquiddick, but spokesmen will praise the candidate as *solid, stable, resolute,* and *responsible.* In such instances, one is expected to recognize the implications of the surface argument.

Often, however, semantic claims are not meant to be penetrated. This is especially true when impressive language is used to mask a negative admission. For example, when government spokesmen announce that a particular recession is *leveling off,* they wish to communicate optimistic reassurance rather than the denotative meaning of the phrase, i.e., that the economy is still sick and is getting sicker. When manufacturers label a garment *shrink-resistant,* they want to suggest that it will not shrink, not what the term literally says, that the garment will resist shrinking and thus that shrinking will probably occur. Advertisements for an inexpensive portable radio wish to imply that it is powerful and can pull in signals from distant stations, but what they say is, *You can take it anywhere.*

This attempt to communicate more than is literally said also occurs when a spokesman uses impressive language to add character to his argument. Couching his views in religious allusions, folksy talk, or esoteric jargon, he argues more with his manner than with his substance. In a letter to the *Saturday Review,* for example, Gelett Burgess maintained that Shakespeare of Stratford did not write the plays attributed to him and began his argument thus:

Sir: My recent communication relative to Oxford-is-Shakespeare elicited responses which evince and hypostatize the bigoted renitency usual in orthodox addicts. For the Stratfordian mythology has engendered a strange nympholepsy like a fanatical religion which is not amenable to reason or logic, and abrogates all scientific method.

Here the writer said more than that his earlier letter received much silly comment. He used pedantic language to make it clear that his response and his whole Shakespearean argument derive from a profoundly learned individual.

One should, of course, judge an argument solely on the evidence brought forward to support a conclusion, not on the effect of connotative language used to describe the issue or to elevate the tone of the discussion.

Connotative language defies meaningful analysis. Is it true that "Education without God produces a nation without freedom," that NATO is "the devil in disguise," that Fleischmann's Gin is "Clean . . . Clean . . . Clean"? Who can say? Until the claims are clarified and documented, such vague language can produce only empty and repetitive argument. Fleischmann advertisements, it should be noted, once offered to explain "What do they mean CLEAN . . . CLEAN . . . CLEAN?" The answer:

They mean that the crispest, brightest drinks under the sun are made with clean-tasting Fleischmann's Gin.

This is about as meaningful as semantic argument gets.

HOW EFFECTIVE ARE THESE SEMANTIC ARGUMENTS?

1. Look morning-lovely all day long. Use Revlon "Love-Pat."

2. Advertisement for *Valley of the Dolls:* "Any similarity between any person living or dead, and the characters portrayed in this film is purely coincidental and not intended."

3. The Russian purges of the 1930s have been too emotionally depicted. What really occurred was a transfer of population, a rectification of frontiers, and an elimination of unreliable elements.

4. Concerned about Foreign Aid Give-a-ways, and Communist Infiltration? *Beat the Washington Crowd!* Vote for JIM ALLEN—Alabama's Candidate for the U. S. Senate.

5. The human organism is a homeostatic mechanism, i.e., all behavior is an attempt to preserve organismic integrity by homeostatic restoration of equilibrium, as that equilibrium is disturbed by biologically significant organizations of energies in the external or internal environments of the organism.

6. Drive a great station wagon—the Chevelle Malibu Classic Estate.

7. Abortion on Demand Is Murder by Request.

8. When a correspondent wrote *Personality Parade* asking whether Elvis Presley had learned to act, columnist Walter

Scott responded, "Mr. Presley has always been good to his mother."

9. There's only one leading shampoo that isn't mostly detergent—GOLD FORMULA BRECK.

Of Ms. and Men

M. J. SOBRAN, JR.

In what magazine can you find both a memoir by Simone de Beauvoir and an ad with Smokey the Bear? Answer: *Ms*. It is *the* feminist magazine, the one with Gloria Steinem, with slick paper, full-color, full-page Chevrolet ads, and lots of articles by and about well known women. It is a rather attractive magazine to look at, and though I don't think highly of it, it avoids most of the invective of the violent "underground" feminist press. I've only seen the phrase "male chauvinist pig" once in the pages of *Ms.*, and I think it was intended rather humorously at that. The magazine's coarseness is intellectual rather than vituperative. *Ms.* seems to be to women's lib what *Vogue* is to the unlib. It is given not only to advocating what it perceives as the cause of women, but also to celebrating women—but in the masculine terms of status and achievement—while denouncing masculinity. A little bizarre; very doctrinaire.

In a way it reminds me of racial theorists. Not that *Ms.* is at all genocidal (or "sexicidal," as it would probably say); I mean something very different. However plausible the theory of, say, Teutonic superiority may seem, you rarely hear it from those who are adduced in proof of it. Mozart doesn't give you a doctrine about the Aryan race; he gives you *Don Giovanni;* just as Goethe produces *Faust,* and Kant his critiques and prolegomena: highly individualized perceptions, reified as richly textured, profoundly ordered works of art and philosophy, each unique. The crude doctrine that lumps such things into a mass comes not from these men, who, even if they agreed with it abstractly, would take no practical interest in it; but from intellectual and moral runts whose very enthusiasm for it reveals their need to cash in on it, to take a derivative self-esteem from the achievements of others to whom they enjoy only an accidental similarity. In the same way, Jane Austen has given us *Pride and Prejudice*: Gloria Steinem gives us *Ms.*

Every dogma has its day, and the dogma *du jour* is that Women Are Oppressed. That notion seems to elicit favorable noises from the least likely people, including such feminist bogeypersons as Pope Paul and Hugh Hefner (though *Playboy*'s notion of sexual

Reprinted from the *National Review*, May 24, 1974, pp. 579–581.

equality probably means no more than going Dutch treat on the abortion). *Ms.* abounds in articles purporting to show how women are oppressed, and how much they have managed to achieve anyway. Many pieces center on feminist heroines—either volunteers like Bella Abzug and Billie Jean King, or conscripts from the past like Gertrude Stein and Marilyn Monroe ("the woman who died too soon," Ms. Steinem calls her); and there are regular short features about "lost women," who have not received their due from male historians—e.g., pirates Anne Bonney and Mary Read.

One's immediate response to this jumble of heroines is to wonder at the magazine's sheer indiscriminancy. If the dignity of women depends upon their having contributed conspicuously to the advance of civilization, what is gained—making all allowances for oppression—by exhuming such as Anne Royall, a feisty nineteenth century publisher who was convicted and fined as a "common scold," granting that the charge was trumped up? It's as if some white supremacist were to support his thesis by citing the invention of the waffle iron. And if the male sex has been historically brutal, one would expect a female victim to tell more poignant atrocity stories than the one recounted by Jane Alpert, who recalled bitterly that her ex-lover had once scrawled her a message in Magic Marker on their refrigerator: "WASH ME." (She went on to say she no longer regretted his death in the Attica revolt.) This in a manifesto embracing everything from prehistory to the apocalypse—a manifesto printed in *Ms.* with great fanfare, including a special introduction. By Gloria Steinem.

The same indiscriminancy appears in the magazine's rhetoric, which often verges on the Symbionese: "sexism," "oppression," "exploitation," "liberation," and so forth, all the jargon of the Seventies assumed complacently, dogmatically, as if it not only corresponded to reality but were also self-explanatory. "WASH ME": that's oppression? Or what? Is all sexual discrimination "sexism"? Is it always bad, or just as a rule? Is any injustice of men to women, as such, "oppressive? (One man wrote in *Ms.,* "I would even [!] argue that in specific situations a woman can oppress a man.") If women are oppressed in the same way Negroes have been—some feminists would say their oppression has been worse—then why isn't this likewise reflected in lower academic scores, shorter life spans, etc.? Oddly enough, even though women *do* live longer than men, and even though our society frowns on men who kill women, one finds in *Ms.* a good deal of talk about "survival," as if merely staying alive and sane were a difficulty of women as such (most of the patients in the mental hospital I used to work in were men), or as if men were waiting to wipe out fractious women at the first opportune moment.

Arlene Croce has observed that the women's liberation movement is the only movement that has to devote full time to convincing its constituents that they are oppressed. Some liberationists acknowledge this, but insist that it merely strengthens their case: that is, women are *so* oppressed that they don't even *know* they're oppressed. Which means that those who don't know the bad news must be told. *Ms.* tells them. It calls this process "consciousness-raising." When a woman learns to throw around words like "sexism"—one of those loathsome neologisms better suited to imprecation than to analysis—her *consciousness* has been certifiably *raised.* I don't much envy that creature whose mind is elevated from what it was by contact with *Ms.*, but she apparently exists, and in profusion. ("There are so many places in this country," Ms. Alpert wrote Ms. Steinem, ". . . where *Ms.* is literally the only thing that stands between a woman and utter insanity.")

Nor is it just her intellect that is enhanced; it is also her sense of herself as put upon by the world, and therefore her self-righteousness too; and consequently her bellicosity. Which is ironic, since *Ms.* depicts women as above all gentle (Lady Macbeth was a male fantasy), and not given to the "male powermongering" that is now "a threat to our survival as a species." They are sensitive Rousseauean essences thrust into a world of Hobbesian brutes, brutes who first paw, then enslave, forcing them to have babies and darn socks. Under the helplessly, unwilling alluring flesh—it is a constant theme of *Ms.*—is the Real Me. Like Yeats's girl in "For Anne Gregory," she wants to be loved "for myself alone and not my yellow hair." Instead the Real Me must fight off the rough attacks and outwit the seductive snares of the male: but it is very hard. Some women are driven to suicide, like Sylvia Plath and Marilyn Monroe; others, like Ingrid Bengis, throw up a lot. The survivors are now politicizing.

Now I have always fancied myself a mighty sensitive fellow, but not ipso facto at odds with other men; in fact I agree with Professor Higgins that "by and large we are a marvelous sex." So I was shocked to find in *Ms.* some expression of doubt about whether men can be reformed, or (as they put it) "humanized." I felt a kind of gratitude to one correspondent who ventured the following surmise: "I think the male can learn to respect and perhaps adopt these [desirable, i.e., feminine] attributes, if trained to do so early in life." That, in *Ms.*, must be taken as a handsome concession, on the order of Dr. Johnson's "Much may be made of a Scotchman, if he be *caught* young."

Still, *Ms.* leaves no doubt that men are, at least for the present, a bad lot. Its writers know some awfully dirty words—I would blush to repeat some of them—but right down there among their devil-terms are *male* and its variants: one reads of *"male* powermonger-ing," or so-and-so's *"masculinist* need to boast," even amid macho butt-kicking talk about what women are going to do to their op-pressors. A woman in a Thurber cartoon coos to a startled man, "I just *love* the idea of there being two sexes, don't you?" And most of us would answer, with a kind of reverent mirth: Yes. But to *Ms.*, there being two sexes shows an annoying want of economy in the Creator. One sex (and maybe a sperm bank)—that would be swell. Three sexes, seven, 41—okay, so long as they were all equal. But it's the stark asymmetries of *these* two sexes—one big and strong, the other small and soft and fertile—they find so vexing. Even a special feature on the "fathering instinct" failed to suggest how it differs from the maternal one; indeed, you gather from it that the two instincts *shouldn't* differ (one subject insists he's not a "fa-ther" but a "parent"). There is nothing admirable or lovable in those things that make men men; there are no *masculine* virtues. Only "human" ones, which men may acquire. Perhaps. Especially if they be *caught* young.

Ms. does want to catch them young. Every issue has "stories for free children," which means children who are "free" of traditional concepts of distinctive sexual roles ("sexist hangups"). A child of either sex may have a healthy interest in sex, but will at least lack masculine ardor, and is therefore humanizable, if not downright human. A recent issue had a special section "for free children," including excerpts from Marlo Thomas' new book *Free to Be . . . You and Me* (the Real You, the Real Me), and a bill of rights for children. The latter listed ten rights: Sexual Freedom, Political Power, Self-determination (a child who wants to run away should have access to a day care center or, if he prefers, a children's com-mune; he shouldn't have to join the circus), and so forth, right down to the right to Responsive Design (an environment without hazards or rough edges; one which would free him from adult con-trol—and, no doubt, free the adult from adult responsibility). The only right missing was the right to be born. But that would have made 11, an awkward number for a bill of rights; and more to the point, would have conflicted with what Ms. Alpert calls "Mother Right."

Sent from underground (she is still a fugitive from the FBI from her Weatherman days), Ms. Alpert's manifesto, the most ambitious *Ms.* has carried to date, combined rancorous memoir with prophetic fury. Its hatred of nature and history, both of which (as Shulamith Firestone has said) are oppressive, produced a corresponding idealization of prehistory (it was matriarchal) and of the future (it *shall* be matriarchal). The world, she wrote, is approaching the final crisis: "Could it not be that just at the moment masculinity has brought us to the brink of nuclear destruction or ecological suicide, women are beginning to rise in response to the Mother's call to save Her planet and create instead the next stage of evolution?" She demanded that "Technology" be "turned over to women *now*," though admitting it would probably have to be taken by force. "Technology," in the right hands, would relieve women of the biological burden of bearing children—inventing the cabbage leaf, as it were—but women would still retain "the power of female consciousness, of the "Mother."

This article "drew more reader reaction than any other piece we have published," the magazine announced a few issues later, and printed seven pages of perfervid letters. There were some demurrals (which, the editors noted, were not really representative), but even they, to judge from the published selection, accepted Ms. Alpert's, and *Ms.*'s, central assumption: that men are good only insofar as they resemble and subserve women. One sex is the norm; the other an aberration. Like *Playboy, Ms.* regards its own gender as the right one, the other a mere extension of it. And indeed if this is so, there is no reason to exalt marriage and procreative sex, which are both suspect for *Ms.* (as for *Playboy*). It is elaborately, tolerant of deviancy, whether in the form of lesbianism, male homosexuality, or abortion; full of blueprints for new "lifestyles," like marriage contracts that divide the husband's income and the wife's household chores, making both partners "equal" (presumably, these equal spouses, hearing a prowler in the night, are to flip a coin to decide who goes downstairs).

Such equality, unfortunately, works only one way, as Dr. Johnson observed: "Your levelers wish to level *down* as far as themselves; but they cannot bear leveling *up* to themselves." *Ms.* confirms this in oddly casual ways, as in a recent article on woman lawyers that approvingly quoted one who represents women in divorce cases. She argued that woman lawyers, questioning "traditional sex roles," were more likely to come up with "creative" new terms of divorce: "For example, most divorce settlements provide that the husband *may* visit his children. I think visitation should be obligatory." Apparently the "traditional sex roles" are not to be so radically changed as to abandon the practice of giving custody to the mother; but let that pass. Let us simply look at the revised roles as the Creative will shape them. John and Jane Doe, say, marry; Jane gets pregnant; John wants the child; Jane doesn't, and exercises her unqualified prerogative of getting it aborted; and that's that. Now take the opposite case: Jane is pregnant; John doesn't want the kid; Jane does, and refuses to abort it; they divorce; John has to support the kid he never wanted. But that's not all: if Jane gets the right lawyer, John may also have to visit the child, or face the penalty of the law. Clearly, John is not free to be . . . him.

"If women's lib wins," Gloria Steinem has written, "perhaps we all do." Perhaps. And if the Equal Rights Amendment passes, perhaps we will all win the thousands upon thousands of lawsuits that will surely ensue. Perhaps a nation's spirit is fortified by a multiplicity of new laws, by vengeful litigation, by frivolous social criticism, by coarse ideological abstractions, and by relentlessly cynical assaults on old customs and civilities. Perhaps anything. If so, then *Ms.* is good for us. Damned good.

DISCUSSION QUESTIONS

1. As the author expresses his opinions and characterizes those of liberated women, he offers a rich collection of words and phrases. These include the following:
   (a) male chauvinist pig
   (b) intellectual coarseness
   (c) bizarre
   (d) doctrinaire
   (e) crude doctrine
   (f) intellectual and moral runts
   (g) dogma *du jour*
   (h) feminist bogeypersons
   (i) sheer indiscriminancy
   (j) Symbionese rhetoric
   (k) sexism
   (l) liberation
   (m) consciousness-raising
   (n) loathsome neologisms
   (o) utter insanity

    (p)   male powermongering
    (q)   sensitive Rousseauean essences
    (r)   the Real Me
    (s)   humanized
    (t)   masculine need to boast
    (u)   macho butt-kicking talk
    (v)   he's not a "father," but a "parent"
    (w)   sexist hangups
    (x)   the right to Responsive Design
    (y)   Mother Right
    (z)   prophetic fury
    (aa) the power of female consciousness
    (bb) perfervid letters
    (cc) creative new terms of divorce

Which of these express definable ideas and which are semantic argument?

2. Evaluate these syllogisms:

Truly gifted people (Mozart, Goethe, Kant, Austen) produce works which show the excellence of their race, sex, or nationality; they do not try to prove it.

Ms. Steinem and her friends try to prove the excellence of their sex.

Ms. Steinem and her friends are not truly gifted people.

Oppressed people (like the blacks) have lower academic scores and shorter life spans.

Women do not have lower academic scores and shorter life spans.

Women are not oppressed people.

3. In presenting examples of "lost women" celebrated by *Ms.*, why did the author select "pirates Anne Bonney and Mary Read"?

4. Why do liberated women call themselves "Ms."?

5. The author says that the Equal Rights Amendment, if passed, would produce "frivolous social criticism," "coarse ideological abstractions," and "relentlessly cynical assaults on old customs and civilities." What does he mean here?

The Watergate Affair

RICHARD M. NIXON

Good evening. I want to talk to you tonight from my heart on a subject of deep concern to every American.

In recent months members of my Administration and officials of the Committee for the Re-election of the President—including some of my closest friends and most trusted aides—have been charged with involvment in what has come to be known as the Watergate affair.

These include charges of illegal activity during and preceding the 1972 Presidential election and charges that responsible officials participated in efforts to cover up that illegal activity.

The inevitable result of these charges has been to raise serious questions about the integrity of the White House itself. Tonight I wish to address those questions.

Last June 17 while I was in Florida trying to get a few days' rest after my visit to Moscow, I first learned from news reports of the Watergate break-in. I was appalled at this senseless, illegal action, and I was shocked to learn that employees of the re-election committee were apparently among those guilty. I immediately ordered an investigation by appropriate Government authorities.

On Sept. 15, as you will recall, indictments were brought against seven defendants in the case.

As the investigation went forward, I repeatedly asked those conducting the investigation whether there was any reason to believe that members of my Administration were in any way involved. I received repeated assurances that there were not. Because of these continuing reassurances, because I believed the reports I was getting, because I had faith in the persons from whom I was getting them, I discounted the stories in the press that appeared to implicate members of my Administration or other officials of the campaign committee.

Until March of this year, I remained convinced that the denials were true and that the charges of involvement by members of the White House staff were false.

The comments I made during this period, the comments made

Televised address given April 30, 1973. Reprinted from *The New York Times*, May 2, 1973.

by my press secretary in my behalf, were based on the information provided to us at the time we made those comments.

However, new information then came to me which persuaded me that there was a real possibility that some of these charges were true and suggesting further that there had been an effort to conceal the facts both from the public—from you—and from me.

As a result, on March 21 I personally assumed the responsibility for coordinating intensive new inquiries into the matter and I personally ordered those conducting the investigations to get all the facts and to report them directly to me right here in this office.

I again ordered that all persons in the Government or at the re-election committee should cooperate fully with the F.B.I., the prosecutors and the grand jury.

I also ordered that anyone who refused to cooperate in telling the truth would be asked to resign from Government service.

And with ground rules adopted that would preserve the basic constitutional separation of powers between the Congress and the Presidency, I directed that members of the White House staff should appear and testify voluntarily under oath before the Senate committee which was investigating Watergate.

I was determined that we should get to the bottom of the matter, and that the truth should be fully brought out no matter who was involved.

At the same time, I was determined not to take precipitive action and to avoid if at all possible any action that would appear to reflect on innocent people.

I wanted to be fair, but I knew that in the final analysis the integrity of this office—public faith in the integrity of this office— would have to take priority over all personal considerations.

Today, in one of the most difficult decisions of my Presidency, I accepted the resignations of two of my closest associates in the White House—Bob Haldeman, John Ehrlichman—two of the finest public servants it has been my privilege to know.

I want to stress that in accepting these resignations I mean to leave no implication whatever of personal wrongdoing on their part, and I leave no implication tonight of implication on the part of others who have been charged in this matter.

But in matters as sensitive as guarding the integrity of our democratic process, it is essential not only that rigorous legal and ethical standards be observed, but also that the public, you, have total confidence that they are both being observed and enforced by those in authority, and particularly by the President of the United States.

They agreed with me that this move was necessary in order to restore that confidence, because Attorney General Kleindienst— though a distinguished public servant, my personal friend for 20 years, with no personal involvement whatever in this matter—has been a close personal and professional associate of some of those who are involved in this case, he and I both felt that it was also necessary to name a new Attorney General.

The counsel to the President, John Dean, has also resigned.

As the new Attorney General, I have today named Elliot Richardson, a man of unimpeachable integrity and rigorously high principle. I have directed him to do everything necessary to insure that the Department of Justice has the confidence and the trust of every law-abiding person in this country. I have given him absolute authority to make all decisions bearing upon the prosecution of the Watergate case and related matters. I have instructed him that if he should consider it appropriate he has the authority to name a special supervising prosecutor for matters arising out of the case.

Whatever may appear to have been the case before, whatever improper activities may yet be discovered in connection with this whole sordid affair, I want the American people, I want you, to know beyond the shadow of a doubt that during my term as President justice will be pursued fairly, fully and impartially, no matter who is involved.

This office is a sacred trust, and I am determined to be worthy of that trust!

Looking back at the history of this case, two questions arise:

How could it have happened—who is to blame?

Political commentators have correctly observed that during my 27 years in politics, I've always previously insisted on running my own campaigns for office.

In both domestic and foreign policy, 1972 was a year of crucially important decisions, of intense negotiations, of vital new directions, particularly in working toward the goal which has been my overriding concern throughout my political career—the goal of bringing peace to America, peace to the world.

And that is why I decided as the 1972 campaign approached that the Presidency should come first and politics second. To the maximum extent possible, therefore, I sought to delegate campaign operations, to remove the day-to-day campaign decisions from the President's office and from the White House.

I also, as you recall, severely limited the number of my own campaign appearances.

Who then is to blame for what happened in this case?

For specific criminal actions by specific individuals, those who committed those actions must of course bear the liability and pay the penalty. For the fact that alleged improper actions took place within the White House or within my campaign organization, the easiest course would be for me to blame those to whom I delegated the responsibility to run the campaign. But that would be a cowardly thing to do.

I will not place the blame on subordinates, on people whose zeal exceeded their judgment and who may have done wrong in a cause they deeply believed to be right. In any organization the man at the top must bear the responsibility.

That responsibility, therefore, belongs here in this office. I accept it.

And I pledge to you tonight from this office that I will do everything in my power to insure that the guilty are brought to justice and that such abuses are purged from our political processes in the years to come, long after I have left this office.

Some people, quite properly appalled at the abuses that occurred, will say that Watergate demonstrates the bankruptcy of the American political system. I believe precisely the opposite is true.

Watergate represented a series of illegal acts and bad judgments by a number of individuals. It was the system that has brought the facts to light and that will bring those guilty to justice.

A system that in this case has included a determined grand jury, honest prosecutors, a courageous judge—John Sirica—and a vigorous free press.

It is essential now that we place our faith in that system, and especially in the judicial system.

It is essential that we let the judicial process go forward, respecting those safeguards that are established to protect the innocent as well as to convict the guilty.

It is essential that in reacting to the excesses of others, we not fall into excesses ourselves.

It is also essential that we not be so distracted by events such as this that we neglect the vital work before us, before this nation, before America at a time of critical importance to America and the world.

Since March, when I first learned that the Watergate affair might in fact be far more serious than I had been led to believe, it has claimed far too much of my time and my attention. Whatever may now transpire in the case, whatever the actions of the grand jury, whatever the outcome of any eventual trials, I must now turn my full attention—and I shall do so—once again to the larger duties of this office.

I owe it to this great office that I hold, and I owe it to you, to my country.

I know that, as Attorney General, Elliot Richardson will be both fair and he will be fearless in pursuing this case wherever it leads. I am confident that with him in charge justice will be done.

There is vital work to be done toward our goal of a lasting structure of peace in the world—work that cannot wait, work that I must do.

Tomorrow, for example, Chancellor Brandt of West Germany will visit the White House for talks that are a vital element of the Year of Europe, as 1973 has been called.

We are already preparing for the next Soviet-American summit meeting later this year.

This is also a year in which we are seeking to negotiate a mutual and balanced reduction of armed forces in Europe which will reduce our defense budget and allow us to have funds for other purposes at home so desperately needed.

It is the year when the United States and Soviet negotiators will seek to work out the second and even more important round of our talks on limiting nuclear arms, and of reducing the danger of a nuclear war that would destroy civilization as we know it.

It is a year in which we confront the difficult tasks of maintaining peace in Southeast Asia and in the potentially explosive Middle East.

There's also vital work to be done right here in America to insure prosperity—and that means a good job for everyone who wants to work; to control inflation that I know worries every housewife, everyone who tries to balance the family budget in America, to set in motion new and better ways of insuring progress toward a better life for all Americans.

When I think of this office, of what it means, I think of all the things that I want to accomplish for this nation, of all the things I want to accomplish for you.

On Christmas Eve, during my terrible personal ordeal of the renewed bombing of North Vietnam which, after 12 years of war, finally helped to bring America peace with honor, I sat down just before midnight. I wrote out some of my goals for my second term as President. Let me read them to you.

To make this country be more than ever a land of opportunity—of equal opportunity, full opportunity—for every American; to provide jobs for all who can work and generous help for those who cannot; to establish a climate of decency and civility in which each person respects the feelings and the dignity in the God-given rights of his neighbor; to make this a land in which each person can dare to dream, can live his dreams not in fear but in hope, proud of his community, proud of his country, proud of what America has meant to himself, and to the world.

These are great goals. I believe we can, we must work for them, we can achieve them.

But we cannot achieve these goals unless we dedicate ourselves to another goal. We must maintain the integrity of the White House.

And that integrity must be real, not transparent.

There can be no whitewash at the White House.

We must reform our political process, ridding it not only of the violations of the law but also of the ugly mob violence and other inexcusable campaign tactics that have been too often practiced and too readily accepted in the past including those that may have been a response by one side to the excesses or expected excesses of the other side.

Two wrongs do not make a right.

I've been in public life for more than a quarter of a century. Like any other calling, politics has good people and bad people and let me tell you the great majority in politics, in the Congress, in the Federal Government, in the state government are good people.

I know that it can be very easy under the intensive pressures of a campaign for even well-intentioned people to fall into shady tactics, to rationalize this on the grounds that what is at stake is of such importance to the nation that the end justifies the means.

And both of our great parties have been guilty of such tactics.

In recent years, however, the campaign excesses that have occurred on all sides have provided a sobering demonstration of how far this false doctrine can take us.

The lesson is clear. America in its political campaigns must not again fall into the trap of letting the end, however great that end is, justify the means.

I urge the leaders of both political parties, I urge citizens—all of you everywhere—to join in working toward a new set of standards, new rules and procedures to insure that future elections will be as nearly free of such abuses as they possibly can be made. This is my goal. I ask you to join in making it America's goal.

When I was inaugurated for a second term this past January 20, I gave each member of my Cabinet and each member of my senior White House staff a special four-year calendar with each day marked to show the number of days remaining to the Administration.

In the inscription on each calendar I wrote these words:

"The Presidential term which begins today consists of 1,461 days, no more, no less. Each can be a day of strengthening and renewal for America. Each can add depth and dimension to the American experience.

"If we strive together, if we make the most of the challenge and the opportunity that these days offer us, they can stand out as great days for America and great moments in the history of the world."

I looked at my own calendar this morning up at Camp David as I was working on this speech. It showed exactly 1,361 days remaining in my term.

I want these to be the best days in America's history because I love America. I deeply believe that America is the hope of the world, and I know that in the quality and wisdom of the leadership America gives lies the only hope for millions of people all over the world that they can live their lives in peace and freedom.

We must be worthy of that hope in every sense of the word.

Tonight, I ask for your prayers to help me in everything that I do throughout the days of my Presidency to be worthy of their hopes and of yours.

God bless America. And God bless each and every one of you.

DISCUSSION QUESTIONS

1. The president began his first major speech on Watergate, "I want to talk to you tonight from my heart," and he closed it "God bless America. And God bless each and every one of you." What tone do such lines give the speech? (Behind Mr. Nixon as he spoke were a statue of Lincoln and a photograph of his family.)

2. "Last June 17 while I was in Florida trying to get a few days' rest after my visit to Moscow. . . ." Why does he mention the Moscow trip? Find other places in the speech where he mentions the achievements and aspirations of his administration. How are these related to Watergate?

3. "The counsel to the President, John Dean, has also resigned."
   How does this line, in context, tell the reader that Mr. Dean
   was out of favor with the president? What does it suggest
   about his relation to Watergate?

4. Mr. Nixon declares, "That responsibility, therefore, belongs
   here in this office. I accept it." What does this mean?

5. Mr. Nixon says that Watergate has taken up too much of his
   time and attention, and "I must now turn my full attention—
   and I shall do so—once again to the larger duties of this office." What is he saying?

6. What is the relation between Watergate and Mr. Nixon's
   "goals for my second term as President"?

7. What is implied in Mr. Nixon's rejection of campaign tactics
   "that have been too often practiced and too readily accepted
   in the past including those that may have been a response by
   one side to the excesses or expected excesses of the other
   side"?

Duty, Honor, Country

DOUGLAS MacARTHUR

No human being could fail to be deeply moved by such a tribute as this, coming from a profession I have served so long and a people I have loved so well. It fills me with an emotion I cannot express. But this award is not intended primarily for a personality, but to symbolize a great moral code—the code of conduct, and chivalry of those who guard this beloved land of culture and ancient descent.

"Duty," "honor," "country"—those three hallowed words reverently dictate what you want to be, what you can be, what you will be. They are your rallying point to build courage when courage seems to fail, to regain faith when there seems to be little cause for faith, to create hope when hope becomes forlorn.

Unhappily, I possess neither that eloquence of diction, that poetry of imagination, nor that brilliance of metaphor to tell you all that they mean.

The unbelievers will say they are but words, but a slogan, but a flamboyant phrase. Every pedant, every demagog, every cynic, every hypocrite, every troublemaker, and, I am sorry to say, some others of an entirely different character, will try to downgrade them even to the extent of mockery and ridicule.

But these are some of the things they build. They build your basic character. They mold you for your future roles as the custodians of the Nation's defense. They make you strong enough to know when you are weak, and brave enough to face yourself when you are afraid.

They teach you to be proud and unbending in honest failure, but humble and gentle in success; not to substitute words for action; not to seek the path of comfort, but to face the stress and spur of difficulty and challenge; to learn to stand up in the storm, but to have compassion on those who fail; to master yourself before you seek to master others; to have a heart that is clean, a goal that is high; to learn to laugh, yet never forget how to weep; to reach into the future, yet never neglect the past; to be serious, yet never take yourself too seriously; to be modest so that you will remember the

Reprinted from the *National Observer*, May 20, 1962. The speech was originally delivered at West Point on May 12, 1962.

simplicity of true greatness, the open mind of true wisdom, the meekness of true strength.

They give you a temperate will, a quality of imagination, a vigor of the emotions, a freshness of the deep springs of life, a temperamental predominance of courage over timidity, an appetite for adventure over love of ease.

They create in your heart the sense of wonder, the unfailing hope of what next, and the joy and inspiration of life. They teach you in this way to be an officer and a gentleman.

. And what sort of soldiers are those you are to lead? Are they reliable? Are they brave? Are they capable of victory?

Their story is known to all of you. It is the story of the American man at arms. My estimate of him was formed on the battlefields many, many years ago, and has never changed. I regarded him then, as I regard him now, as one of the world's noblest figures; not only as one of the finest military characters, but also as one of the most stainless.

His name and fame are the birthright of every American citizen. In his youth and strength, his love and loyalty, he gave all that mortality can give. He needs no eulogy from me, or from any other man. He has written his own history and written it in red on his enemy's breast.

In 20 campaigns, on a hundred battlefields, around a thousand campfires, I have witnessed that enduring fortitude, that patriotic self-abnegation, and that invincible determination which have carved his statue in the hearts of his people.

From one end of the world to the other, he has drained deep the chalice of courage. As I listened to those songs in memory's eye I could see those staggering columns of the First World War, bending under soggy packs on many a weary march, from dripping dusk to drizzling dawn, slogging ankle deep through mire of shell-pocked roads; to form grimly for the attack, blue-lipped, covered with sludge and mud, chilled by the wind and rain, driving home to their objective, and for many, to the judgment seat of God.

I do not know the dignity of their birth, but I do know the glory of their death. They died unquestioning, uncomplaining, with faith in their hearts, and on their lips the hope that we would go on to victory.

Always for them: Duty, honor, country. Always their blood, and sweat, and tears, as they saw the way and the light. And 20 years after, on the other side of the globe, again the filth of dirty fox-holes, the stench of ghostly trenches, the slime of dripping dugouts, those boiling suns of the relentless heat, those torrential rains of devastating storms, the loneliness and utter desolation of jungle trails, the bitterness of long separation of those they loved and cherished, the deadly pestilence of tropical disease, the horror of stricken areas of war.

Their resolute and determined defense, their swift and sure attack, their indomitable purpose, their complete and decisive victory—always victory, always through the bloody haze of their last reverberating shot, the vision of gaunt, ghastly men, reverently following your password of duty, honor, country.

You now face a new world, a world of change. The thrust into outer space of the satellite spheres and missiles marks a beginning of another epoch in the long story of mankind. In the five or more billions of years the scientists tell us it has taken to form the earth, in the three or more billion years of development of the human race, there has never been a more abrupt or staggering evolution.

We deal now, not with things of this world alone, but with the illimitable distances and as yet unfathomed mysteries of the universe. We are reaching out for a new and boundless frontier. We speak in strange terms of harnessing the cosmic energy; of making winds and tides work for us; of creating synthetic materials to supplement or even replace our old standard basics; to purify sea water for our drink; of mining ocean floors for new fields of wealth and food; of disease preventatives to expand life into the hundreds of years; of controlling the weather for a more equitable distribution of heat and cold, or rain and shine; of space ships to the moon; of the primary target in war no longer limited to the armed forces of an enemy, but instead to include his civil populations, of ultimate conflicts between a united human race and the sinister forces of some other planetary galaxy; of such dreams and fantasies as to make life the most exciting of all times.

And through all this welter of change and development your mission remains fixed, determined, inviolate. It is to win our wars. Everything else in your professional career is but corollary to this vital dedication. All other public purpose, all other public projects, all other public needs, great or small, will find others for their accomplishments; but you are the ones who are trained to fight.

Yours is the profession of arms, the will to win, the sure knowledge that in war there is no substitute for victory, that if you lose the Nation will be destroyed, that the very obsession of your public service must be duty, honor, country.

Others will debate the controversial issues, national and international, which divide men's minds. But serene, calm, aloof, you stand as the Nation's war guardians, as its lifeguards from the raging tides of international conflict, as its gladiators in the arena of battle. For a century and a half you have defended, guarded, and protected its hallowed traditions of liberty and freedom, of right and justice.

Let civilian voices argue the merits or demerits of our processes of government: Whether our strength is being sapped by deficit financing indulged in too long, by Federal paternalism grown too mighty, by power groups grown too arrogant, by politics grown too corrupt, by crime grown too rampant, by morals grown too low, by taxes grown too high, by extremists grown too violent; whether our personal liberties are as firm and complete as they should be.

These great national problems are not for your professional participation or military solution. Your guidepost stands out like a tenfold beacon in the night. Duty, honor, country.

You are the lever which binds together the entire fabric of our national system of defense. From your ranks come the great captains who hold the Nation's destiny in their hands the moment the war tocsin sounds.

The long, gray line has never failed us. Were you to do so, a million ghosts in olive drab, in brown khaki, in blue and gray, would rise from their white crosses, thundering those magic words: Duty, honor, country.

This does not mean that you are warmongers. On the contrary, the soldier above all other people prays for peace, for he must suffer and bear the deepest wounds and scars of war. But always in our ears ring the ominous words of Plato, that wisest of all philosophers: "Only the dead have seen the end of war."

The shadows are lengthening for me. The twilight is here. My days of old have vanished—tone and tints. They have gone glimmering through the dreams of things that were. Their memory is one of wondrous beauty, watered by tears and coaxed and caressed by the smiles of yesterday. I listen then, but with thirsty ear, for the witching melody of faint bugles blowing reveille, of far drums beating the long roll.

In my dreams I hear again the crash of guns, the rattle of musketry, the strange, mournful mutter of the battlefield. But in the evening of my memory I come back to West Point. Always there echoes and re-echoes: Duty, honor, country.

Today marks my final roll call with you. But I want you to know that when I cross the river, my last conscious thoughts will be of the corps, and the corps, and the corps.

I bid you farewell.

DISCUSSION QUESTIONS

1. " 'Duty,' 'honor,' 'country'—those three hallowed words reverently dictate what you want to be, what you can be, what you will be. . . . They teach you to be proud and unbending in honest failure, but humble and gentle in success; not to substitute words for action; not to seek the path of comfort, but to face the stress and spur of difficulty and challenge." This kind of rhetoric was more impressive several decades ago than it is today. What are its strengths and weaknesses as argument?

2. Comment on the author's description of "the American man at arms."

3. "I have witnessed . . . that invincible determination which [has] carved his statue in the hearts of his people." Show examples where the author's metaphors are more and less effective.

4. "Let civilian voices argue the merits or demerits of our processes of government." Does the author follow his own recommendation?

5. Why are the final lines, where the author comments on his own military career, the most effective of the speech?

Money... love... power... friends... everything you want!

The amazing miracle of

PSYCHO-COMMAND POWER

can automatically bring you the things you most desire.

Find out how!

Scott Reed—Master Researcher—has just made what may well be one of the most exciting revelations in the history of Psychic Research. For the first time anywhere, he reveals an amazing **materialization** method . . . in a thrilling new book called THE MIRACLE OF PSYCHO-COMMAND POWER: The New Way to Riches, Love, and Happiness.

The Discovery that Could Change Your Life

Scott Reed says, "For years I dreamed of an automatic way to do things, that would make life a heaven on earth. I spent all my time in scientific and occult libraries, searching for the secret . . . until one day it happened! I discovered THE SUPREME COMMAND FOR SUMMONING DESIRES OUT OF THIN AIR . . . and I found that I could actually materialize desires and make things happen automatically! Everything I asked for I received, with this secret . . . a new home . . . a new car . . . thousands of dollars, and more! All problems seemed to dissolve. I felt a mysterious aura around me . . . a feeling of power!"

The Words of the SUPREME COMMAND:

"I B······ I· M····· A··T··H····· P···· T··R·······

M··· I·M··M··· A··I·T··M··· O·T··E······

O·· A·····"

"Into those blanks fit the opening words of THE SUPREME COMMAND, as I discovered it," says Scott Reed—and he gives you the words, in this new book. Then, Reed says, "you'll have a secret that is **guaranteed** to bring about any event or condition you desire, **starting immediately! Anything** is within the realm of possibility!"

Scott Reed Gives Startling Proof!

"On nearly every page of this book," Reed says, "I show you how ordinary men and women from all walks of life —no better, no smarter, no luckier or harder working than you—got what they wanted, easily and automatically, with the Miracle of Psycho-Command Power. If it worked for them—it will work for you, too!"

Reed tells of Phillip O., who—desperate for money— sent up THE SUPREME COMMAND with Psycho-Command Power! A short while later, staring at the kitchen table, empty moments before, he noticed an envelope with a thick bulge in it. It contained $600, the exact amount he needed!

And he tells of Bradford D., who achieved love and companionship with THE SUPREME COMMAND . . . of Bill N., who found a steady stream of money . . . Jill H., who made her boyfriend say "Yes!" instead of no . . . Gloria D., who brought her mate to her without asking.

Find Out for Yourself How to Gain This Power!

Accept Our 10-Day, No-Risk Trial Offer

Put to work in your own life THE MIRACLE OF PSYCHO-COMMAND POWER. Just fill out and return the coupon below, and we'll send you a copy of Scott Reed's amazing book, for ten days at no risk or obligation. This is the book that will enable you to ask for anything and expect to receive it. This is the book that will change your life—instantly.

Don't waste another minute. You have nothing to lose and everything to gain! Fill out the coupon and mail it right now!

--------- NO RISK, MAIL COUPON TODAY ---------

PSYCHO-COMMAND POWERS, Dept. **B-75**
380 Madison Ave., New York, N.Y. 10017

Yes! Send me a copy of Scott **Reed's** THE MIRACLE OF PSYCHO-COMMAND POWER for 10 days' no-risk trial. I enclose *$7.95* as payment in full. If after ten days I am not delighted with this book, I will simply return it for a complete refund.

Name_____

Address_____

City_____State_____Zip_____

YOU RISK NOTHING! Send *$7.95* with coupon—publisher pays all tax, postage, shipping and handling charges for you! Refund guaranteed if you decide to return book.

Advertisement reprinted from *Baer's Agricultural Almanac for the Year 1975* (Lancaster, Pa.: John Baer's Sons, 1974).

DISCUSSION QUESTIONS

1. The discoverer of Psycho-Command Power is Scott Reed. Would the discovery be equally credible if it were made by—
   (a) Irving Reed
   (b) Nancy Reed
   (c) Maharishi Krishna
   (d) Bruno Kinkade
   (e) Ashley Poindexter III
   (f) Donald Sniegowski
   Would the addition of "Dr." or "Professor" or "Major" or "Rev." to these names make them more worthy of belief?

2. What is a "Master Researcher"? What (or perhaps where) are "scientific and occult libraries"?

3. Discuss the denotative and connotative meaning of these terms:
   (a) amazing miracle
   (b) Psycho-Command Power
   (c) automatically
   (d) an amazing materialization method
   (e) the secret

4. How persuasive are the experiences of Phillip O., Bradford D., Jill H., and Gloria D.?

5. "I   B------   I-   M-----   A--   T--   H-----. . . ."
   Why are such "words" effective as persuasion?

6. The book is sold as a "10-Day, No-Risk Trial Offer." Why the 10-day feature?

6

Fallacies

Where there's smoke, there's fire.
Luther left the priesthood to get married.
Is it true blondes have more fun?
If guns are outlawed, only outlaws will have
guns.
Governor Reagan is divorced; he'd make a
poor president.

Certain forms of misleading argument occur so commonly that they have been specifically isolated and labeled. Though most could be analyzed as faulty induction, deduction, and so on, they are treated separately here because the terms describing them are frequently encountered. They are part of the language of argument.

FALSE ANALOGY

To argue by analogy is to compare two things known to be alike in one or more features and to suggest they will be alike in other features as well. This method constitutes reasonable argument if the compared features are genuinely similar. (Jim Dorrill is an *outstanding player-coach;* he will make a fine *manager.*) It is fallacious if the features are essentially dissimilar. (You have *fruit* for breakfast; why not try *Jell-O* for breakfast?)

One tests an analogy by asking if the assumed statement is true and if the elements compared in the argument are sufficiently alike. The assumed assertion is particularly questionable when it exists as an adage. Reelection campaigns regularly submit, for example, that "You wouldn't change horses in the middle of a stream." But the smallest consideration will remind one of situations in which he would be eager to change horses. Equally vulnerable are arguments insisting, "You can lead a horse to water but you can't make him drink"; "Where there's smoke, there's fire"; and "There's no use locking the barn door after the horse has been stolen."

More commonly, one challenges an analogy by showing the fundamental dissimilarity of the things compared. A common argument insists "We have Pure Food and Drug laws, why can't we have comparable laws to keep movie makers from giving us filth?" Here, one must examine the definitions relating to *Pure* and *filth*. Food is called *impure* when the person eating it suffers demonstrable physical distress. Because the individual who devours pornography suffers no such distress, there is no comparable definition of *filth*. Thus, the analogy fails. Similarly, facing the argument, "We should no more teach communism in the schools than we should teach safe-cracking," one can respond that knowing a thing is not practicing it and that, while safe-cracking is a crime, being a communist is not.

Some analogies are more complex. An instance is this argument which appears in most temperance campaigns.

There are 10,000 deaths from alcohol poisoning to 1 from mad-dog bites in this country. In spite of this, we license liquor but shoot the dogs.

Since it is desirable to get rid of any dogs or any liquor which proves deadly, this analogy seems reasonable. But the argument hinges on the implicit recommendation that *all* liquor be outlawed. And this action is reasonable only if one is willing to pursue the comparison and get rid of certain diseased examples by shooting *all* dogs. Similarly, one should scrutinize popular arguments which compare independent nations with dominoes, and federal deficit spending with a family budget.

In argument, an analogy is valuable for illustrating a point or for speculating on an event. But, by itself, it can do little more than that.

Presumed Cause-Effect

Relating an event to its cause can lead to three different fallacies.

Argument in a Circle occurs when a spokesman offers a restatement of his argument as a reason for accepting it. He offers his conclusion, adds *because*, then repeats the conclusion in different words. ("Smoking is injurious because it harms the human body." Or "One phone is not enough in the modern home because modern homes have plenty of phones.") Sometimes the expression is more oblique, with the *because* implied rather than stated. (William Jennings Bryan once declared "There is only one argument that can be made to one who rejects the authority of the Bible, namely, that the Bible is true.") It is pointless to argue that a thing is true because it is true. Repetition is not evidence.

Post Hoc Ergo Propter Hoc ("After this, therefore because of this," commonly shortened to *post hoc*) occurs when someone cites two past events and insists that because one occurred first, it necessarily caused the second. On such evidence he can argue that Martin Luther left the Catholic priesthood in order to get married, that President Hoover caused the Depression, and that continuing attacks by the news media forced the resignation of President Nixon. Such logic can make much of trivial events: in 1964, an anti-Jewish newspaper found sinister implications in the fact that President Johnson had breakfast with Supreme Court Justice Arthur Goldberg shortly before he announced Hubert Humphrey as his running mate.

Post-hoc reasoning is fallacious because it ignores the more complex factors which contribute to an event. A successful advertisement announced, for example, that students who type their schoolwork get 30 percent higher grades than those who do not, then suggested that buying one's child a typewriter would improve his grades. The fallacy here is in the implication that simply owning a typewriter caused the higher grades. Other factors seem more likely to account for the higher grades: the parents who would buy their child a typewriter were those concerned about his education, those who took pains to see that he learned his lessons, those who could afford to give him other cultural advantages, and so on. The typewriter alone gave no one higher grades.

Recognizing the post-hoc fallacy keeps one from jumping to unwarranted conclusions. No one can doubt, for example, that there exist people wearing copper bracelets who no longer suffer arthritis pain; patients treated with L-DOPA who have experienced aphrodiasiac effects; individuals related to John Kennedy's assassination who have died in a variety of ways; and heroin addicts who have been shown to have significantly fewer accidents than other drivers. Nevertheless, sensational cause-effect conclusions are unjustified. A post-hoc judgment would ignore the range of other factors involved.

Non Sequitur ("it does not follow") occurs when a person submits that one fact has led or must inevitably lead to a particular consequence. He can take a present fact (Senator Tom Eagleton underwent shock treatments to relieve mental fatigue) and project a conclusion (He would have been a poor vice-president). Or he can take an anticipated fact (If sex education is offered in American school . . .) and spell out the consequences (Student morals will suffer). The response, of course, is that the conclusion does not necessarily follow from the cited cause.

The term "non sequitur" is widely used. And it lends itself to describe either a multiple-cause argument ("The more you know— the more you do—the more you tax your nerves—the more important it is to relax tired nerves. Try safe, non-habit-forming Sedquilin") or to an argument so extreme that it falls outside the usual categories (Of course the Jehovah Witnesses are communists; otherwise there wouldn't be so many of them). But the term has little value in defining general argument; almost any kind of fallacious reasoning is a non sequitur.

BEGGING THE QUESTION

One begs the question by assuming what it is his responsibility to prove; he builds his argument on an undemonstrated claim. Generally this takes the form of a question. ("Have you stopped beating your wife?" Or "Is it true blondes have more fun?") But it can appear as a declaration. ("Busing is no more the law of the land than is any other communist doctrine.")

Another form of begging the question is to make a charge and then insist that someone else disprove it. ("How do you know that flying saucers haven't been visiting the Earth for centuries?") In all argument, the burden of proof is on the individual making the assertion. It is foolish to try to disprove a conclusion which was never proven in the first place.

IGNORING THE QUESTION

One can ignore the question in two ways: he can leave the subject to attack his opponent, or he can leave the subject to discuss a different topic.

Argumentum ad Hominem is attacking the opposing arguer, not the question at issue. ("You favor resumption of the draft because you're too old to have to serve." Or "The district attorney wants to become famous prosecuting my client so he can run for governor.") The speaker says nothing of the facts; he ignores the question by attacking his adversary.

To avoid confusion, it should be added that an argument about a particular individual—a candidate, a defendant—is probably not *ad hominem* argument; in such a case, the man *is* the issue.

Extension has the same effect. Here one "extends" the question until he is arguing a different subject altogether. (Invoking Senator Kennedy and Chappaquiddick, pro-Nixon bumper stickers proclaimed, "Nobody Drowned at the Watergate!") Invariably the new subject is one the speaker finds it easier to discuss. Regularly, opponents of gun *registration* begin their argument, "If guns are *outlawed*. . . ."

Either-Or is a form of extension. Here a spokesman distorts the question by insisting that only two alternatives exist, his recommendation and something much worse. He will describe a temperance resolution as a decision between Christianity and debauchery, and abortion as a choice between American family life and murder. Should one question America's military involvement in a foreign war, he can challenge, "Which side are you on, anyway?"

This technique is common in presidential elections where political statements regularly pit a favored candidate against a vulnerable figure who can be associated with his opponent. In 1952, for example, Eisenhower ran against Hiss; in 1956, Stevenson challenged Nixon; in 1960, Nixon opposed Pope John XXIII; and in 1964, the Republicans ran against Bobby Baker. In 1968, the Democrats challenged Spiro Agnew; and in 1972 McGovern opposed the Watergate burglars. Like most either-or argument, this straw-man approach oversimplifies the situation.

To all such examples of ignoring the question, the reasonable response is, "Let's get back to the issue."

CONCLUSION

Most of the fallacies cited can be dissected as examples of induction, deduction, semantic argument, and so on. Any false analogy, for example, is deduction with invalid form. Any post-hoc error is induction with an insufficient sample. And any kind of false argument can be called a non sequitur. But special terms do exist for these fallacies, and it is perhaps valuable to have two different ways of looking for them.

IDENTIFY THE FALLACY IN THESE ARGUMENTS

1. So you don't like this story; I suppose you could write a better one.

2. Major Claude Eatherly must be honored as a man of upright conscience. After partaking in the atomic raid on Hiroshima, he left the Air Force and suffered a mental breakdown.

3. Black Power vs. White Power! The War against the white race has already begun. Which side are you on?

4. Arguing from the principle that a person is sick "when he fails to function in his appropriate gender identification," Dr. Charles Socarides, a New York psychoanalyst, concludes that homosexuality is a form of emotional illness.

5. If evolution is true, why has it stopped?

6. No one in his right mind would give a baby a loaded machine gun to play with. Why then do so many people keep urging academic freedom on campuses?

7. Of course, alcoholics lack will power. That's why they're alcoholics.

8. The West wasn't won with a registered gun.

The essays in this section either illustrate or respond to particular fallacies.

Michigan Trial Reveals
FBI Plot To Frame Klansmen

FBI Joins Jew Judge To Frame Klansmen

On August 30, 1971 the nation was electrified by the news that 10 school buses in Pontiac, Michigan were blown up just before the beginning of court ordered busing. Shortly thereafter five patriotic Michigan Klansmen were charged with *"conspiracy"* to bomb the busses. The FBI has never named which individuals actually did the bombing. In fact they had no case at all except for a paid informer who is well known as *"the biggest liar in Pontiac."*

A year and a half passed and still no date for the trial had been set. Finally the defendants made a formal demand *"for a quick and speedy trial."* Little did they know that the courts would maneuver their case before Jewish Federal Judge, Laurance Gubow of Detroit. Also, on poor legal advice, (in this editor's opinion) they waived their right to a jury trial.

The defendants are Robert Miles, 47, Wallace R. Fruit, 31, Dennis C. Ramsey, 25, Alexander J. Distel, Jr., 29, and Raymond Quick, 25.

The chief witness against *"The Michigan Five"* is a Pontiac fireman named Jerome Lauinger, 38. He claims to have overheard Rev. Miles say on July 4 of 1971 that: *"If they are going to bus the blacks, we are going to have to do something about it."* (Nothing illegal here, many folks express such views all the time.)

Then he claims that on Aug. 17 there was a discussion on the *"best way to blow up the busses."* The defendants say no such talk ever took place.

The above is about all the FBI has been able to produce in the case. They spent the rest of two weeks parading FBI agents across the witness stand testifying about all the Klan paraphenalia they found in the homes of the defendants when they arrested them— BUT NOTHING THEY FOUND WAS ILLEGAL!

Biggest Liar in Town

The FBI pimp Lauinger admitted that he sold his soul cheap to the enemy. He said that the FBI only gave him about $700 for his

Reprinted from *The Thunderbolt* (July 1973), pp. 8–9.

expenses. Of course the FBI often tells pimps not to report such payments on their income taxes as much more could have actually been paid. Sometimes they will offer a "bonus" at the end of a trial if the pimp is able to help them gain a conviction of an innocent patriot. Defense Attorney James E. Wells told the court that he would prove Lauinger to be a *"pathological liar."*

The Assistant Fire Chief of Pontiac, Samuel M. James testified that the FBI informer, Jerome Lauinger, was a *"habitual liar."* Mr. James said that he told so many lies that most of the other firemen would walk away from him rather than listen to his *"bull."*

Even the pimp's own brother, William Lauinger, 30, admitted on the witness stand that his brother was such a story teller that he would have to doubt his testimony in this case.

One of the lies that several testified to was Lauinger's claim that some scars on his arms were from combat wounds suffered in World War II. Under cross examination Lauinger admitted, *"Yes, that was a lie."* The fact was that he entered the Navy after the end of that war and never saw combat. This entire case boiled down to whose word should be believed—sincere patriots or this "notorious liar" and paid pimp!

PIMP ALSO A PROVACATEUR

It is even possible that the FBI pimp Lauinger may have bombed the busses himself in order to frame these Patriots. The Thunderbolt has exposed in the past one so-called minister, "Rev." Wesley Pruden, Sr., of Little Rock, Arkansas. Some years back he bombed a building in that city in an FBI plot to frame local patriots. The FBI lost that case and the defense exposed the FBI pimp.

Several Klansmen testified that it was Jerome Lauinger of 699 Clara St., Pontiac, Michigan who talked about bombings. One said that Lauinger boasted that he purchased dynamite in the latter part of 1970 or the early part of 1971 on the pretext of blowing up stumps. A Klansman named Leon Jake testified that the government pimp offered him explosives in May of 1971. Mr. Jake stated:

"Lauinger said he had some (dynamite) in his possession . . . that if I wanted some he'd give me half of it."

FBI Caught in Big Lie

FBI agents testified that they knew the Pontiac buses were going to be bombed 10 days before the event took place. They claimed to have warned the local fire department. Pontiac Fire Chief Charles Marion took the witness stand to flatly swear that the FBI never gave his department any advance knowledge of the bombing. Neither were the Pontiac Police Department alerted. Actually, since bombing is a federal crime, the FBI itself could legally have stood guard over the buses to prevent the bombing.

The FBI is caught in a lie of major proportions when they say they warned local officials of the bombing. This means two things, either their "notorious lying" pimp made up this entire story after the bombings and none of the federal agents had prior knowledge—OR THE PIMP DID THE BOMBING FOR THE FBI TO FRAME FIVE INNOCENT MEN!

More FBI Pimps

The FBI produced two more pimps they had paid to infiltrate the Michigan Klan. One was Wendell Evans. Because of his feigned "activism" in the Klan, Evans had become a local Kligrap and even editor of the "Michigan Klan Newsletter." Here we have a perfect illustration of how low a man must sink when he becomes a professional lying pimp for the FBI. Wendell Evans is related by marriage to two of the defendants, Wallace E. Fruit and Alexander J. Distel, Jr.

He is helping to place his two brothers-in-law in prison by telling the preposterous lie that he once saw dynamite at Fruit's sign shop. Seeking to cover for the lie, he said that Fruit was not there when he peeked in and saw dynamite!

Evans was caught in another lie which should have resulted in his testimony being thrown out of court. Under oath, and penalty of perjury, he testified on the witness stand that he had never discussed this knowledge with government officials. At this point the chief Prosecutor Robert Murphy had to stand up and tell the court that Evans was lying and was just another paid pimp. Murphy said Evans had gone over all of his testimony with the FBI and the prosecutor's office long before the trial.

Another FBI pimp was James O. Vanderver of 792 Blaine, Pontiac, Michigan. The FBI paid him to join the Klan after the bombing. His testimony was to the effect that the KKK believed in violence. He charged that Dennis C. Ramsey had vowed to kill the star FBI pimp, Jerome Lauinger, if he was sent to prison.

Rev. Robert Miles, the former head of the Michigan Klan, said he was shocked at Vanderver's testimony stating: *"He's been to my house. He's eaten there and slept there. His kids played with mine. The government may win the case, but it's lost the moral issue."*

Dennis Ramsey flatly denied Vanderver's story as just more concocted FBI lies.

One FBI Pimp Backs Out

All of this was just too much for one FBI informer named Kenneth R. Petty. He is a student at Macomb County Community College. He said that he joined as a sincere Klansmen to serve his country and the White race. Later Petty said he was pressured by FBI agents who used communist police state tactics. They pressured him to give FBI prompted testimony to the Grand Jury that indicted Miles and the others. He said:

"I was so scared I would have confessed to crimes at the Nuernberg trial. They (FBI) were coming down on the Klan and I thought I would be swept up."

Petty said his testimony before the September, 1971 Grand Jury was all a product of *"coercion."*

Federal Prosecutor Murphy was shaken by Kenneth Petty's testimony and then let an even bigger cat out of the bag. He said that FBI agents had been visiting Petty regularly since 1970 to get information on the Klan out of him. They even gave him money to go to Washington, D.C. to spy on a convention held by Matt Koehl in September, 1971.

Defense Attorney Wells put Petty back on the stand and he said he did these things against his will, because if he refused, he feared the FBI or other government agents would have him killed.

FBI agents during this trial made the amazing admission that they had been able to hire as pimps or frighten into cooperation 10 out of the 18 Klansmen who constituted the total membership of the Pontiac Klavern. In other words, the FBI used illegal acts of terrorism to physically take control of this anti-communist, anti-race mixing, Christian organization!

This is the first time we have ever heard such an admission. This should put every Patriot on guard against the FBI as they are the worst enemy the White Race has. Actually the FBI is out to destroy every organization that actively opposes communism because it goes against our government's formal policy of building an alliance with Russia.

Recent Watergate hearings revealed that the FBI long ago dropped such activities against communist and militant black groups in America. Instead they have applied the "Red Secret Police" methods toward right wing Christian Patriots for the avowed purpose of silencing anti-communism in America! This has been one of the very highest orders from within the FBI. They came from the Jew Mark Felt who has just announced his forthcoming retirement as number two man within the FBI.

FBI THREATENS KLAN WITNESS

It is a criminal offense to intimidate or coerce any witness in a Federal proceeding. Herb Hay, a Pontiac fireman, had agreed to testify for the defense about the FBI's chief pimp Lauinger being a well known liar. Hay backed out because two FBI agents came to his home. They threatened that a drunk and disorderly arrest record of 20 years ago would be brought out in court to embarrass him if he testified for the Klan.

He said the FBI agents remained in his home for 45 minutes making innuendoes that he had better not testify for the Klan. A Grand Jury should be immediately impaneled and the two FBI agents and their superiors who sent them should be indicted, tried and imprisoned for intimidating a witness. The biased Jew Judge Gubow said: *"I haven't heard anything that would be implied threats. All I heard was testimony that these men (FBI) were doing their job."*

(Note: All members of the Jew establishment are strong backers of the FBI. They know the FBI holds down opposition to the Jew plan to make America into a Marxist state. That is why "The FBI Story" on T.V. has so many Jewish sponsors. Jews who help direct and produce the program, as well as its main star, Efrem Zimbalist, Jr., who is also a Jew. The network which carries the program is ABC which is headed by the Jew Goldenson.

Every motion to dismiss the charges against the defendants was overruled by the Jew Judge Gubow. Actually this obviously biased Orthodox Jew should have voluntarily removed himself from the trial because of his prejudice against these Christian defendants.

The defendants have all taken and passed lie detector tests proving that they did not bomb the busses. Gubow refused to allow this entered as evidence. The FBI has never said which one they thought did the bombing. They just charged a "conspiracy." This is one reason the NSRP has long advocated that all "conspiracy" laws be abolished. They are so vague they allow the government to obtain convictions without having to prove anyone did any specific illegal act!

The federal government has no case against Rev. Robert Miles and the other four innocent defendants. Gubow should have tossed the entire government's case out of court for the many illegal and underhanded acts of the FBI. Never has any left wing organization been victim of such tactics as has the Klan. The FBI is quick to admit to the wire tapping of Reds like Daniel Ellsberg so his case could be thrown out of court. Everyone knows the FBI had Rev. Miles phone tapped during this frameup, but they will not admit to it to help him like they did the Jew Ellsberg. Unfortunately Rev. Miles has no friends high up in the FBI like the Jew Mark Felt to help him out.

Jew Judge Finds Klansmen Guilty

The Jew Federal Judge Lawrence Gubow waited over two weeks to announce his verdict "GUILTY ON ALL COUNTS." But guilty of what? The hysterical Jew judge did not stand up in court and say which man was guilty of bombing the busses. Instead he delivered a hate spawned verbal barrage blasting the Klan as a *"racist organization which advocates White Supremacy"* and said he believes the five defendants were still members despite their denials. He said the bombing represented *"the fruit of your conspiracy."*

In other words Judge Gubow has branded himself an enemy of the White race. He is admitting that he has found these five Christian Patriots GUILTY because they are "racists" and "advocates of White Supremacy." Judge Gubow also does not believe in the U.S. Constitution because it gives us the right to hold such views.

Judge Gubow again extended this case by postponing his sentencing of the Patriots. They can be given as much as a $10,000 fine and 10 years in prison for "conspiracy." By the time this newspaper reaches its readers you no doubt will have read in the daily press and on T.V. their gloating over the sentences imposed by Judge Gubow.

*This outrageous frameup case will be appealed, of course. Jus-
tice may still be obtained for these men. We will continue to keep
you informed as to the eventual disposition of this case.*

DISCUSSION QUESTIONS

1. "This entire case boiled down to whose word should be believed—sincere patriots or this 'notorious liar' and paid pimp!"
Name the fallacy here. Identify examples of begging the
question, ad hominem argument, either-or, and post hoc
fallacy as they appear in the essay.

2. The essay contains several arguments. Trace through the article to find evidence for each of the following:
    (a) that Jerome Lauinger lied in court
    (b) that the Government had a weak case against the five
        Klansmen
    (c) that the FBI worked to frame these and other Klansmen
    (d) that there is an active "Jewish establishment"
    (e) that the FBI is heavily influenced by the Jews

3. How would *Occam's razor* (see p. 12) lead one to judge this
case?

4. Was Judge Gubow's Jewish bias demonstrated by his refusal
to allow lie-detector tests as evidence in court?

5. The author treats Jews, communists, race-mixers, and the
FBI as a common enemy. How are these related?

This Thing Called Love Is Pathological

LAWRENCE CASLER

> Men have died from time to time,
> and worms have eaten them,
> but not for love.
> —Act IV, Scene I, *As You Like It*

Magazines, movies and television teach us the joys of love. Advertisers insist that we must look good and smell good in order to escape loveless solitude. Artists, philosophers and hippies urge their varying versions of Love; and most psychotherapists hold that the ability to love is a sign—sometimes *the* sign—of mental health.

To suggest that this emphasis on lovingness is misplaced is to risk being accused of arrested development, coldness, low self-image, or some unmentionable deficiency. Still, the expanding frontiers of psychology require a reconsideration of love at this time.

We shall be concerned, chiefly, with what is generally called "romantic" love. But many of these observations may be applicable to other varieties as well.

Love, like other emotions, has causes, characteristics and consequences. Temporarily setting aside an inquiry into why, or whether, love makes the world go 'round, makes life worth living, and conquers all, let us consider the somewhat more manageable question of causality. Love between man and woman has many determinants, but instinct is not one of them. Anthropologists have described entire societies in which love is absent, and there are many individuals in our society who have never loved. To argue that such societies and individuals are "sick" or "the exception that proves the rule" (whatever *that* means) is sheer arrogance. Love, when it exists, is a learned emotion. Explanations for its current prevalence must be sought elsewhere than in the genes.

Most individuals in our society, beset by parent-bred, competition-bred insecurity, need acceptance, confirmation, justification. Part of this need is inescapable. Life requires continual decision-

Reprinted from *Psychology Today*, December 1969, pp. 18–20, 74–76.

making: white vs. red wine, honesty vs. dishonesty, etc. In the presence of uncertainty, most of us need to know that we are making the right decisions, so we seek external validation. We are, therefore, absurdly pleased when we meet someone who shares our penchant for Palestrina or peanut butter. Should we find one person whose choices in many different matters coincide with our own, we will value this buttress of our self-esteem. This attachment to a source of self-validation constitutes one important basis for love.

While the relationship between loving and being loved is an intimate one, this is not to say that love is automatically reciprocated. Indeed, it may lead to feelings of revulsion if the individual's self-image is already irretrievably low: "Anyone who says he loves *me* must be either a fool or a fraud." Still, a person is relatively likely to love someone who loves him. Indirect support for this generalization comes from a number of experiments in which persons are falsely informed that they are liked (or disliked) by other members of their group. This misinformation is enough to elicit congruent feelings in most of the deceived subjects. A similar kind of feedback often operates in the elaborate American game of dating. The young woman, for any of several reasons, may pretend to like her escort more than is actually the case. The man, hungry for precisely this kind of response, responds favorably and in kind. And the woman, gratified by this expression of affection, now feels the fondness she had formerly feigned. Falling in love may be regarded, in cases such as these, as a snowball with a hollow core.

Nevertheless, we do not fall in love with everyone who shows acceptance of us. Other needs clamor for satisfaction. And the more needs that one person satisfies, the more likely are we to love that person. One of the foremost needs is called, very loosely, sex. Our love is elicited not simply by the ego-booster, but by the ego-booster with sex appeal.

The mores of our society discourage us from seeking sexual gratification from anyone with whom we do not have a preexisting relationship. As a result, the more ego-boosting a relationship is, the greater the tendency will be for the booster to serve—actually or potentially—as a sex-satisfier. But it is also true that a person who gives one sexual pleasure tends to boost one's ego. Once again, the snowball effect is obvious.

Society emphasizes, furthermore, the necessity for love to precede sex. Although many disregard this restriction, others remain frightened or disturbed by the idea of a purely sexual relationship.

The only way for many sexually aroused individuals to avoid frustration or anxiety is to fall in love—as quickly as possible. More declarations of love have probably been uttered in parked cars than in any other location. Some of these surely are nothing more than seduction ploys, but it is likely that self-seduction is involved in many cases.

For most of us, the internal and external pressures are so great that we can no longer "choose" to love or not love. Loving becomes inevitable, like dying or getting married. We are so thoroughly brainwashed that we come to pity or scorn the person who is not in love. (Of course, the pity or scorn may be self-directed, but not for long: anyone who does not have the inner resources to stand alone can usually impose himself upon somebody else who is equally incapacitated.)

Our society, besides being love-oriented, is marriage-oriented. From early childhood on, we hear countless statements beginning, "When (not *if*) you get married. . . ." And, just as love is regarded as a prerequisite for sex, it is regarded as a prerequisite for marriage. Consequently, the insecurity and the fear of social punishment that force most of us into marriage provide additional powerful motives for falling in love. (The current value of marriage as a social institution, while open to question, is beyond the scope of this essay.)

To summarize, the *causes* of love are the needs for security, sexual satisfaction, and social conformity. Thus viewed, love loses its uniqueness. Hatred, too, in societies that are as aggression-oriented as ours is love-oriented, may reflect these same needs. To state that love is a superior emotion is to express a current cultural bias. Nothing is good or bad but culture makes it so.

We can study the *characteristics* of love by using techniques of the laboratory psychologist. Several of our emotions trigger specific, distinguishable biochemical reactions. Fear, for example, can be reliably inferred from adrenal and other secretions. However, no physiological indices have been discovered for love. Perhaps there is no biological correlate of love. Perhaps there *is* a correlate, but one so subtle that it has not yet been observed. Or perhaps love is accompanied by other emotions so that its own particular signs are cancelled.

This last possibility seems especially attractive. Love involves need-satisfaction, and need-satisfaction typically is associated (as a cause or an effect) with physical relaxation. But physical relaxation is not a usual concomitant of love. Perhaps the relaxation is being neutralized by sexual arousal or by such tension-producing emotions as anger or fear. The intrusion of either of these latter emotions is easily explicable. The lover may well be angry because he resents his increasing dependency. (Recall that the loved person is likely to be viewed as the actual or potential gratifier of more and more needs—self-esteem, sex, etc.—and therefore becomes more and more indispensable.) A man can come to hate his mistress or his wife as he hates the cigarettes or race track to which he is addicted.

Another likely accompaniment of need-satisfaction is fear. Every increase in dependency increases the fear of losing the source of gratification. There is always the chance of loss through death, but the fear is more usually based, in competitive societies, on the possibility that the loved one will find someone else more gratifying. The fear of loss of the beloved thus fuses with the fear of loss of self-respect. Jealousy, generally regarded as a destructive emotion, thus appears to be a well-nigh inevitable component of love.

While both fear and anger seem to be inextricably involved in love, fear is probably the more fundamental. Indeed, the anger may be viewed as a reaction to fear. This being the case, a working definition emerges: love is the fear of losing an important source of need gratification.

Up to now, my emphasis has been on so-called romantic love. But the same four-letter word is used in an almost infinite variety of other contexts. Besides loving his wife, one may love his parents, his children, his dog, the New York Mets, and God. (We shall return to God later.) One may also, following the lead of psychotherapists and adolescents of all ages, love love. Hopefully, the emotion is somewhat different in each of these cases, but there is considerable overlap. For example, whatever is loved is likely to be a satisfier of multiple needs. Also, it may be that only those experiences that are believed, or feared, to be transitory can inspire love.

Another characteristic shared by many types of love is the primacy of the skin. The mother wishes to touch her child almost constantly, young lovers are obsessed by desire for physical contact, the vain person (the lover of self) continually engages in hair-patting and other self-touching activity. Even the rhesus monkeys in Harlow's experiments demonstrate that whatever love may be, it is likely to be found in the presence of something soft and cuddly.

The skin is richly endowed with nerve endings, and neurophysiologists have found that the nerve fibers connecting the skin and the central nervous system are better developed at birth than any others. Most of the newborn's experiences are, therefore, tactile. His first contact with his mother is skin contact, and, as other receptive modes develop, they become associated with cutaneous stimulation. Thus, if the baby is held during feeding, he will probably associate skin contact with the satisfaction of hunger. Touching another person acquires linkages with an expanding number of needs and finally becomes an independent source of gratification. The progression may be viewed as beginning with *skin* love, broadening to *kin* love, and culminating in that mildly pathological state of being *in* love.

Recent experiments suggest a relationship between the skin and pleasure centers in the brain. Should this research continue to be fruitful, we will have an explanation of love in terms of the workings of the central nervous system. Meanwhile, we may content ourselves with the observation that when love finds its ultimate physical expression in sexual intercourse, more square inches of skin are stimulated than in any other conceivable joint activity. Love is, undoubtedly, a touching experience.

But love is more than skin deep. If we examine the language of love, we find intimations of yet another of its components. At varying levels of discourse, we encounter such terms as "adoration," "heavenly transport," and "soul kiss." The loved one is an angel, a goddess, a divine creature. Perhaps the most seminal assertion in the Bible is that "God is love." Clearly, the interpenetration of love and religion is too pervasive to be accidental.

The virtual deification of the beloved can be traced to the era of courtly love. In *The Natural History of Love,* Morton Hunt provides several examples: The lady of the troubadors (who was often addressed as "Madonna") was an "inert, icon-like figure." Duke Louis of Bourbon is described as "a very amorous knight, first towards God and then towards all ladies and highborn girls." And one writer of the period portrayed "Lancelot coming to Guinevere's room . . . and then bowing and genuflecting at her door as he leaves, precisely as if before a shrine."

Perhaps the persistent influence of courtly love can be understood in terms of this trinity of love, sex and religion. The linkage of the three has received particularly vivid documentation in religious writings. To give but one instance, St. Theresa of Avila offers this description of a visionary experience:

I saw an angel . . . in bodily form. . . . He was most beautiful—his face burning as if he were one of the highest angels, who seem to be all of fire. . . . I saw in his hand a long spear of gold and at the iron's point there seemed to be a little fire. He appeared to me to be thrusting it at times into my heart, and to pierce my very entrails: when he drew it out, he seemed to draw them out also and to leave me all on fire with a great love of God. The pain was so great that I cried out, but at the same time the sweetness which that violent pain gave me was so excessive, that I could not wish to be rid of it. . . .

This closely resembles the plea to "sheathe in my heart sharp pain up to the hilt," in a love poem by Coventry Patmore, as well as the phallic "sheathings" and "thrustings" that loom so large in the avid descriptions in *Fanny Hill*. Worthy of note, too, is the fact that a nun who has sexual intercourse is regarded by the Church as an adulteress.

Let us turn now to a consideration of the *consequences* of love. First, being in love makes it easier to have guilt-free sex, to marry, and to view oneself as a normal, healthy citizen of the Western world. Love also tends to alter certain psychological processes. According to a charming quotation that I've been able to trace back no further than its utterance in an old movie called *Mr. Skeffington,* "A woman is beautiful only when she is loved." The statement, however, is not quite accurate. A woman (likewise a man, a worm, a grain of sand) may become beautiful when the perceiver has been primed with LSD, hypnosis, or anything else that can induce hallucinations. In short, love may create the error of over-evaluation. The doting lover is doomed either to painful disillusion or to the permanent delusion that so closely resembles psychosis.

Some may argue that I am speaking of immature infatuation, rather than real love. Mature love, they may insist, is a broadening, deepening experience. This postulation of the salutary effects of love is so pervasive that we must examine its validity. First, there is the matter of evidence. Subjective reports are notoriously unreliable, and experimental studies are nonexistent. The claim that love promotes maturity is unpersuasive without some indication that the individual would not have matured just as readily in the absence of love. Indeed, to the extent that love fosters dependency, it may be viewed as a deterrent to maturity.

I am not asserting that the effects of love always border on the pathological. I *am* saying that the person who seeks love in order to obtain security will become, like the alcoholic, increasingly dependent on this source of illusory well-being. The secure person who seeks love would probably not trap himself in this way. But would the secure person seek love at all?

One inference to be drawn from the material here is that the nonloving person in our society is likely to be in a state of either very good or very poor mental health. The latter possibility requires no extended explanation. One of the standard stigmata of emotional disturbance is the inability to love. Most schools of psychotherapy aim specifically at the development of this ability. Some therapies go so far as to designate the therapist himself as a proper recipient of the patient's newly released love impulses (perhaps on the assumption that if the patient can love his therapist, he can love anybody).

The other part of the statement—that a love-free person can be in excellent mental health—may seem less acceptable. But if the need for a love relationship is based largely on insecurity, conformity to social pressures, and sexual frustration, then the person who is secure, independent, and has a satisfying sex life will not need to love. He will, rather, be a person who does not find his own company boring—a person whose inner resources are such that other persons, although they provide pleasure and stimulation, are not absolutely necessary. We have long been enjoined to love others as we love ourselves. But perhaps we seek love relationships with others only because we do not love ourselves sufficiently.

What would a healthy love-free person be like? One might assume that coldness would be among his most salient characteristics. But a cold person is simply one who does not give us the warmth we want or need. The attribution of coldness says more about the person doing the attributing than it does about the person being characterized. Absence of warmth is responded to negatively only by those insecure persons who interpret it as rejection. (Similarly, a nymphomaniac has been defined as a woman whose sex drive is stronger than that of the person who is calling her a nymphomaniac.)

Would the love-free person be egotistical? Perhaps, but only if that term is relieved of its ugly connotations. To be self-centered does not mean to disregard the worth of other people. It does imply that other people are reacted to within a frame of reference that is centered on the self. There is nothing reprehensible about this. In fact, most psychologists would probably accept the position that we are *all* self-centered. No matter how other directed our actions may appear, they are functions of *our* perception of the world, based, in turn, on *our* previous experiences. Since every act is a "self-ish" one, evaluative criteria should be applied only to the effects of selfishness, rather than to selfishness, *per se*.

This essay has not been anti-love, but pro-people. I view society's emphasis on love as both an effect and a cause of the insecurity, dependency, and frightened conformity that may be the death of us all. To love a person means, all too often, to use that person. And exploitation, even if mutual, is incompatible with human growth. Finally, like a crutch, love may impede the exercise of our own potential for growth, and thus tend to perpetuate itself.

Perhaps the goal of social reformers should be not love, but respect—for others and, most of all, for self.

DISCUSSION QUESTIONS

1. The author describes a lover as a product of social pressure and sexual frustration and defines a love-free person as honest, secure, and independent. Can the argument as a whole be said to express a common fallacy?

2. Consider the language used to describe the two conditions (love: "dependency," "ego-boosting," "exploitation" vs. non-love: "inner resources," "independent," "excellent mental health"). Distinguish terms which have a specific meaning from those which simply convey a snarl or purr effect.

3. Love is said to derive from the need for security, sex, and social conformity. The author adds, "Hatred, too, in societies that are as aggression-oriented as ours is love-oriented, may reflect these same needs. To state that love is a superior emotion is to express a current cultural bias." Discuss the kinds of definition necessary before one can begin to argue this statement.

4. "We can study the *characteristics* of love by using techniques of the laboratory psychologist." Among the characteristics, the author mentions physical relaxation, anger, fear, and the desire for tactile stimulation. Could one shape a laboratory experiment to demonstrate that love produces these effects? Which fallacy of argument would be likely to result?

5. In discussing what might be called religious love, the author quotes the writings of Morton Hunt, St. Theresa of Avila, Coventry Patmore, and John Cleland (*Fanny Hill*). How persuasive is this argument by authority?

6. The author says that love creates "the error of overevaluation" as does LSD and hypnosis and that, like alcohol, it can gratify an insecure person. Discuss this either as argument by analogy or as a deductive syllogism.

7. The essay rejects the claim that genuine love (as opposed to infatuation) produces a broadening, maturing effect: "Subjective reports are notoriously unreliable, and experimental studies are nonexistent." Would it be possible to shape a controlled experiment to test this question? Does the lack of experimental data preclude drawing any conclusions in the area?

8. The author refuses to distinguish romantic love from the love one might have for his children, for his dog, for God, for the New York Mets, or for love itself. Is this identification self-evident? Is it subject to evidence?

Teaching As a Subversive Activity

NEIL POSTMAN AND CHARLES WEINGARTNER

Picture this scene: Dr. Gillupsie has grouped around him several of the young resident surgeons at Blear General Hospital. They are about to begin their weekly analysis of the various operations they have performed in the preceding four days. Gillupsie nods in the direction of Jim Kildear, indicating that Kildear's cases will be discussed first:

GILLUPSIE: Well Jim, what have you been up to this week?

KILDEAR: Only one operation. I removed the gall bladder of the patient in Room 421.

GILLUPSIE: What was his trouble?

KILDEAR: Trouble? No trouble. I believe it's just inherently good to remove gall bladders.

GILLUPSIE: Inherently good?

KILDEAR: I mean good in itself. I'm talking about removing all gall bladders *qua* removing gall bladders.

GILLUPSIE: Oh, you mean removing gall bladders *per se*.

KILDEAR: Precisely, Chief. Removing his gall bladder had intrinsic merit. It was, as we say, good for its own sake.

GILLUPSIE: Splendid, Jim. If there's one thing I won't tolerate at Blear, it's a surgeon who is merely practical. What's in store next week?

KILDEAR: Two frontal lobotomies.

GILLUPSIE: Frontal lobotomies *qua* frontal lobotomies, I hope?

KILDEAR: What else?

GILLUPSIE: How about you, young Dr. Fuddy? What have you done this week?

FUDDY: Busy. Performed four pilonidal-cyst excisions.

GILLUPSIE: Didn't know we had that many cases.

FUDDY: We didn't, but you know how fond I am of pilonidal-cyst excisions. That was my major in medical school, you know.

GILLUPSIE: Of course, I'd forgotten. As I remember it now, the prospect of doing pilonidal-cyst excisions brought you into medicine, didn't it?

FUDDY: That's right, Chief. I was always interested in that. Frankly, I never cared much for appendectomies.

GILLUPSIE: Appendectomies?

FUDDY: Well, that seemed to be the trouble with the patient in 397.

GILLUPSIE: But you stayed with the old pilonidal-cyst excision, eh?

Reprinted from *Teaching as a Subversive Activity* (New York: Delacorte Press, 1969), pp. 39–43.

FUDDY: Right, Chief.

GILLUPSIE: Good work, Fuddy. I know just how you feel. When I was a young man, I was keenly fond of hysterectomies.

FUDDY [*giggling*]: Little tough on the men, eh, Chief?

GILLUPSIE: Well, yes [*snickering*]. But you'd be surprised at how much a resourceful surgeon can do. [*Then, solemnly.*] Well, Carstairs, how have things been going?

CARSTAIRS: I'm afraid I've had some bad luck, Dr. Gillupsie. No operations this week, but three of my patients died.

GILLUPSIE: Well, we'll have to do something about this, won't we? What did they die of?

CARSTAIRS: I'm not sure, Dr. Gillupsie, but I did give each one of them plenty of penicillin.

GILLUPSIE: Ah! The traditional "good for its own sake" approach, eh, Carstairs?

CARSTAIRS: What were you treating them for?

CARSTAIRS: Well, each one was awful sick, Chief, and I know that penicillin helps sick people get better.

GILLUPSIE: It certainly does, Carstairs. I think you acted wisely.

CARSTAIRS: And the deaths, Chief?

GILLUPSIE: Bad patients, son, bad patients. There's nothing a good doctor can do about bad patients. And there's nothing a good medicine can do for bad patients, either.

CARSTAIRS: But still, I have a nagging feeling that perhaps they didn't *need* penicillin, that they might have needed something else.

GILLUPSIE: Nonsense! Penicillin never fails to work on good patients. We all know that. I wouldn't worry too much about it, Carstairs.

Perhaps our playlet needs no further elaboration, but we want to underscore some of its points. First, had we continued the conversation between Dr. Gillupsie and his young surgeons, we could easily have included a half dozen other "reasons" for inflicting upon children the kinds of irrelevant curricula that comprise most of conventional schooling. For example, we could have had one doctor still practicing "bleeding" his patients because he had not yet discovered that such practices do no good. Another doctor could have insisted that he has "cured" his patients in spite of the fact that they have all died. ("Oh, I taught them that, but they didn't learn it.") Still another doctor might have defended some practice by reasoning that, although his operation didn't do much for the patient now, in later life the patient might have need for exactly this operation, and if he did, *voilà!*, it will already have been done.

The second point we would like to make is that we have not

"made up" these "reasons." Our playlet is a parody only in the sense that it is inconceivable for doctors to have such conversations. Had we, instead, used a principal and his teachers, and if they discussed what was "taught" during the week, and why, our playlet would have been a documentary, and not a heavy-handed one, either. There are thousands of teachers who believe that there are certain subjects that are "inherently good," that are "good in themselves," that are "good for their own sake." When you ask "Good for whom?" or "Good for what purpose?" you will be dismissed as being "merely practical" and told that what they are talking about is literature *qua* literature, grammar *qua* grammar, and mathematics *per se*. Such people are commonly called "humanists."

There are thousands of teachers who teach "subjects" such as Shakespeare, or the Industrial Revolution, or geometry because *they* are inclined to enjoy talking about such matters. In fact, that is why they became teachers. It is also why their students fail to become competent learners. There are thousands of teachers who define a "bad" student as any student who doesn't respond to what has been prescribed for him. There are still thousands more who teach one thing or another under the supposition that the "subject" will do something for their students which, in fact, it does not do, and never did, and, indeed, which most evidence indicates, does just the opposite. And so on.

The third point we would like to make about our analogy is that the "trouble" with all these "reasons" is that they leave out the (patient) learner, which is really another way of saying that they leave out reality. With full awareness of the limitations of our patient-learner metaphor, we would assert that it is insane (literally or metaphorically, take your pick) to perform a pilonidal-cyst excision unless your patient requires it to maintain his comfort and health; *and* it is also insane (again, take your pick as to how) for a teacher to "teach" something unless his students require it for some identifiable and important purpose, which is to say, for some purpose that is related to the life of the learner. *The survival of the learner's skill and interest in learning is at stake.* And we feel that, in saying this, we are not being melodramatic.

Recently, we attended a state convention of supervisors of teachers of English. The state in question has had a troubled and ugly history of racial crisis. Its people are struggling, against themselves, to adopt attitudes America desperately needs. Like other states, this one has had many of its young men in Vietnam, killing and being killed for reasons not all Americans support. Poverty is no stranger to this state. Nor is censorship, The John Birch Society, or a dozen other issues and quarrels that separate Americans from each other and from a satisfactory meeting with the future. Since all of these problems are human problems, in one way or another they are touched, shaped, even created by language. Could there be, then, a more interesting meeting to attend than one convened by supervisors of teachers concerned primarily with language and its uses? Early in the proceedings a man rose to ask a question about linguistics, for that was the main topic of the conference. "What we want to know," he asked the assembled experts, "is which grammar should we teach?" Now, what would you suppose to be the response of an audience of mature, responsible educators to such a question? Laughter perhaps, at a feeble attempt at irony? Annoyance maybe, for the time it wastes? Disgust, in a measure equal to the seriousness of the questioner? Wrong. There was applause. Warm, fully approving applause. The man was right. That was exactly what the audience wanted to know, and the answer it received was also warmly appreciated: teach all of the grammars, and prepare yourself to teach, as well, those yet to come.

Where is the learner in all of this? Where is his world?

DISCUSSION QUESTIONS

1. This argument hinges on an analogy between instructors teaching students and doctors treating patients. Is this a reasonable comparison from which to draw a conclusion? Are there essential differences?

2. In the analogy, it is obvious that the surgeon relates to the teacher and the patient to the student. What elements of teaching are related to these features:
   (a) frontal lobotomies
   (b) hysterectomies
   (c) the patient with appendicitis
   (d) deaths
   (e) bad patients

3. "There are thousands of teachers who teach 'subjects' such as Shakespeare, or the Industrial Revolution, or geometry because *they* are inclined to enjoy talking about such mat-

ters." Are the authors saying that Shakespeare, the Industrial Revolution, and geometry should not be taught?

4. The authors say it is a mistake to emphasize a kind of grammar in a state that is troubled with questions of race, Vietnam, poverty, and the John Birch Society. They insist nothing should be taught which is not "related to the life of the learner." What areas do they think should be taught?

There Is No Middle Ground!

Reprinted from *The Thunderbolt*, April 1969, p. 6.

DISCUSSION QUESTIONS

1. The terms of this argument tend to be largely snarl words and purr words:
   (a) White American
   (b) Freedom
   (c) Racial Purity
   (d) Christianity
   (e) Patriotism
   (f) Communism
   (g) Mongrelization
   (h) Jewish Corruption
   (i) Treason
   Are some of these more subject to specific definition than others?

2. Is this a straightforward example of the either-or fallacy?

3. Is there an instance or two of begging the question?

7

Statistics

One-third of Johns Hopkins coeds wed
professors.
Smoke Viceroy; it has 20,000 filters.
In May 1973, Americans reported 361 UFO's.
There are 9 million rats in New York City.
My candidate will be lucky to win 15 percent of
the vote.

There are a number of ways in which statistics can be used to
distort argument. A spokesman can cite impressive averages, irrelevant totals, and homemade figures. He can present his numbers
in a context which will make them appear large or small, according to his wish.

A common fallacy involves the use of "average" figures: e.g.,
average income, average price, average audience size. It is easy to
argue from such statistics, because the word "average" can mean
three things. What, for example, is the average if a group of 15
housewives interviewed respond that they watch television 41, 32,
28, 25, 21, 18, 12, 10, 9, 5, 5, 5, 1, and 0 hours per week? From
this data, it can be said that the group watched television an
average of 14.533 hours per week, or 10 hours per week, or 5
hours per week. The figure 14.533 is the *mean* (the total number
of hours watched divided by the number of viewers); the figure 10
is the *median* (the middle number in the list); and the figure 5 is
the *mode* (the number which appears most frequently). Each kind
of average has its value, according to the kind of data being measured. But all three are available to the spokesman seeking to ma-
nipulate an argument.

Questionable data can produce impressive averages. Numbers
derived from memory, guesswork, and exaggeration can be
averaged with exquisite precision. (The figure 14.533 in the preceding paragraph was calculated after 15 housewives made rough
guesses of their TV viewing time.) Dr. Kinsey interviewed American men and reported that those without a high-school education

163

averaged 3.21 sex experiences per week. The annual FBI report, *Crime in the United States,* compiling data from police departments across the country, showed that Baltimore in one year suffered a crime increase of 71 percent. But police departments report crimes differently and with different degrees of accuracy; the sensational Baltimore figure derived, not from a huge increase in crime, but from more accurate police reporting in the second year.

Similarly, notable results can be produced from a small or partial sample. Some years ago, a survey reported that 33 and one-third percent of all coeds at Johns Hopkins University had married faculty members. Johns Hopkins had only three women students at the time. Similarly, advocates for extrasensory perception like to report cases where a gifted individual (Hubert Pearce, Basil Shackleton, etc.) has produced laboratory results in which the odds were 10 million to one against chance as the explanation. Routinely, it is discovered that such cases were *part* of a longer series of tests and that the results of the entire experiment were not given.

An argument can be bulwarked with irrelevant statistics. Some years ago, cigarette companies responded to evidence that smoking causes cancer by counting filter traps. Viceroy boasted 20,000 filters ("twice as many as the other two largest-selling brands") until Parliament began claiming 30,000, and Hit Parade overwhelmed both with 400,000. These were impressive figures, but totally pointless; there was no evidence that *any* filter protected one from the pernicious effects of smoking, and no one had defined "filter trap." This practice of putting large numbers to undefined elements has been particularly notable in those given to counting communist-front citations, UFO's, and angels.

Even when counting clearly defined entities, a spokesman can offer irrelevant numbers. In a period of high unemployment, he can proclaim that more Americans are employed than ever before. Responding to a demonstrated statistical relationship between cigarettes and lung cancer, he can observe that the vast majority of smokers do not get cancer. In a time of rising crime, he can oppose gun-control legislation by computing that only 34/10,000ths of 1 percent of American handguns are involved in homicides.

There is also a kind of irrelevancy in statistics derived from a singular example. Hollywood Bread, for example, advertised that it had fewer calories per slice than other breads; this occurred because its slices were cut thinner. Carlton Cigarettes boasts it has regularly been tested as lowest in "tar" of all filter kings; one reason is that it measures 2 mm. shorter than the other cigarettes, and therefore contains less tobacco. Television personality Hugh Downs announced that he got 28.3 miles per gallon driving a Mustang II from Phoenix to Los Angeles; the trip is largely downhill.

The preceding examples indicate that one does not have to make up statistics to create a misleading argument. But, of course, one *can* make up statistics, too. For example, the temperance spokesman who built an analogy on the claim that there were 10,000 deaths from alcohol poisoning to 1 from mad-dog bites, was using figures which exist nowhere else.

Homemade statistics usually relate to events that have not been measured or which are impossible to measure. Authorities can be suspiciously precise about events too trivial to have been counted. (*Esquire* reported that, as of February 1964, Judy Garland had sung "Over the Rainbow" 10,478 times. Dr. Joyce Brothers declared that "the American girl kisses an average of seventy-nine men before getting married.") They can be glibly confident about obscure facts. (A *Nation* article said there were 9 million rats in New York City. A Lane cedar chest advertisement warned that moths destroy $400 million worth of goods each year.) And even in instances where a measure of scientific computation has occurred, resulting statistics often seem singularly creative. (Recent news stories have announced that 17 percent of babies born to near-affluent parents are unwanted, that 5 percent of Americans dream in color, and that men ages 35–50 average one sexual thought every 25 minutes.) With a little practice, one can identify such statistics with the naked eye.

By careful presentation, a spokesman can make any statistic seem bigger or smaller, as his argument requires. For example, many newspapers reported the 1968 Oberlin College poll which revealed that 40 percent of the unmarried coeds had engaged in sex, that 1 in 13 of these became pregnant, and that 80 percent of the pregnancies were terminated by abortion. Relatively modest statistics appear sensational when given as percentages of percentages of percentages.

More commonly, a person changes the character of a statistic by simple comparison. He relates it to a smaller number to make it appear larger and to a larger number to make it seem small. The contrasting figure need have no relevance aside from offering an advantageous comparison. In 1968 when Senator Eugene McCarthy was running in state presidential primaries, for example, his spokesmen would regularly point out that the contest was not in his strongest state, that official duties had limited his public appearances, and that—all in all—the senator would be lucky to win 15 percent of the vote. Then when he won 22 percent, they announced, "He did well. His vote far exceeded expectations." (Russell Baker called this technique "poor-mouthmanship.") One reverses the process to dwarf a statistic. In the same primaries, when George Wallace—the law-and-order candidate—had to face the fact that Alabama had the highest murder rate in the nation (11.4 per 100,000), it was explained that this figure was not nearly as high as that for Detroit, Los Angeles, and other major cities.

In a summary statement on statistical manipulation, Darrell Huff (*How to Lie with Statistics*, 1954) counseled the business community:

There are often many ways of expressing any figure. You can, for instance, express exactly the same fact by calling it a one percent return on sales, a fifteen percent return on investment, a ten-million-dollar profit, an increase in profits of forty percent (compared with 1935 – 39 average), or a decrease of sixty percent from last year. The method is to choose the one that sounds best for the purpose at hand and trust that few who read it will recognize how imperfectly it reflects the situation.

In a society subject to political controversy, social argument, and Madison Avenue rhetoric, such misleading statistics are common.

HOW RELIABLE ARE THESE STATISTICAL ARGUMENTS?

1. If you begin having your hair styled, are people going to think you've gone soft? Half the Los Angeles Rams' line has theirs styled. If you want to laugh at them, go ahead. We don't.

2. Listerine Antiseptic stops bad breath 4 times better than tooth paste.

3. When presidential candidate George Wallace toured Chicago in 1968, the crowd on the street was estimated at "20,000 to 30,000" (by liberal students), at "50,000" (by Chicago police), and at "2 million" (by Mr. Wallace).

4. *One in Twenty* by Bryan Magee. Adult, plainly written study of male and female homosexuality.

5. Leo Guild's book *What Are the Odds?* reports that a young person with a broken engagement behind him is "75 percent as happy" as one who was never engaged.

6. Antismoking advertisements announce that cigarette smoking, on the average, reduces a smoker's life by 8.3 years, and that every cigarette he smokes takes one minute from his life.

7. Wartime statistics: Last week the Viet Cong lost 1231 men. American and Vietnamese losses were moderate.

8. Arguing that the period of American Prohibition did reduce the level of crime, a Michigan prohibitionist compared Census Bureau figures for 1910 with 1923, showing that vagrancy decreased by 52 percent, larceny by 42 percent, assault by 53 percent, and disorderly conduct by 51 percent. He added that during prohibition there were fewer than two arrests for drunkenness per 100,000 population, whereas by 1956 there were 1939 arrests for each 100,000 of population.

Report by Cancer Society Finds Higher Death Rate for Smokers

WILLIAM L. LAURENCE

A massive report on the statistical relationship between the smoking of cigarettes and an increase in the death rate from various diseases, such as heart disease and cancer of the lung, was presented last week at the annual clinical meeting of the American Medical Association in Portland, Oregon.

The report was presented by Dr. E. Cuyler Hammond, director of statistical research for the American Cancer Society, who described it as "the first real analysis" of information gathered by the society in a huge health study that began Oct. 1, 1959.

Altogether, some 1,078,894 men and women have been enrolled in the study, but the report presented last week was devoted to the data for men only, analyzing the records of 422,094 between the ages of 40 to 79. From this number of men, Dr. Hammond and his colleagues culled, with a high speed computer, 36,975 smokers who were matched in many points in their history, habits and health with 36,975 non-smokers.

Findings Confirmed

The results, Dr. Hammond reported, fully confirm findings in previous prospective studies. Death rates were found: (1) to be far higher in cigarette smokers than in men who did not smoke cigarettes: (2) to increase with the amount of cigarette smoking and (3) to be lower in ex-cigarette smokers who had given up the habit for a year or longer than in men who were currently smoking cigarettes at the time of enrollment.

The study also showed that death rates from the following diseases were greatly higher in cigarette smokers than in non-smokers: cancer of the lung; cancer of the mouth and pharynx; cancer of the larynx; cancer of the bladder and the pancreas; gastric ulcer, emphysema (overdistention of the air spaces in the lungs) and aortic aneurysm (dilation of the wall of the main artery).

Reprinted from *The New York Times*, December 8, 1963, p. E7.

168

"Death rates from coronary artery disease," the report states, "were considerably higher in cigarette smokers than in non-smokers and this accounted for nearly half of the difference in the total rates between cigarette smokers and non-smokers.

HIGHER DEATH RATES

Lung cancer death rates were 11 times as high among current cigarette smokers as among men who never smoked regularly and 18 times as high among very heavy smokers as among men who never smoked regularly. Lung cancer death rates were considerably lower among ex-cigarette smokers who had given up the habit for several years than among current cigarette smokers.

Death rates were found to be highly related to degree of inhalation of cigarette smoke and age at start of cigarette smoking. Age at start of cigarette smoking appears to be particularly important in this respect.

Non-smokers were matched, individually with men who smoked 20 or more cigarettes a day, the two men in each matched pair being similar in respect to: age, height, race, nativity, religion, marital status, residence (rural or urban), certain occupational exposures, education, drinking habits, nervous tension, use of tranquilizers, sleep, exercise, well or ill at time of enrollment, the past history in respect to cancer, heart disease, stroke and high blood pressure.

This kind of evidence was gathered, it was explained, to test the possibility, suggested by critics of previous statistical studies, that the smokers and non-smokers differed from each other in fundamental ways other than smoking and that it was these other differences that accounted for the disparity in the death rates.

The possibility that the association between cigarette smoking and higher death rates might conceivably result from an accidental association, Dr. Hammond said, was extremely unlikely in the light of (1) the quantitative relationship between death rates and the degree of exposure to cigarette smoke; (2) the finding that among ex-cigarette smokers death rates diminish with the length of time since last smoking; (3) the known biological effects of some of the components of cigarette smoke, and (4) pathologic evidence of the effects of cigarette smoking upon bronchial epithelium (tissue lining the air passages leading to the air sacs in the lungs) and the tissues of the lung parenchyma (lungs' air sacs).

Nevertheless, Dr. Hammond said, "we decided to investigate the matter by studying the death rate of cigarette smokers and non-smokers who were alike in respect to many characteristics other than their smoking habits."

During the course of the study, 1,385 of 36,975 cigarette smokers died, while only 662 of the non-smokers died. Of the cigarette smokers, 110 died of lung cancer and 654 died of coronary artery disease, while of the non-smokers only 12 died of lung cancer and 304 died of coronary artery disease.

ONE TO FIFTEEN

Emphysema accounted for the death of 15 cigarette smokers but only one of the non-smokers. Far more of the cigarette smokers than the non-smokers died of cancer of the buccal cavity (mouth), pharynx, larynx and esophagus; cancer of the pancreas; cancer of the liver, aortic aneurysm and several other diseases.

Following Dr. Hammond's report, the House of Delegates, policy-making body of the American Medical Association, voted to undertake an all-out study on smoking by its education and research foundation, to determine which human ailments are "caused or aggravated by smoking" and which part of the cigarette was responsible. Once before, the AMA attempted to start such a study but dropped it when the U. S. Public Health Service undertook to review the subject. The Public Health Service is expected to release its report in the near future.

DISCUSSION QUESTIONS

1. What is the conclusion to be drawn from this essay?
2. This kind of statistical argument must be analyzed as induction:
    (a) Is the sample sufficient?
    (b) Can a study of 73,950 individuals lead to a reliable conclusion about hundreds of millions of smokers?
    (c) Is four years long enough to get meaningful results from such a study?
    (d) Is the sample representative?
       Why does the test only concern men?
       Why only men aged 40–79?
       Can the study have any relevance for young female smokers?

3. Each pair of subjects (the smoker and the nonsmoker) was matched on the basis of age, height, race, nativity, religion, and at least 14 other areas. How could such factors as height, nativity, or religion be relevant? Why were there so many areas of comparison?

4. The report reads, "Lung cancer death rates were 11 times as high among current cigarette smokers as among men who never smoked regularly. . . ." Is this figure substantiated by the statistics given later in the essay?

5. How reliable as argument by authority is a report made by the American Cancer Society and read to the annual clinical meeting of the American Medical Association?

6. Contrast this essay with the two other arguments in this book which concern smoking and health: "100,000 Doctors Have Stopped Smoking Cigarettes (p. 260) and "Smoking Is Very Glamorous" (p. 223). Which of these would you consider most effective as argument? Which least effective?

Crime Higher in Gun Control Cities

ASHLEY HALSEY, JR.

The city of Toledo, Ohio, once garishly described as the wide-open "gun capital of the Midwest," is now being acclaimed by anti-gun spokesmen as a community where a local handgun control law reduced violent crime.

Toledo is being held up to Cincinnati, Los Angeles, and other large cities as a shining example of the wonders that can be worked by gun control.

Without question, violence in Toledo has decreased since the city enacted, in August 1968, a whole package of anti-crime measures including an ordinance requiring an I.D. card of anyone who would buy or own a handgun. Comparing the first half of 1969 with the first half of 1968, in Toledo murders decreased 57% from 14 to 6; rapes 37% from 51 to 32; robbery 37% from 562 to 352, and aggravated assaults 12% from 210 to 183.

A glowing account of Toledo's conquest of crime was read into the *Congressional Record* (Oct. 20, 1969, p. S12797) by Sen. Joseph D. Tydings (Md.) and has been widely quoted. Those who quote the account seldom stress the seventh paragraph, which frankly says: "Toledo's experience is unique. It may be traceable in part to special restrictions on gun dealers as well as owners, to a tough, well-publicized court crackdown on violators of the control law and to the other city efforts against crime."

The "other city efforts" include such things as increasing the 700-man Toledo police force by 100, a sizable increase.

Toledo, population 400,000, is not among the 12 largest cities in the land. Of those 12 cities, four were covered by total firearms registration during the first half of 1969. Four more were under local or State laws requiring permits to buy or transfer handguns. Yet another had an ordinance covering all firearms transfers. Three more, by contrast, had no local or State laws rigidly restricting the sale of firearms.

In the four cities requiring registration of all firearms, murders increased anywhere from 6% (New York City) to 102% (San Francisco). In the four cities covered by handgun controls only, the

Reprinted from *The American Rifleman*, December 1969, p. 43.

murder increase varied from 2% (Baltimore) to 53% (Cleveland). In the three cities without firearms restrictions, murders went up 14% in one instance (Los Angeles) and went down in the other two (Houston—5%, Milwaukee—18%).

The same FBI Uniform Crime Reports that periodically list violence statistics also report the strength of local police departments. From the latter figures, it appears that Houston, Los Angeles, and Milwaukee increased their police forces (1968 compared with 1967) by an average of 6% whereas the other nine largest cities in the U.S. reinforced their police by only 2 to 4% on the average during that time.

Because factors other than firearms control laws obviously enter into the crime control picture, a detailed comparison of violent crimes in these 12 largest cities is given here. It is based on figures from the FBI Uniform Crime Reports, in turn assembled from city police reports and like sources. So it may be assumed that they are authentic.

The four cities requiring firearms registration of rifles, shotguns and handguns during the first half of this year all reported sharp rises in violent crimes compared with the first half of 1968. They are as follows:

New York City—Murders up 6% from 436 to 464; rapes up 15% from 907 to 1047; robberies up 23% from 24,255 to 30,002, and aggravated assaults up 7% from 13,570 to 14,552.

Chicago—Murders up 10% from 288 to 317; rapes up 34% from 482 to 650; robberies up 11% from 8576 to 9569. Aggravated assaults decreased 2% from 6118 to 5939.

Washington, D. C.—Murders up 42% from 88 to 125; rapes up 50% from 100 to 150; robberies up 45% from 3491 to 5096, and aggravated assaults up 15% from 1489 to 1725.

San Francisco—Murders up 102% from 36 to 73; rapes up 183% from 85 to 241; robberies up 13% from 2801 to 3184, and aggravated assaults up 18% from 1239 to 1471.

Another group of large cities, three in the Midwest and one in the East, come under laws requiring permits for handguns to change ownership. Cleveland, Ohio's largest city, passed an ordinance making a permit necessary to purchase (though not to possess) a handgun. A similar law in Detroit is reinforced by a Michigan law requiring a license to buy or carry a handgun. In St. Louis, a Missouri law requires a permit to buy a handgun. In Baltimore, a police order signed by the Police Commissioner, and involving registration of the arm and owner, is necessary to transfer a handgun. Here are crime rates in those four cities for the first half of 1969 compared with the first half of 1968:

Cleveland—Murders up 53% from 76 to 117; rapes up 59% from 86 to 137; robberies up 61% from 1440 to 2327, and aggravated assaults up 70% from 565 to 964.

Detroit—Murders up 13% from 176 to 200, and robberies up 29% from 5648 to 7297. Rapes decreased 7% and aggravated assaults dropped 1%.

St. Louis—Murders up 50% from 83 to 125; rapes up 63% from 188 to 308; robberies up 27% from 1786 to 2273, and aggravated assaults up 27% from 1299 to 1651.

Baltimore—Murders up 2% from 115 to 118; robberies up 9% from 4072 to 4451; aggravated assaults up 25% from 4231 to 5210. Rapes decreased 4% from 321 to 308.

Philadelphia, somewhat in a class by itself, passed a city ordinance in 1965 involving registration of all firearms that change hands or are brought into the city. Pennsylvania has a longstanding State law making it illegal to sell handguns to undesirables. The crime score there:

Philadelphia—Murders up 18% from 107 to 127; rapes up 24% from 203 to 253; robberies up 32% from 1840 to 2431, aggravated assaults up 1% from 1832 to 1865.

The three largest cities having the least restrictive gun laws are Los Angeles, Houston, and Milwaukee. The figures there:

Los Angeles—Murders up 14% from 158 to 181; rapes up 20% from 829 to 998; robberies up 8% from 5440 to 5918, aggravated assaults up 12% from 6571 to 7373.

Houston—Murders decreased 5% from 125 to 118; rapes increased 20% from 154 to 186; robberies increased barely from 2093 to 2101, and aggravated assaults decreased 5% from 1483 to 1395.

Milwaukee—Murders decreased 18% from 22 to 18; rapes decreased 15% from 44 to 37; robberies decreased 39% from 421 to 254; aggravated assaults decreased 13% from 381 to 330.

Milwaukee was the only one of the 12 most populous cities ·to show decreases in all forms of violent crime, but decreases were registered in several categories in the other cities without restrictive gun laws.

DISCUSSION QUESTIONS

1. What conclusion is one likely to draw from this essay?

2. The author denies the claim that Toledo's new gun-control law was responsible for the decrease in crime. Name the fallacy he is rejecting. What is paradoxical about his rejecting this kind of argument?

3. The central argument here discusses crime and gun laws in "the 12 largest cities in the land." Why did the author choose 12 rather than 8 or 20?

4. "[The argument] is based on figures from the FBI Uniform Crime Reports, in turn assembled from city police reports and like sources. So it may be assumed they are authentic." Is this a reasonable claim?

5. "In the four cities requiring registration of all firearms, murders increased anywhere from 6% (New York City) to 102% (San Francisco). In the four cities covered by hand-gun controls only, the murder increase varied from 2% (Baltimore) to 53% (Cleveland)." How might these statistics have been presented to make the difference less impressive?

6. The author notes that the three cities without firearms restriction increased their police forces "by an average of 6% whereas the other nine largest cities in the U. S. reinforced their police by only 2 to 4% on the average during that time." Clarify the meaning here.

7. "Because factors other than firearms control laws obviously enter into the crime control picture, a detailed comparison of violent crimes in these 12 largest cities is given here." How does the second half of this sentence relate to the first?

8. Do the four crimes cited have much relationship to gun laws? Do they have equal relationship? Is the author arguing that, in San Francisco, rapes went up 183% *because* the city requires registration of firearms?

Overpopulated America

WAYNE H. DAVIS

I define as most seriously overpopulated that nation whose people by virtue of their numbers and activities are most rapidly decreasing the ability of the land to support human life. With our large population, our affluence and our technological monstrosities the United States wins first place by a substantial margin.

Let's compare the U. S. to India, for example. We have 203 million people, whereas she has 540 million on much less land. But look at the impact of people on the land.

The average Indian eats his daily few cups of rice (or perhaps wheat, whose production on American farms contributed to our one percent per year drain in quality of our active farmland), draws his bucket of water from the communal well and sleeps in a mud hut. In his daily rounds to gather cow dung to burn to cook his rice and warm his feet, his footsteps, along with those of millions of his countrymen, help bring about a slow deterioration of the ability of the land to support people. His contribution to the destruction of the land is minimal.

An American, on the other hand, can be expected to destroy a piece of land on which he builds a home, garage and driveway. He will contribute his share to the 142 million tons of smoke and fumes, seven million junked cars, 20 million tons of paper, 48 billion cans, and 26 billion bottles the overburdened environment must absorb each year. To run his air conditioner we will strip-mine a Kentucky hillside, push the dirt and slate down into the stream, and burn coal in a power generator, whose smokestack contributes to a plume of smoke massive enough to cause cloud seeding and premature precipitation from Gulf winds which should be irrigating the wheat farms of Minnesota.

In his lifetime he will personally pollute three million gallons of water, and industry and agriculture will use ten times this much water in his behalf. To provide these needs the U. S. Army Corps of Engineers will build dams and flood farmland. He will also use 21,000 gallons of leaded gasoline containing boron, drink 28,000 pounds of milk and eat 10,000 pounds of meat. The latter is produced and squandered in a life pattern unknown to Asians. A steer

Reprinted from *The New Republic*, January 10, 1970, pp. 13–15.

on a Western range eats plants containing minerals necessary for plant life. Some of these are incorporated into the body of the steer which is later shipped for slaughter. After being eaten by man these nutrients are flushed down the toilet into the ocean or buried in the cemetery, the surface of which is cluttered with boulders called tombstones and has been removed from productivity. The result is a continual drain on the productivity of range land. Add to this the erosion of overgrazed lands, and the effects of the falling water table as we mine Pleistocene deposits of groundwater to irrigate to produce food for more people, and we can see why our land is dying far more rapidly than did the great civilizations of the Middle East, which experienced the same cycle. The average Indian citizen, whose fecal material goes back to the land, has but a minute fraction of the destructive effect on the land that the affluent American does.

Thus I want to introduce a new term, which I suggest be used in future discussions of human population and ecology. We should speak of our numbers in "Indian equivalents". An Indian equivalent I define as the average number of Indian citizens required to have the same detrimental effect on the land's ability to support human life as would the average American. This value is difficult to determine, but let's take an extremely conservative working figure of 25. To see how conservative this is, imagine the addition of 1000 citizens to your town and 25,000 to an Indian village. Not only would the Americans destroy much more land for homes, highways and a shopping center, but they would contribute far more to environmental deterioration in hundreds of other ways as well. For example, their demand for steel for new autos might increase the daily pollution equivalent of 130,000 junk autos which *Life* tells us that U. S. Steel Corp. dumps into Lake Michigan. Their demand for textiles would help the cotton industry destroy the life in the Black Warrior River in Alabama with endrin. And they would contribute to the massive industrial pollution of our oceans (we provide one third to one half the world's share) which has caused the precipitous downward trend in our commercial fisheries landings during the past seven years.

The per capita gross national product of the United States is 38 times that of India. Most of our goods and services contribute to the decline in the ability of the environment to support life. Thus it is clear that a figure of 25 for an Indian equivalent is conservative. It has been suggested to me that a more realistic figure would be 500.

In Indian equivalents, therefore, the population of the United States is at least four billion. And the rate of growth is even more alarming. We are growing at one percent per year, a rate which would double our number in 70 years. India is growing at 2.5 percent. Using the Indian equivalent of 25, our population growth becomes 10 times as serious as that of India. According to the Reinows in their recent book *Moment in the Sun,* just one year's crop of American babies can be expected to use up 25 billion pounds of beef, 200 million pounds of steel and 9.1 billion gallons of gasoline during their collective lifetime. And the demands on water and land for our growing population are expected to be far greater than the supply available in the year 2000. We are destroying our land at a rate of over a million acres a year. We now have only 2.6 agricultural acres per person. By 1975 this will be cut to 2.2, the critical point for the maintenance of what we consider a decent diet, and by the year 2000 we might expect to have 1.2.

You might object that I am playing with statistics in using the Indian equivalent on the rate of growth. I am making the assumption that today's Indian child will live 35 years (the average Indian life span) at today's level of affluence. If he lives an American 70 years, our rate of population growth would be 20 times as serious as India's.

But the assumption of continued affluence at today's level is unfounded. If our numbers continue to rise our standard of living will fall so sharply that by the year 2000 any surviving Americans might consider today's average Asian to be well off. Our children's destructive effects on their environment will decline as they sink ever lower into poverty.

The United States is in serious economic trouble now. Nothing could be more misleading than today's affluence, which rests precariously on a crumbling foundation. Our productivity, which had been increasing steadily at about 3.2 percent a year since World War II, has been falling during 1969. Our export over import balance has been shrinking steadily from $7.1 billion in 1964 to $0.15 billion in the first half of 1965. Our balance of payments deficit for the second quarter was $3.7 billion, the largest in history. We are now importing iron ore, steel, oil, beef, textiles, cameras, radios and hundreds of other things.

Our economy is based upon the Keynesian concept of a continued growth in population and productivity. It worked in an underpopulated nation with excess resources. It could continue to work only if the earth and its resources were expanding at an annual rate of 4 to 5 percent. Yet neither the number of cars, the economy, the human population, nor anything else can expand indefinitely at an exponential rate in a finite world. We must face this fact *now*. The crisis is here. When Walter Heller says that our economy will expand by 4 percent annually through the latter 1970s he is dreaming. He is in a theoretical world totally unaware of the realities of human ecology. If the economists do not wake up and devise a new system for us now somebody else will have to do it for them.

A civilization is comparable to a living organism. Its longevity is a function of its metabolism. The higher the metabolism (affluence), the shorter the life. Keynesian economics has allowed us an affluent but shortened life span. We have now run our course.

The tragedy facing the United States is even greater and more imminent than that descending upon the hungry nations. The Paddock brothers in their book, *Famine 1975!,* say that India "cannot be saved" no matter how much food we ship her. But India will be here after the United States is gone. Many millions will die in the most colossal famines India has ever known, but the land will survive and she will come back as she always has before. The United States, on the other hand, will be a desolate tangle of concrete and ticky-tacky, of strip-mined moonscape and silt-choked reservoirs. The land and water will be so contaminated with pesticides, herbicides, mercury fungicides, lead, boron, nickel, arsenic and hundreds of other toxic substances, which have been approaching critical levels of concentration in our environment as a result of our numbers and affluence, that it may be unable to sustain human life.

Thus as the curtain gets ready to fall on man's civilization let it come as no surprise that it shall first fall on the United States. And let no one make the mistake of thinking we can save ourselves by "cleaning up the environment." Banning DDT is the equivalent of the physician's treating syphilis by putting a bandaid over the first chancre to appear. In either case you can be sure that more serious and widespread trouble will soon appear unless the disease itself is treated. We cannot survive by planning to treat the symptoms such as air pollution, water pollution, soil erosion, etc.

What can we do to slow the rate of destruction of the United States as a land capable of supporting human life? There are two approaches. First we must reverse the population growth. We have far more people now than we can continue to support at anything near today's level of affluence. American women average slightly over three children each. According to the *Population Bulletin* if we reduced this number to 2.5 there would still be 330 million people in the nation at the end of the century. And even if we reduced this to 1.5 we would have 57 million more people in the year 2000 than we have now. With our present longevity patterns it would take more than 30 years for the population to peak even when reproducing at this rate, which would eventually give us a net decrease in numbers.

Do not make the mistake of thinking that technology will solve our population problem by producing a better contraceptive. Our problem now is that people want too many children. Surveys show the average number of children wanted by the American family is 3.3. There is little difference between the poor and the wealthy, black and white, Catholic and Protestant. Production of children at this rate during the next 30 years would be so catastrophic in effect on our resources and the viability of the nation as to be beyond my ability to contemplate. To prevent this trend we must not only make contraceptives and abortion readily available to everyone, but we must establish a system to put severe economic pressure on those who produce children and reward those who do not. This can be done within our system of taxes and welfare.

The other thing we must do is to pare down our Indian equivalents. Individuals in American society vary tremendously in Indian equivalents. If we plot Indian equivalents versus their reciprocal, the percentage of land surviving a generation, we obtain a linear regression. We can then place individuals and occupation types on this graph. At one end would be the starving blacks of Mississippi; they would approach unity in Indian equivalents, and would have the least destructive effect on the land. At the other end of the graph would be the politicians slicing pork for the barrel, the highway contractors, strip-mine operators, real estate developers, and public enemy number one—the U. S. Army Corps of Engineers.

We must halt land destruction. We must abandon the view of land and minerals as private property to be exploited in any way economically feasible for private financial gain. Land and minerals are resources upon which the very survival of the nation depends, and their use must be planned in the best interests of the people.

Rising expectations for the poor is a cruel joke foisted upon them by the Establishment. As our new economy of use-it-once-and-throw-it-away produces more and more products for the affluent, the share of our resources available for the poor declines. Blessed be the starving blacks of Mississippi with their outdoor privies, for they are ecologically sound, and they shall inherit a nation. Although I hope that we will help these unfortunate people attain a decent standard of living by diverting war efforts to fertility control and job training, our most urgent task to assure this nation's survival during the next decade is to stop the affluent destroyers.

DISCUSSION QUESTIONS

1. Considering the first sentence of this essay, show how the author's argument is essentially a syllogism.

2. How impressive is his comparison of "The average Indian" and the equivalent American?

3. "An American . . . will contribute his share to the 142 million tons of smoke and fumes, seven million junked cars, 20 million tons of paper, 48 billion cans, and 26 billion bottles the overburdened environment must absorb each year." Trace the use of such statistics through the essay. Do all seem equally reliable?

4. The author says that an "extremely conservative" Indian equivalent is 25, but that "It has been suggested to me that a more realistic figure would be 500." What does one infer from such varying estimates?

5. "A civilization is comparable to a living organism. Its longevity is a function of its metabolism." Is this a reasonable analogy?

6. Twice the author mentions "the starving blacks of Mississippi": "they are ecologically sound, and they shall inherit a nation." Does this seem simplistic?

7. "If the economists do not wake up and devise a new system for us now, somebody else will have to do it for them." In a number of references, the author proposes what seem to be strict and imposed solutions for America. Trace these and comment on them.

"We're a big company."

We're a big company.

We sell thousands of products ranging from natural gas and asphalt to gasoline and gear oil.

In 1972 we made $574 million. But our average profit was slightly more than a cent and a half a gallon.

$$\frac{\text{1972 NET PROFITS}}{\text{1972 PETROLEUM PRODUCTS SOLD (GALLONS)}} \quad \frac{\$574,199,000}{37,031,000,000} = 1\tfrac{1}{2}\text{¢}$$

Even though we don't have all the 1973 figures as this goes to press, we know that last year we sold more and we made more.

But our average profit still was only about two cents a gallon.

That's not so much when you consider how much we invest, the risks we take, and the products and services we provide.

Advertisement reprinted from the *Washington Post,* January 20, 1974, p. C2.

DISCUSSION QUESTIONS

1. What motivated this statement from Mobil Oil Corporation?
2. Is it excessive for the corporation to be making merely a $^1/_2$ cent a gallon more than last year?
3. What does net profit mean?
4. What will be Mobil's net profit for 1973?
5. What is the percentage of increase in profit per gallon sold?
6. Can one estimate the percentage of increase in net profits?
7. How do the amount of money invested and the kinds of products and services provided justify this level of increase?

8

Exercises for Review

How valid are these arguments? Identify examples of induction, deduction, expert testimony, semantic argument, analogy, argument in a circle, *post hoc ergo propter hoc,* begging the question, *argumentum ad hominem,* extension, the either-or fallacy, and statistical manipulation.

1. Of course you support federal aid to education. You're a teacher; you stand to profit on the deal.

2. "Ever wonder why kids instinctively go for soft drinks in bottles?"—Glass Container Manufacturers Institute

3. Register Communists, not Guns!

4. Naval ROTC should be abolished; I'm learning nothing from it.

5. America's greatest danger is not from without but from the traitors within. It was from these United States that 20 million dollars in gold was carried by Trotsky and 276 revolutionists in their nefarious mission to overthrow the czar and take over Russia.

6. It's not safe to walk the streets in New York City; I'm glad I live in Los Angeles.

7. As you go to the polls to decide this temperance issue, ask yourself, "How does Jesus want me to vote?"

8. I disagree with Abby Van Buren when she says no woman should be forced to have a baby she does not want. A lot of people are forced to have parents they do not like, but we don't let them go around murdering their parents.

9. "There is no proof that sugar confectionary gives rise to dental cavities."—*Association International Des Fabricants De Confiserie*

10. "Seven out of every ten Americans cheat on their income tax."—Professor R. Van Dyke Ellington

11. In 1936, the *Literary Digest* chose 10 million names at random from telephone books and lists of registered automobile owners. The magazine sent preelection ballots to these per-

sons and received over 2 million responses. The resulting prediction: Landon would defeat Roosevelt.

12. A *Saturday Review* article on the Middle East carried the subtitle: "Do the Arabs Have a Case?"

13. "Obscene material is material which deals with sex in a manner appealing to prurient interest."—Justice Brennan, delivering the opinion of the Supreme Court, *Roth v. United States*, June 24, 1957.

14. *The Husband* (a novel by Sol Stein). "The dilemma of countervailing demands on the sensual man of good will. . . . rich and true. . . . modulated with a respectful reserve . . . handled with hardly a false note."—*New York Times*

15. I never knew a University of Alabama varsity football player who could read or write beyond the eight-grade level.

16. *Miss MacIntosh, My Darling* by Marguerite Young. "What we behold is a mammoth epic, a massive fable, a picaresque journey, a Faustian quest and a work of stunning magnitude and beauty . . . some of the richest, most expressive, most original and exhaustively revealing passages of prose that this writer has experienced in a long time. . . . It is a masterpiece."—William Goyen, *New York Times*

17. We scientists working with astrological data do not mind being criticized. We know that Newton and Einstein were ridiculed in the past.

18. All this effort to register and confiscate guns will not help us fight crime. Violence arises from the souls of men.

19. On a typical television poll, an early-evening newscaster poses a yes-or-no question, asking viewers to phone one number to vote "yes" and another to vote "no"; and a late-evening newscaster gives the result, e.g., 71 percent oppose socialized medicine.

20. Homosexuality is no illness. It is a widespread practice like vegetarianism. The homosexual has a sexual preference for members of the same sex; the vegetarian has an alimentary preference for noncarnivorous foods. In neither case is there any impairment of function or any disease.

21. Athletics teaches our young people good sportsmanship and how to play the game of life.

22. *Miss MacIntosh, My Darling* by Marguerite Young. "In fact, this is an outrageously bad book, written by an author with very little of interest to say, and very little skill in saying it . . . wholly unreadable."—*Time*

23. Charlie's a gorgeous, sexy-young smell. (*Concentrated!*) And full of surprises. Just like you.

24. If your name is Mackay, Malloy, or Murray, beware of drink. According to John Gary, director of the Council for Alcoholism in Glasgow, Scotland, people whose surname begins with the letter "M" may be eight times more prone to alcoholism than others.

25. A clever magician can always perform his tricks; but a genuine psychic can sometimes produce paranormal effects and sometimes not. Uri Geller produced no effects at all when he appeared on the "Tonight Show." He is a true psychic.

26. What I want to know is who masterminded the plan to get President Nixon impeached?

27. "To find her [Lizzy Borden] guilty, you must believe she is a fiend. Gentlemen, does she look it?"

Part II

ARGUMENT
FOR ANALYSIS

Where there is much desire to learn,
there of necessity will be much arguing, much writing, many opinions; for
opinion in good men is but knowledge
in the making.

John Milton, *Areopagitica* (1644)

Professor Durant
Demonstrates Psychokinesis

Dr. James Durant, Professor of Psychology at Millburn University, demonstrates to a companion his celebrated powers of psychokinesis. The photograph was taken at the Faculty Club before a dozen professors. The event was supervised by Dr. Xavier Crosert, dean of the College of Arts and Sciences. (Redstone Wire Service photo)

Advertisement for *Jane*
by Dee Wells

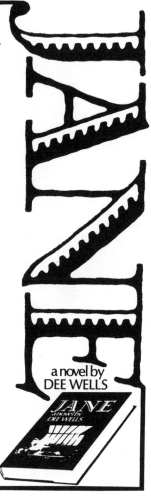

"JANE is a magnificently engaging novel. ...Makes us murmur, 'Yes, this is what it's like; I've felt it—this is true.'"
—PENELOPE MESIC,
CHICAGO TRIBUNE BOOK WORLD

"One of those books that one can't put down....One is left reading in the small hours, longing in rather an old-fashioned way to know how it is going to end."
—MARGARET DRABBLE,
NEW YORK TIMES BOOK REVIEW

"By the time I was halfway through I hated to put it down....Her *ménage à quatre* seems not only believable but also conventional."   —HAL BURTON, *NEWSDAY*

"Dee Wells has created one of the finest and most sympathetic characters since Yossarian won the war in *Catch-22*."
—ELIZABETH CODY,
CHICAGO DAILY NEWS PANORAMA

"Immensely entertaining and engrossing ...the most vivacious and witty heroine since Holly Golightly."   —ELENA K. VASILEV,
SAN FRANCISCO CHRONICLE

"Because JANE is a book about making love, instead of a book about making war, it is called a 'woman's novel'....[It is] a very good novel about women."
—JULIA CAMERON,
WASHINGTON POST BOOK WORLD

"Read it."
—*THE VIKING PRESS*

$6.95

THE VIKING PRESS

a novel by
DEE WELLS

Viking Press advertisement by Waterman Getz Niedelman.

The Welfare Dollar Goes 'Round and 'Round

CLAYTON THOMAS

The welfare rolls in the United States currently number 15 million Americans, and the annual cost is approximately $20 billion. But welfare is not just statistics. It is synonymous with poverty, and poverty means drugs, crime, and deteriorating cities. A drug addict dies on a lonely Harlem street. A building superintendent bashes down a door in a dank tenement and rapes a woman. A welfare mother screams obscenities because she cannot get the money to feed her children.

Despite the massive social and economic effects of welfare, no solution seems forthcoming, partly because sharply conflicting analyses logjam reform. Liberals see the problem as economic: those on relief are excluded from the mainstream, unable to help themselves; higher payments are in order. Conservatives see the problem in moral terms: those on relief are "cheaters" and "loafers"; financial cutbacks and stricter regulations are in order.

Some of the contradictory attitudes are no doubt illusions believed by various people for political or personal reasons. My own opinion is that there are indeed many myths about welfare, and that these must be exploded before a solution to the problem of public assistance can come into sight. Among the most significant are these:

Welfare is an economic phenomenon caused by a lack of jobs.

The rapid growth of Northern welfare rolls results from the immigration of blacks and Puerto Ricans who, frustrated in their search for jobs, are forced onto the welfare rolls.

Welfare clients are disabled by their social environment and will leave the relief rolls when they are given better housing, education, job training.

Welfare clients are not loafers, cheaters, and baby producers, and their aspirations and values closely resemble those of middle class working people; but because of social deprivation and alienation, they have never had the opportunity to get jobs and become self-sufficient.

Reprinted from *The National Review*, January 18, 1974, pp. 78–81.

"Unemployable"

During a year as a caseworker in the New York City Department of Social Services (formerly known as the Welfare Department), I dealt with hundreds of welfare clients—black, white, and Puerto Rican—in all welfare categories. I pounded the pavements of hard-core ghettos and visited dilapidated tenement apartments, welfare hotels, and boarding houses. My own experiences did not support the above myths.

Although welfare regulations required that single employable individuals (Home Relief) look for jobs, only two of the 60 on my caseload made any effort to find work. The rest turned down employment, avoided interviews and job training like the plague (they usually got sick on the day of their appointment with prospective employers or job counselors), and tried desperately to produce medical excuses indicating that their ability to work was limited or that they were incapacitated.

In one case, a white welfare client admitted to me that he was physically able to work, and he subsequently passed a city health examination with flying colors. Then, apparently panicking at the thought of a job, he brought in a letter from a physician stating that he had numerous ailments and was not employable. (The doctor who had written the report specialized in welfarites and mentioned that this patient would be coming to him for a substantial amount of treatment.) The welfare department, fearing legal suits if they made the man work and it turned out that he really was ill, decided to classify him unemployable. When I asked him about his sudden change in health, he merely looked at the floor, shuffled his feet, and said nothing.

A Puerto Rican male on my caseload, classified as employable until he brought a letter from a doctor alleging a disabling kidney ailment, somehow maintained an excellent wardrobe; once he was picked up by the police for robbery and held for five days; after his release he explained to me that "I had no idea this friend of mine standing next to me in the department store was stealing all that stuff. I thought we were just going in to do some legitimate shopping."

In another case of health impairment, a white client had been badly slashed with straight razors and left for dead on a desolate street. After intensive hospital care he recovered, but he claimed that the psychological effects of his "accident" incapacitated him for work. By his own account, however, he did have the energy to hunt down black and Puerto Rican addicts and beat them with a lead pipe. (He was eventually arrested and held on $20,000 bail.)

Fifty-seven of my 60 Home Relief recipients had no job histories within the previous three years that I could verify, and only two could qualify for unemployment benefits. When I suggested to one client, who had complained that he could not find work, that he might be able to get a position as a janitor, he replied, "You can go f——— yourself, Mr. Thomas, if you think I'll do s——— work like that." This man, who had deserted his family, eventually found a job of his own: he sold narcotics.

Most of these clients came in off the streets and were narcotics and cocaine addicts, alcoholics, and prostitutes (male and female). Others were referrals from hospitals (often addicts) and prisons (usually addicts and/or pushers).

Home Relief clients and narcotics addicts were the most dangerous to deal with, and employees in my center were periodically beaten for refusing to give them funds to which they were not entitled. On the other hand, the welfare center's guards frequently beat up recipients (usually frail ones), and one floored a female supervisor one day with a punch in the face. Another was arrested for selling heroin to the welfarites. Though nearly all of them were black or Puerto Rican, they hated the recipients and the system itself. One, a Negro, told me, "Rockefeller and Lindsay give these f———ers assistance, but they won't give us a decent salary. The best way to clean up this city is to assassinate the mayor."

Welfare mothers had fundamentally the same attitude toward work as the Home Relief clients. Nor were they interested in gaining employment skills. Only one of 30 mothers on my caseload could be persuaded to apply for the Work Incentive Program (WIN), then voluntary, which granted cash incentives and baby-sitting fees to trainees, and only gradually reduced a woman's welfare payments once she found a job. Of those who enrolled in WIN citywide, only 10 percent finished the course; of these, only a small number took employment. Why such a poor success rate? In my opinion, many mothers enrolled only for the extra cash and for a variation in their daily routine. Then, as time went on, they began to resent the restriction on their freedom, and they quit. A mother of four told me, "I'll go to school or job training, but I don't want to work."

From such experiences, I concluded that supplying more jobs would hardly resolve the welfare problem, or even significantly reduce the rolls. On the contrary, the rolls would remain static, because the vast majority of welfarites would do whatever they could to escape the employment created for them.

How, then, do sociologists manage to conclude that welfarites want to work? My guess is that, after years of interrogation by their caseworkers, welfare clients know full well what values they are *supposed* to have, and how they are supposed to respond to questions posed by middle class interviewers. When asked how he feels about working, the client automatically responds, "I want to work." I ran into this phenomenon constantly on my job; some recipients even falsified their life and work histories according to what they felt was expected of them, and I often held erroneous views of a welfare family's status because of the fabricated answers I got. Researchers do not realize that welfare clients feel psychological pressure to conform, or to pretend to conform, to traditional middle class values.

MIGRATING TO JOBS?

Another mistaken theory, as I mentioned, is that blacks and Puerto Ricans generally came north in search of employment, and were instead forced onto the relief rolls by the shortage of jobs. My own experience is that they generally migrated specifically to get public assistance. Two years ago, when food budgets in New York were reduced 10 percent by the state legislature, an irate mother of five told me, "If you people keep cutting back the budgets, I'll tell my relatives in Puerto Rico not to come over here." A black client told me, "I want to go back to the South, but the welfare there is way too low. The only way I would do it is if I got my New York welfare checks sent down to me in South Carolina." When I told her that was impossible, she decided to stay in New York. A carload of prospective clients drove straight through from California and arrived, one day, at the front door of my welfare center, got out of their jalopy, and got right on the rolls. They made no bones about it. Ronald Reagan was cutting back welfare in California, and they had come to New York for higher payments.

Many advocates of welfare fail to realize that migrants from the South and Puerto Rico are far better off in New York slums than in the hovels from which they came (four to eight times better off, in dollars). But the point is not lost on the South and Puerto Rico. A white welfare employee with friends in Mississippi and Louisiana told me, "The Southerners are laughing in their boots as the blacks flow north for welfare. They're only too glad to let us have them." And the local government in San Juan has erected signs in the slums: "Go to New York and Have the Baby Free."

WHAT CAUSES SLUMS?

The civic-minded, alarmed by the degradation in which welfarites live, often call for new housing. The usual assumption is that dilapidated neighborhoods result from the negligence of slumlords. But I found the primary reason the sheer active destruction by tenants themselves. A member of the mayor's Hotel Task Force, who spent his time rehousing hotel welfarites in apartments all over New York, told me: "The continuing decay of the city and the condemning and razing of city blocks is due to welfare recipients. The working poor have a stake in their property, and they care for their homes. Welfarites don't. They know that whatever happens, the welfare department will take care of them." Welfarites, I found, move into neighborhoods, bring crime and violence, rout the working poor and middle class, occupy the buildings, then physically destroy them. The process takes only a few years; the cycle merely begins anew when welfarites are moved to new housing, as is now happening with low income model housing and Model Cities buildings.

How does the destruction occur? One family with 12 children was rehoused four times. Each time, one of the children, a firebug, burned down their accommodations. In another case, a mother of four who wanted better housing simply burned her own apartment down. A physically ill welfare client who had lived four years in the Hamilton Hotel, one of the first of a series of welfare hotels to be condemned in the city during 1971, gave this account of how his building deteriorated: "About a year ago, the management formally opened the doors to welfare to get more money. That was the end of the place. The clients burned out whole wings of the structure. Most of the people are addicts and prostitutes. We have muggings and murders in the hallways. The junkies ring the fire alarms to attract the guards to one area of the building and then break down doors, beat and rob people in another. I've seen the kids bashing away at the marble on the walls with hammers." Why do they do that? "For the same reason that people climb mountains. Because they're there. These people aren't civilized enough to live in organized society." A black welfare recipient who lived in the Broadway

Central Hotel told me: "Last week they gang-raped the maid on the seventh floor, and two nights ago a seven-year-old was raped on the fifth. I can take the rats, Mr. Thomas, but I can't take the people. I have to barricade my doors at night to stay alive." Equally shocking accounts were given me by members of the Hotel Task Force.

In order to visit the homes of my welfare clients, I entered what were, undoubtedly, some of the most dangerous neighborhoods in the world—the South Bronx, Harlem, and East New York. I dodged addicts in doorways, confronted heroin users about to "shoot up," and was followed through lonely streets by muggers eager for my wallet. Other caseworkers in my center were less fortunate; they were assaulted, robbed, and, in one case, held down on the top floor of a dilapidated building and injected with heroin. It is hard for most of us even to imagine the day to day terror in which slum residents live. One family, living in a building that seemed to be on the verge of collapse, told me: "The addicts trade drugs and shoot up every night in our building. Last week we heard a bad fight in the hallway at about 3 A.M. The next morning, when we got up, a corpse blocked our front door. The man had been stabbed to death." I once ran for my life from a hotel, pursued by one of my own clients, a huge, crazed black man who assaulted and robbed the other tenants, but was tolerated for a time by the terrified couple who ran the place.

Reform-minded people often hope that better schooling for the children of welfarites will prepare them for jobs and a decent future. But unfortunately the decline of ghetto schools has paralleled the rise of the welfare rolls and the expansion of slum areas. The role of the teacher is no longer to teach, but to maintain at most minimal order; as one teacher put it: "My two jobs are to keep myself alive and to keep my students alive." Drugs, crime, and violence permeate the junior high and high schools in poor neighborhoods. A talented 12-year-old welfare child, going to a half-black and half-Puerto Rican junior high school in Manhattan, said: "I keep quiet in the classroom and don't make trouble. That way the teacher gives me Bs. The troublemakers get Cs and Ds. Whatever I learn, I learn on my own. I'm under a lot of pressure to take heroin, and kids try to beat me up because I won't. The high school I'll end up going to is worse. I hang out with the white kids, who get in much less trouble." A Puerto Rican mother, whose two children attend a primary school in the South Bronx, told of a gang war among 12-year-olds that resulted in one child's being shot in the face.

To exacerbate the situation, poor parents have recently grown self-righteous and militant toward established authority. Discipline is next to impossible. One teacher told me: "Whereas, in the past, parents would be angry at their children when they got into trouble at school, most blacks and Puerto Ricans vent their hatred on the system when the kids do something wrong. The children are rarely taken to task."

Abuses Unchecked

A recent survey revealed that the working American tends to see welfarites as loafers, cheaters, and baby producers. Despite the protestations of many social commentators and politicians that this is an unfair stereotype, my own experiences support this view. Cheating was virtually universal. One mother of six, who had secretly moved to New Jersey, came into the city for over a year to collect undeserved public assistance checks at a Manhattan mailbox. Several of my clients held full-time jobs they had not acknowledged. Others were getting financial support from boyfriends or fathers of their children and did not report it. Some recipients had gotten on the rolls at a number of different welfare centers and were receiving from two to six checks at a time.

The computer checkup system which was designed to detect such abuses was in a state of chaos. Even when fraud was somehow discovered, welfare officials in my center, fearing that they would be held responsible, took no action against the offenders and quietly ordered the records sent to the dead files.

In one case of gross embezzlement, a supervisor was so infuriated he decided to prosecute; but when he brought his evidence to the courthouse, the Assistant District Attorney asked him to drop the charges, explaining that the strong support the clients would get from groups like the Legal Aid Society would make the litigation interminable. Besides, he added, his office had to deal with more important criminal cases than welfare offenses. The charges were dropped. Two days later, the family was back at the social service center demanding assistance. Payments were quickly resumed.

In most court cases, ironically, it was not the welfare department but clients themselves who did the prosecuting. One man who had concealed an income double the amount of his welfare payments demanded, upon being detected, a hearing. He flatly denied the facts, which welfare officials proceeded to establish. The court ruled against the client, who, enraged, threw a chair at the judge. A supervisor then had to grab the recipient in a hammerlock to prevent further violence.

The "missing" father of a welfare family turned out to be living at the family address, fully employed, and claiming the family as dependents on the tax form. Armed with full proof, the caseworker terminated the mother's checks—whereupon she demanded a hearing. She claimed in court that her husband had deserted her since the termination. The welfare department, caught off guard, had no way of proving otherwise. Payments were ordered resumed. When the husband's name was referred to the Division of Legal Services for tax evasion, the detectives showed no interest in pursuing the matter. Contrary to City Hall press releases, the Legal Services Division showed the same reluctance to track down missing fathers of welfare children.

These cases typify the casual fraud and belligerency of welfare clients, but they also point up the fantastic craving of welfarites for their checks and the difficulty of getting them off the rolls. Welfare has become a social right as unchallengeable as the right to life itself. Such fraud was actively assisted by the mayor's aides. Pro-welfare organizations, like Mobilization for Youth and the West Side Community Alliance, constantly put pressure on the city to give illegal grants to bitterly vociferous clients. Lindsay's appointed political officials, especially Jule Sugarman and his associates at the Human Resources Administration (which governs the city welfare system), usually buckled and ordered the money handed out. In one case, a welfarite decided he wanted an apartment for which the rent was far in excess of normal public assistance levels. Rather than waste time with the welfare department, the man opened a small bank account and purposely bounced $450 worth of checks for the rent, security, and broker's fee needed to secure the accommodations. While the various defrauded parties considered legal action against him, antipoverty agencies pressured city administrators to help him out, and I was finally ordered to issue welfare funds to cover the bogus checks.

In another case, when a political aide authorized illegal grants of money to a public assistance family on my caseload, I asked the director of my welfare center to complain to the Human Resources

Administration. He did. The response he got over the phone was "Lay off these people." This answer seems natural enough, since the welfare mother involved had a long list of appointed officials to call whenever she needed help. Once I was even directed to give money to an unauthorized alien who was being deported, even though welfare officials at my social service center admitted he was totally ineligible for funds.

Fraud is now harder than ever to expose, since the new income maintenance affidavit system has all but eliminated checkup visits to welfare homes. A prospective recipient simply comes into a welfare center, states his case, signs an affidavit form attesting that the facts he has given are true, gives some documented proof, and the checks start rolling off the computer. To qualify for further aid, he has only to reappear periodically to reiterate his need for funds.

When it came to reproducing children, welfare clients justified the worst suspicions of conservative cynics. Not only were there many children; in large families, there were often many fathers. Instances of deserting husbands were rare; transient boyfriends begot most of the children, and mothers usually claimed they knew little or nothing about their vanishing mates. Some children resulted from casual pickups. I had no success in getting any of the mothers on my caseload to practice contraception. Exasperated, I finally asked several Puerto Rican mothers if their resistance was on religious grounds; the answer was always a flat no. Most of the welfare mothers were single and knew about contraceptives; but apparently they just could not be bothered to use them.

The high birth rate would be less disturbing if welfare children were raised in a healthier atmosphere. But though a few mothers showed great concern for their offspring, most let their four-year-olds roam the streets unattended and left their children home alone. Physical violence and child abuse was commonplace. I observed whippings and clubbings of three- and four-year-olds, and saw one infant picked up and thrown across a room. One welfare mother's boyfriend would hold her five-year-old 'daughter's hands over the flames of a gas stove for punishment; eventually the child's fingers became maimed lumps of scar tissue. Another mother poured boiling water over her small son; the social worker told me that this was not a serious enough abuse to warrant placing the boy in a foster home.

Many social theorists think that a father's presence would help to stabilize public assistance families. Accordingly, the welfare department tried not to break up mothers and their lovers. But it is doubtful whether this theory is entirely realistic; in many cases, the presence of the lover was clearly a negative influence on the family, but the mother—out of loneliness, simple affection, or an inability to handle his brute force—did not put him out. One woman got a new hairdo and hat to celebrate when she heard that her common law husband had died in a gutter.

Costs Grow and Grow

Though welfare requirements in New York have been made more stringent over the past two years, the cost of the welfare program continues to grow. This is largely due to increasing rents and medical costs, and to the general inefficiency of the system; college-educated caseworkers have lately been replaced by incompetent, untrained, and often truculently lazy affidavit clerks, and the recently installed computer system is chaotically disorganized.

The Nonscience of Human Nature

STEPHEN JAY GOULD

When in the seventeenth century a group of girls simultaneously suffered seizures in the presence of an accused witch, the justices of Salem explained the girls' behavior as demonic possession. In 1971, when the followers of Charles Manson attributed occult powers to their leader, no judge took them seriously. During the nearly 300 years separating the two incidents, we have learned quite a bit about the psychological determinants of group behavior. A crudely literal interpretation of such events now seems ridiculous.

An equally crude literalism has prevailed in the past in interpreting human nature and the differences among human groups. Human behavior was simply attributed to innate biology. We do what we do because we are made that way. The first lesson of an eighteenth-century primer stated the position succinctly: In Adam's fall, we sinned all. A progressive advance from this biological determinism has been a major trend in twentieth-century science and culture. We have come to see ourselves as a learning animal; we have come to believe that the influences of class and culture far outweigh the weaker predispositions of our genetic constitution.

Nonetheless, we have been deluged during the past decade by a resurgent biological determinism, ranging from "pop ethology" to outright racism.

With Konrad Lorenz as godfather, Robert Ardrey as dramatist, and Desmond Morris as raconteur, we are presented with the behavior of man, "the naked ape," descended from an African carnivore, innately aggressive and inherently territorial.

Lionel Tiger and Robin Fox try to find a biological basis for outmoded Western ideals of aggressive, outreaching men and docile, restricted women. In discussing cross-cultural differences between men and women, they propose a hormonal chemistry inherited from the requirements of our supposed primal roles as group hunters and child rearers.

Carleton Coon offered a prelude of events to come with his claim (*The Origin of Races*, 1962) that five major human races evolved

Reprinted from *Natural History*, April 1974, pp. 21–24.

independently from *Homo erectus* ("Java" and "Peking" man) to *Homo sapiens*, with black people making the transition last. More recently, the I.Q. test has been (mis)used to infer genetic differences in intelligence among races (Arthur Jensen and William Shockley) and classes (Richard Herrnstein)—always, I must note, to the benefit of the particular group to which the author happens to belong.

All these views have been ably criticized on an individual basis; yet they have rarely been treated together as expressions of a common philosophy—a crude biological determinism. One can, of course, accept a specific claim and reject the others. A belief in the innate nature of human violence does not brand anyone a racist. Yet all these claims have a common underpinning in postulating a direct genetic basis for our most fundamental traits. If we are programmed to be what we are, then these traits are ineluctable. We may, at best, channel them, but we cannot change them, either by will, education, or culture.

In various guises, the political function of biological determinism has been to serve the supporters of class, sex, and race distinctions at home and of conquest or domination of supposedly inferior peoples abroad. In the context of Western history, this means that biological determinism has served as a tool of state and commercial power.

If we accept the usual platitudes about "scientific method" at face value, then the coordinated resurgence of biological determinism must be attributed to new information that refutes the earlier findings of twentieth-century science. Science, we are told, progresses by accumulating new information and using it to improve or replace old theories, but the new biological determinism rests upon no recent fund of information and can cite in its behalf not a single fact. Its renewed support must have some other basis, most likely social or political in nature.

Science is always influenced by society, but it operates under a strong constraint of fact as well. The Church eventually made its peace with Galilean cosmology. In studying the genetic components of such complex human traits as intelligence and aggressiveness, however, we are freed from the constraint of fact, for we are sure of practically nothing about these traits. In these questions, "science" follows (and indirectly exposes) the social and political influences of the time.

What, then, are the nonscientific reasons for the resurgence of biological determinism? They range, I believe, from pedestrian pursuits of high royalties for best sellers to pernicious attempts to reintroduce racism as respectable science. Their common denominator must lie in our current malaise. How satisfying it is to fob off the responsibility for war and violence upon our presumably carnivorous ancestors. How convenient to blame the poor and the hungry for their own condition—lest we be forced to blame industry or government for our abject failure to secure a decent life for all people. And how convenient an argument it is for those who control government and, by the way, provide the money that current science requires for its very existence!

The deterministic arguments divide neatly into two groups—those based on the supposed nature of the human species in general and those based on presumed differences among "racial groups" of *Homo sapiens.* . . . I shall treat the first subject here and reserve the second for my next column.

Summarized briefly, mainstream pop ethology contends that two lineages of hominids inhabited Pleistocene Africa. One, a small, territorial carnivore, evolved into us; the other, a larger, presumably gentle herbivore, became extinct. Some carry the analogy of Cain and Abel to its full conclusion and accuse our ancestors of fratricide. The "predatory transition" to hunting established a pattern of innate violence and engendered our territorial urges: "With the coming of the hunting life to the emerging hominid came the dedication to territory" (Ardrey, *The Territorial Imperative*).

According to this view, although clothed, citified, and civilized, we carry deep within us the genetic patterns of behavior that served our ancestor, the "killer ape." In *African Genesis* Ardrey champions Raymond Dart's contention that "the predatory transition and the weapons fixation explained man's bloody history, his eternal agression, his irrational self-destroying, inexorable pursuit of death for death's sake."

Tiger and Fox extend the theme of group hunting to claim a biological basis for the differences between men and women that Western cultures have traditionally valued. Men did the hunting; women stayed home with the kids. Men are aggressive and combative, but they also form strong bonds among themselves that reflect the ancient need for cooperation in the killing of big game and now find expression in touch football and rotary clubs. Women are docile and devoted to their own children. They do not form intense bonds among themselves because their ancestors needed none to tend their homes and their men: sisterhood is an illusion. "We are wired for hunting. . . . We remain Upper Paleolithic hunters, fine-honed machines designed for the efficient pursuit of game" (Tiger and Fox, *The Imperial Animal*).

The pop ethology story has been built on two lines of supposed evidence, both highly disputable:

1. Analogies with the behavior of other animals (abundant but imperfect data). No one doubts that many animals (including some, but not all, primates) display innate patterns of aggression and territorial behavior. Since we exhibit similar behavior, can we not infer a similar cause? The fallacy of this assumption involves a basic difference in evolutionary theory between homologous and analogous features. Homologous aspects of two species are due to a common descent and a common genetic constitution. Analogous traits evolved separately.

Comparisons between human beings and other animals can yield causal assertions about the genetics of our behavior only if they are based on homologous traits. But how can we know whether similarities are homologous or analogous? It is hard to differentiate even when we are dealing with concrete structures, such as muscles and bones. In fact, most classic arguments in the study of phylogeny involve the confusion of homology and analogy, for analogous structures can be strikingly similar (we call this phenomenon evolutionary convergence). How much harder it is to tell when the similar features are only the outward motions of behavior!

Baboons may be territorial; their males may be organized into a dominance hierarchy—but is our quest for Lebensraum and the hierarchy of our armies an expression of the same genetic makeup or merely an analogous pattern that might be purely cultural in origin? And when Lorenz compares us with geese and fish, we stray even further into pure conjecture; baboons, at least, are second cousins.

2. Evidence from hominid fossils (scrappy but direct data). Ardrey's claims for territoriality involve the assumption that our African ancestor *Australopithecus africanus,* was a carnivore. The evidence is based on accumulations of bones and tools at the South African cave sites and on the size and shape of teeth. The bone piles are no longer seriously considered; they are more likely the work of hyenas or leopards than of hominids.

Teeth are granted more prominence, but I believe that the evidence is equally poor if not absolutely contradictory. The relative size of grinding teeth (premolars and molars) is the basis of the argument. Herbivores need more surface area to grind their gritty and abundant food. *A. robustus,* the supposed gentle herbivore, possessed grinding teeth relatively larger than those of the presumed carnivore, our ancestor *A. africanus.*

But *A. robustus* was the larger of the two species. As size increases, an animal must feed a body growing as a cube of length by chewing with tooth areas that would increase only as the square of length if they maintained the same relative size. This will not do, and larger mammals must have differentially larger teeth than smaller relatives. I have tested this assertion by measuring tooth areas and body sizes for species in several groups of mammals (rodents, piglike herbivores, deer, and several groups of primates). Invariably, I find that larger animals have relatively larger teeth—not because they eat different foods, but simply because they are larger.

Moreover, the "small" teeth of *A. africanus* are not at all diminutive. They are *absolutely larger* than ours (although we are three times as heavy), and they are about as big as those of gorillas weighing nearly ten times as much! The evidence of tooth size indicates to me that *A. africanus* was primarily herbivorous.

The issue of biological determinism is not an abstract matter to be debated within academic cloisters. These ideas have important consequences, and they have already permeated our mass media. Ardrey's dubious theory is a prominent theme in Stanley Kubrick's film *2001.* The bone tool of our apelike ancestor first smashes a tapir's skull and then twirls about to transform into a space station of our next evolutionary stage. Kubrick's next film, *Clockwork Orange,* continues the theme and explores the liberal dilemma inspired by claims of innate human violence. (Shall we accept totalitarian controls for mass deprogramming or remain nasty and vicious within a democracy?) But the most immediate impact will be felt as male privilege girds its loins to battle a growing women's movement. As Kate Millett remarks in *Sexual Politics:* "Patriarchy has a tenacious or powerful hold through its successful habit of passing itself off as nature."

"It's hard to ignore one medical study"

**It's hard to ignore one medical study.
It's even harder to ignore two.**

Two important medical research
studies (one at a leading university
and another at a major hospital) have
provided evidence that Excedrin is
significantly more effective against pain than the
common aspirin tablet.
Don't ignore this evidence. Try Excedrin.
The extra-strength pain reliever.

Advertisement for Excedrin.

How about Him?

"A thing isn't a sin unless it harms some-body."

The SITUATIONAL THEOLOGIANS

Reprinted from *The Catholic Week,* July 25, 1969, p. 6. Cartoon by E. H. Wolf.

Review of Louis Nizer's
The Implosion Conspiracy

SARA SANBORN

In the absence of other sources, an illuminating political history of postwar America could be constructed out of writings on the Rosenberg case alone. As books have followed one another into print over a period of twenty years, the raging accusations of fascism and frameup by Rosenberg partisans have given way to cold-eyed scrutinies of the evidence and the witnesses. On the other side, even before the end of the 1950s, writers who considered the Rosenbergs guilty no longer presented them as the arch-villains that the prosecutor and the popular press had made them out to be, the symbols of a godless menace that threatened every American, but rather as contemptible neurotics whose personal inadequacies made them easy cat's-paws. Before he passed sentence on the accused, Judge Irving R. Kaufman's mail is said to have run 99 percent in favor of a death penalty. Only a few years later, no writer could find a way to defend the sentence or the judge's infamous statement that he held the Rosenbergs responsible for the Korean War and 50,000 American casualties.

With the appearance in 1971 of E. L. Doctorow's fine novel, *The Book of Daniel,* the Rosenbergs passed into the timeless realm of emotion recollected in tranquillity. They would have been pleased, for whatever else they were or were not, Ethel and Julius Rosenberg were avid for immortality. Whether they achieved it in their own perverse way or had it thrust upon them remains the question.

The case also acts as a glass to the authors who treat it, reflecting their values, concerns and assumptions about themselves and others. We have had the austere condescension of Jonathan Root and the all-pervading radical suspicion of Miriam and Walter Schneir. Though Louis Nizer's new study is occasionally marked by the footprints of earlier authors, it also faithfully mirrors his preoccupations and public personality. To Nizer, the Rosenberg case is essentially a courtroom drama, a battle between legal adversaries, with the outcome depending on the canniness and daring of one side or the other, and lots of crowd-pleasing human interest

Reprinted from *The Nation,* May 7, 1973, pp. 598–600.

thrown in free. One senses that he would like to have had a hand
in the arguments—and that he wouldn't have cared greatly which
side he represented. Nizer occasionally tries to lend weight to his
account by ritual invocations of the most destructive weapon ever
devised and the most important secret ever stolen, but his heart
isn't really in it. Neither the circumstances nor the outcome seems
to mean much to him, except in their possibilities for facile drama.
And an audience that measures death in megatons isn't likely to
freeze with horror at America's loss of the "secret" of the Naga-
saki-pattern bomb. What is left when the public thrills and chills
are removed is compelling enough: the history of three outcasts
battling the massed weight of society for their lives, and, although
Nizer seems happily unaware of the implications of some of his
materials, a morality play parading hypocrisy, vanity and cruelty,
occasionally redeemed by generosity and devotion.

Nizer set himself a large task in telling the Rosenbergs' story
again. He pledged himself to master "the internal facts such as the
psychological motivations," as well as the external ones. "I was not
going to write a word until research had put me under their skins,
the prosecutors', the defense counsels', the judge's, the appellate
judges', the witnesses'." It is an impossibly ambitious, indeed pre-
sumptuous, undertaking—unless one has a very simplistic notion
of psychological motivation. When Nizer tries to get under the
Rosenbergs' skins, his conclusions are generally thin, hackneyed,
and condescending. We understand them most fully and painfully
as human beings when the author intrudes least, in the last sections that describe their lives in the death house. The death sentence itself seems scarcely less terrible than the gratuitous and
hypocritical cruelties of prison life. When Ethel Rosenberg's children brought her a bouquet at their last meeting, she was not
allowed to accept it. Elaborate precautions were taken to see that
the couple never touched each other: at joint meetings with their
lawyer (and their children), they wore handcuffs and were separated by the length of a conference table; in their last meeting on
the night they died, a wire screen was meticulously placed between them. In a particularly hideous torture, federal officials let
them know down to the moment each sat in the electric chair that
their lives would be spared if, and only if, they confessed and
implicated others. The author reports these grotesque inhumani-
ties quite uncritically: it seems that to him they merely add local
color.

Nizer makes no effort to get "under the skin" of his professional colleague, Judge Kaufman. Of the chief prosecutor (late judge) Irving H. Saypol, who built a career prosecuting such public enemies as Alger Hiss, William Remington and Abraham Brothman, Nizer observes only, "Saypol was effective because of an inner conviction that he was fighting a wicked enemy. It armed him with sincerity. There is no more effective weapon to pierce a jury's doubts." Here there is no pretense of understanding the traits of character that contributed to the tragic outcome.

As to the witnesses: who can penetrate the psychological motivations of a David Greenglass, who swore his older sister into the electric chair? Greenglass confessed in copious detail that, at the instigation of the Rosenbergs, he had taken advantage of his position as a machinist at Los Alamos to pass on information about the detonating device of the atom bomb. He and his wife, who acted as a courier, testified that they had known from the beginning that their activities were "wrong"; however, they had been kept in the conspiracy by his "hero-worship" for the older Julius. The Greenglasses were rewarded handsomely for their testimony: David was sentenced to fifteen years, getting off the lightest of all the defendants though he was the only one who had actually had access to secret government data; Ruth, who by her own confession was as deeply involved as Ethel, was never indicted. Probably we need not seek much further for their motivations.

Nizer is most successful in creating as a personality the defense attorney, Emmanual Bloch, whom he regards as "the hero of the book." With no help except that of his father, Ethel's attorney, and one assistant, Bloch carried the main burden of the defense, pressed the record number of appeals, attended rallies, and took charge of the tormented Rosenberg children, accompanying them on harrowing visits to Sing Sing. A few months after the execution, having finished a coast-to-coast speaking tour to raise funds for the children, and facing proceedings by the New York City Bar Association for his intemperate public remarks ("I am ashamed to be an American"), Emmanual Bloch died of a heart attack at the age of 51.

Bloch's devotion to his clients was exemplary and his appeal briefs, Nizer says, were brilliant. Unfortunately, "apparently the Blochs were better brief writers than trial lawyers." With the loving care of a successful artist commenting on a lesser man's work, Nizer points out all the missed opportunities in cross-examination, in the presentation of evidence and witnesses, and in the final summations, as well as the spectacular errors of commission made by Bloch in what were, transparently, efforts to placate the judge and jury. This is a perspective on the case we have never had before, and an illuminating one. It is Nizer's expert if self-satisfied commentary on the courtroom events and his re-creation of the advocate's ordeal that give this otherwise unoriginal and thinly researched book its interest.

The real question we should ask about the trial, the author says, is not whether the Rosenbergs were guilty—we will probably never know—but whether the jury had sufficient ground for its verdict of guilty "beyond a reasonable doubt." Nizer claims he began his study with no opinion either way, and he purports to give the reader the same opportunity to judge for himself. In fact, what in a trial judge would be reversible prejudice appears throughout the book, and we are not surprised when Nizer declares the verdict legitimate on the basis of his study of the trial transcript. Nonetheless, the reader will probably agree that the verdict did not fly in the face of the evidence. The Rosenbergs testified, feebly, in their own behalf, while against them appeared half a dozen witnesses. Most, to be sure, had something to gain by their testimony, but none was discredited by cross-examination. The case of Morton Sobell, whose grievances have been obscured by the more sensational fates of the Rosenbergs, is different. Sobell was tied to the conspiracy by the word of one man, who had something to fear from the government for having perjured himself in swearing that he was not a Communist, and there seems substantial room for reasonable doubt here. Nizer seems rather to feel that Sobell, on whom he expends little attention, deserved the thirty years he got for having mounted an optimistically incomplete defense.

In any case, it is not the *jury*'s honesty which those with continuing doubts about this case question, as Nizer must know perfectly well. His bright conclusion that all is well because the evidence can support the verdict and there were no gross improprieties in the conduct of the trial, seems either naive or disingenuous. It is precisely the quality of the evidence presented to the jury that has been persistently questioned. We are not content to be assured of what most of us never doubted, that the jury acted in good faith. We would like to know if the prosecutors and investigators did too. It is extraordinary that Nizer does not list among the few books he consulted the Schneirses' *Invitation to an Inquest,* in which the authors presented what appeared to be new facts. To cite only one example, the testimony of Harry Gold, the self-confessed spy-courier, is thrown into doubt by the Schneirses' investigation, during which they heard tapes of Gold's interviews with his lawyers describing his interrogation by the FBI. These tapes make clear that Gold's story was incomplete in many respects until the FBI "helped" him recall such details as Greenglass' name and address and, apparently, the damning password, "I come from Julius." Many facts of Gold's history make it hard to believe that those who interrogated him could have found him completely credible, except by wishful thinking.

Appellate courts do not rule on matters of fact or the credibility of witnesses, considered the province only of the jury, nor may they review sentences, set by the trial judge alone. Bloch pressed twenty-three applications for relief of one kind or another, and 112 judges (counting some more than once as they ruled on different occasions) found the proceedings unimpeachable under prevailing federal law and practice, while only twelve dissented. Nizer calls on us to witness and rejoice in how many safeguards America grants her accused. Everything including sentencing was done according to law and precedent, and Nizer makes clear his scorn of amateurs who dare to question the law itself or suggest that it may be subject to abuse. While he considers the death sentence "unfortunate" (especially in the propaganda opportunities it gave the Communists), he is satisfied that the Rosenbergs got their full measure of justice in this best of all possible legal worlds.

Hence, this is ultimately a cheap book. It is cheap in its meticulous avoidance of the real issues in the Rosenberg case, in its smugness about American legal institutions, in the complacency of its author, and in his indifference to the Rosenbergs as human beings except insofar as their incredible emotional ordeal can be exploited for the screenplay he says he is writing. A study that attacked the issues and personalities of the case head-on and then straightforwardly found against the Rosenbergs would be more worth while than this, for Nizer is not really objective; he is merely morally absent. The book is stuffed with routine pieties about the jury system, but even here the author's professions fail to carry conviction. The hymns to American jurisprudence ring false when Nizer describes with a craftsman's delight what kind of jurors the defense should try to seat and how counsel should behave to make the best impression. These sections, and those in which Nizer elucidates (quite uncritically and with a sneer for amateurs who presume to have an opinion) such legal monstrosities as the law of conspiracy, are enlightening as they relate to the Rosenberg case, and they add to the education of the armchair advocate. But they do not build faith in the law's majestic impartiality, nor in Nizer's ethical sensibilities.

It is unfortunate that this book fails in the ways it does, because it is time for another study of the Rosenbergs. It would be good to have a study that instead of trying once again to prove a case one way or the other, could put the whole complex of events into perspective for us, could help us understand what it meant to and about us as Americans. Even if we consider the Rosenbergs to have been guilty, the conduct of the trial and the surrounding events still have important implications for us. The sentence and the accompanying public blood-lust, for example, remain as painful souvenirs of our immaturity, reminders of what we are capable when roused. But we have also traveled beyond that: it seems possible that the Rosenberg verdict might be set aside by a higher court today, if only because the jury in this most sensational of all cases was not sequestered during the trial.

Such a treatment will have to await the appearance of a writer of much greater stature than Nizer. What we will probably get in the meantime is his screenplay, a measure of what the Rosenberg case has become to us twenty years after: "A great spy story! A great love story!"

What a Catholic Wishes
to Avoid in Marriage

JOHN S. BANAHAN

Tall stories are not the exclusive property of Texans. Men have enjoyed stretching the truth at least as long as they have been able to write. One of the earliest prototypes of Paul Bunyan was a character of Greek mythology named Cyclops. He was a tremendous giant employed in Vulcan's blacksmith shop to forge thunderbolts for Zeus to hurl down from the heavens at the mortals who might defy him. He was a being of gigantic size and immeasurable strength. He was gifted with acute senses. And his only defect was that he had but one eye placed squarely in the midst of his forehead. This weakness was fatal. For he was brought to his knees by one far smaller in stature than he who was clever enough to deprive him of his eyesight. Thus being blinded, his great strength was useless.

In a way, modern man is an image of Cyclops. For though he possesses two eyes and two ears, he has only one intellect. It is this mind of his that gives man the power to look deep into things and understand them. And yet today millions of men have suffered a cyclopean wound. Their mind's eye is blinded. They are deprived of the vision that their intellect should give them.

Tiny objects can deprive us of sight. A cinder or a cataract are infinitesimal but nonetheless they can blind us. And there are things less substantial than these which can darken the light of the mind. A strong emotion has this ability. Quite commonly men are blinded by anger, love, or desire. The company of those blinded by desire is perhaps the largest in world history. Among its membership are such men as Adolf Hitler, Joseph Stalin, and Benito Mussolini. Now, these three men were not the incarnate devils that the cartoonists of the past decade pictured them. They were men of at least ordinary intelligence who were blinded with their desire for power. Desire of wealth can lead men to steal. Desire for liquor can cause drunkenness. Desire for property can bring men to murder. Whenever men are ruled by their desires they become something less than men. Animals have no higher faculties than

Reprinted from *Instructions for Mixed Marriages* (Milwaukee: Bruce Publishing Company, 1955), pp. 78–89.

their desires. But men have within them the spark of divinity—the ability to think and will. The more a man is influenced by his thoughts, the more a man is he. Now, marriage has been made for man, not for animals, and when men forget this the slow cancer of unhappiness threatens their lives.

One of the most prominent signs that man has forgotten his nature is the practice of artificial birth control. Everyone knows that Catholics aren't supposed to use birth prevention devices, but few realize that this applies likewise to the rest of the world. Catholics are not the only ones forbidden to steal or murder. No one should do these things. They are not "Catholic Sins" any more than is artificial birth prevention.

Before we go much farther, let us point this out. There is nothing wrong with birth control! The word "control" implies the correct use of mind and will. It implies that a man acts like a man and not as a blind animal force. The Church favors such control! She encourages men to practice control of their lives, of their faculties, and of their desires. But a further question is just how this control is to be achieved. A man has a right and duty to clothe and feed his family. Suppose he chooses a career of armed robbery to accomplish this end. Certainly the Church would try to dissuade him from adopting such a means of livelihood. But it would be the means that she would criticize, and not the purpose for which he steals. Likewise, with birth prevention by artificial means, she criticizes the measures adopted, not the policy of control of marital relations. The Church has never commanded her members to have two, twelve, or twenty children. The size of a family is something to be determined by husband and wife, not by pastor or bishop. But what the Church says is this: It is improper to use the human faculty of procreation and then deliberately exclude and frustrate its natural purposes by some artificial means. There are three reasons for this condemnation:

I. Reason Tells Us That This Is Wrong

Nothing that exists in this world is evil. Everything is good. The use of things is not wrong, but the *misuse* of things is. A Cadillac in itself is good. But if I drive it at top speed through a crowded street and bring injury and death to several bystanders, my actions are evil. The auto is still good, but I have misused it. Or, if I employ a shotgun to shoot not pigeons but people, then the misuse of this weapon is something evil.

Of course, we cannot determine if a thing is misused unless we know its correct use. This is true of the smallest atom and the largest skyscraper. They all have a proper purpose and a correct usage. Our eyes, our ears, and our voices all are designed for definite purposes. When we frustrate these purposes, we do wrong. For instance, our voices have been given us that we might communicate honestly and truthfully what we are thinking. Every time we read a paper or listen to a news analyst, we accept this principle. We trust men to tell us what they think is true. But when we tell a deliberate lie, then we consciously frustrate the purpose for which the power of speech was given us. We have misused this tremendous faculty; we have thereby done wrong.

Paramount among the wonderful activities man is capable of is procreation. Besides the powers to think and will which are replicas of God's faculties, He has given man the ability to co-operate with Him in creating new life. These generative powers are given to all normal men and women for the purpose of perpetuating the human race. It is axiomatic that those who bring such life into existence should assume responsibility for it. And since this obligation is not a light one, mankind must be encouraged to assume it and be rewarded for doing so.

Thus God has attached to this faculty a deep and instinctive drive and a unique physical pleasure. These things are normal and good. There is nothing evil or warped about sex instinct or pleasure. Only their misuse is wrong. Did you ever start to cross a street, then barely see the flicker of an approaching vehicle and find that you have automatically, without thinking at all, jumped back to the safety of the curbstone? If you have had this experience, then you witnessed the subconscious drive all men have of self-preservation. Equal to this in unrelenting intensity is the drive for self-perpetuation, more popularly identified as the sex instinct. This leads mankind to discount the burdens of parenthood and to co-operate again and again with God in bringing human life to exist for all eternity. Besides this, parents experience a unique reward called sexual pleasure. These feelings are attached to the use of the generative faculty. And although all of our senses bring us pleasure, they do not match in any way the sensations evoked by the use of the creative faculty. This is proportionate because none of the others involve us in such tremendous responsibilities.

Thus instinct and pleasure co-operate to encourage men to use their generative powers. But observe, the purpose of these faculties is the production of new life, not pleasure. Therefore, when a man deliberately excludes the proper purpose and makes this godlike act of procreation an act of mere pleasure, he does wrong.

Among the sins of man there is no parallel of this. A crime it approximates is an opprobrious custom of the ancient past. In the days when Roman culture had flowered and then began to decay the aristocracy built huge and lovely villas in renowned spas such as Pompeii. There they lived in overnourished luxury. It was then that the practice of all night dinner parties began, made up of twenty or thirty of the richest courses imaginable. And since the human body could not consume such quantity and variety of food, the guests would occasionally retire to a room adjacent to the dining area where they would regurgitate and then return to continue feasting. Such a practice appalls the modern man whose acts parallel the sins of the Romans when he practices artificial birth prevention to enjoy the pleasures of marriage while excluding its proper purpose.

Do not misunderstand! The Church does not say that those who practice planned parenthood today are degenerate. She does not say that they are decadent. But she does say that the two actions are equivalent and that people today can be excused only because they lack the proper information or have not thought deeply on the question. Reason, if correctly employed, should tell all men that this practice is morally wrong.

II. The Bible Tells Us That It Is Wrong

Most Christians today believe in Holy Scripture. Some believe it to be the inspired Word of God, as do Catholics. Others at least admit it to be a collection of profound truths of dubious authorship. But most Christians believe that the statements of the Bible are true.

In the very first book of Holy Writ we find a passage which deals clearly and specifically with this practice. In the Book of Genesis, we can read the tragic story of Onan. In the early days of history, the Jews were a nomadic group with no fixed land to call their own. One of their sociological problems was the care of widows and orphans. In their primitive society, there was no employment suitable for women who had lost their husbands. Therefore, a law was passed requiring the deceased's brother to marry the widow and care for her and her children. This misfortune befell Onan, and it is recounted that as a result of his dissatisfaction with this regulation he proceeded to practice artificial birth prevention with his new wife. The very next verse of Holy Scripture recounts: "Therefore the Lord slew him because he did a detestable thing." [1]

Notice the two points of this citation:

a) God *detests* this practice. In other words, He regards it as sinful.

b) He detests it to such an extent that He *slew* Onan in punishment. Therefore, this practice cannot be regarded as something merely mischievous or naughty, but as something which is very seriously wrong. Catholics call it mortal sin.

This is not the only mention of artificial birth prevention in the Bible, for the Book of Tobias and certain of the Pauline Epistles [2] abound in instructions on the nature of marriage. However, if you are one who accepts the truth of the biblical quotations the story of Onan should be sufficient.[3]

III. THE CHURCH SAYS IT IS SERIOUSLY WRONG

A clergyman is as prone to error as the butcher, the baker, or the candlestick maker. Even when said clergyman is a priest, bishop, or even pope, he can still blunder. But the first chapter of this booklet mentioned that there was a percentage of religious teaching that was guaranteed to be true by no less an authority than God Himself, acting through His own institution of which He has said: "He who hears you, hears me." [4] In twenty centuries, this organization has occasionally made public and official statements and given the world assurance that they were true. Among these infallible statements is listed the condemnation of artificial birth control as being a serious sin. There is as much possibility that ecclesiastical teaching on this subject will change as there is that the Church's opposition to murder will change. Birth prevention has always been practiced; it has always been wrong. Possibly it always will be practiced, and if so, it always will be wrong!

[1] Gen. 38:10.

[2] Tob. 6:16; Rom. 1:26.

[3] St. Augustine writes: "Marital relations even with a lawful wife, are unlawful and degrading when the conception of a child is deliberately frustrated. This was the sin of Onan, and God struck him dead because of it" (*De Adulterio*, 2:12).

[4] Lk. 10:6.

WHY

There are various reasons why people indulge in this practice. Let us enumerate three classes:

a) Those Who Are Selfish. There are married folk who prefer a new Frigidaire or Ford to a filled bassinet. There are wives who fear to lose their figures. There are couples who treasure their adult privacy overmuch. Of course, people who have such a warped and dwarfed appreciation of human life should never be allowed to be parents. Their unborn children are fortunate for there is nothing more pitiful than to be an unwanted child. To them we cite the words of our Saviour who spoke thus to those who maltreated children: "It is better for him to have a great millstone hung around his neck, and to be drowned in the depths of the sea." [5]

b) Those Who Cannot Afford Children. There are several varieties of this excuse.

1. There are the teen-agers who marry though penniless and unemployed! This should not be allowed to happen. Parents, clergy, and judiciary should close ranks in an attempt to prevent boys and girls from entering marriage without the proper financial resources. The mistake having been made, these same authorities should be just as solicitous and co-operative in providing these couples with temporary subsidies.

2. There are those who confuse luxuries and necessities. Some parents feel that their families should be limited to the few whom they can afford to send to college or finishing school. Little do they realize that their children may not wish to attend the schools selected for them. The child that remains unborn might have been the one to treasure and use well the education and physical advantages wasted by the living. Benjamin Franklin was the eighth child of his parents. There were six in the Washington family, and Abraham Lincoln had seven brothers and sisters. The Jeffersons numbered ten, the Madisons twelve, the Longfellows eight, and the Beethovens twelve. There were eight Shakespeares, twelve Tennysons and Scotts, and nine Carlyles. God bestows talent and genius where He wills; it is not arrived at by selective breeding!

3. Those who actually have a serious financial problem. To these the Church will give sympathy, encouragement, and assis-

[5] Mt. 18:6.

tance. Sometimes priests are criticized for their interest in trade unionism and collective bargaining. Their policy is founded on the belief that a man cannot live the moral life the Church demands of him unless he receives wages proportionate to his obligations and dignity as the head of a household. Empty bellies make poor Christians. The Church is realistic enough to know that greed and avarice can affect union leaders as well as the rest of mankind. She knows that her concern for her people can be twisted by the unscrupulous. But she will continue to use every possible means to enable parents to afford their families.

Remember the famous fairy tale of Cinderella? In the closing chapter, the Prince comes searching his kingdom for the owner of the dainty glass slipper. He proffers it to one of the ugly sisters who lives with Cinderella, who in an effort to make her foot fit the shoe, cuts off her toes! This is a dreadful way to acquire footwear of the proper size, but it is rather reminiscent of what occurs each year in many American homes. Because the size of the family won't fit the current budget, the family is pared down a member or two. The Church suggests an alternative solution. Instead of decreasing the family, why can't men increase their budgets? Perhaps this is more difficult than purchasing prophylactics at the corner drugstore, but the Church attempts to give the *correct* solution and not just the easiest one. What is right is very often difficult!

c) Those Who Are Told That Pregnancy Will Endanger Their Lives. The sympathy and solicitude of the Church is aroused by the plight of these worried husbands and wives. But while she understands the concern of these couples the Church points out that medical opinion is not infallible. We all know of women who have defied their physician's orders and safely raised large families. We do not therefore recommend wholesale rebellion against all medical authority, but merely point out that sometimes a doctor's diagnosis is incorrect and sometimes perhaps God Himself suspends the laws He has made for us. Very great wonders have been worked by the sincere prayers of ordinary husbands and wives.

However, there certainly are some cases when it is not safe for a woman to become a mother. What suggestions does the Church make to a married couple troubled with such a burden? The only remedy that can be suggested to such people is a life of virtuous abstinence. This is impossible except for couples who accept the philosophy that God has made them for eternal happiness and earthly problems are the price we pay for everlasting felicity. It was impossible for Peter to walk on the waters of the Sea of Galilee until God gave him that ability. God can likewise give married couples the strength to live lives of complete abstinence if such people would devoutly ask it of Him.

"Smoking Is Very Glamorous"

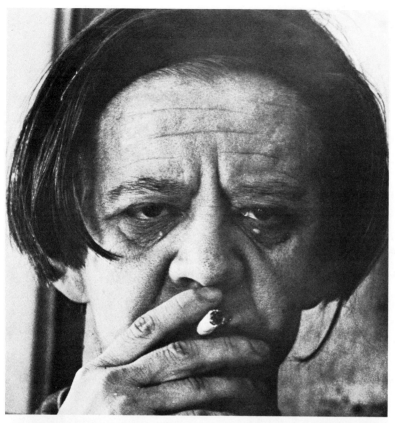

Reprint of an American Cancer Society poster.

"They'll Go Away . . ."

"They'll Go Away if You Put the Light Out."

Reprinted from *The American Rifleman*, September 1973, p. 60. Cartoon by Ted Robins.

O What Is that Sound

W. H. AUDEN

O what is that sound which so thrills the ear
  Down in the valley drumming, drumming?
Only the scarlet soldiers, dear,
  The soldiers coming.

O what is that light I see flashing so clear
  Over the distance brightly, brightly?
Only the sun on their weapons, dear,
  As they step lightly.

O what are they doing with all that gear,
  What are they doing this morning, this morning?
Only their usual manoeuvers, dear,
  Or perhaps a warning.

O why have they left the road down there,
  Why are they suddenly wheeling, wheeling?
Perhaps a change in their orders, dear.
  Why are you kneeling?

O haven't they stopped for the doctor's care,
  Haven't they reined their horses, their horses?
Why, they are none of them wounded, dear,
  None of these forces.

O is it the parson they want, with white hair,
  Is it the parson, is it, is it?
No, they are passing his gateway, dear,
  Without a visit.

O it must be the farmer who lives so near.
  It must be the farmer so cunning, so cunning?
They have passed the farmyard already, dear,
  And now they are running.

O where are you going? Stay with me here!
  Were the vows you swore deceiving, deceiving?

Reprinted from W. H. Auden, *Collected Shorter Poems, 1927–1957* (New York: Random House, 1965).

No, I promised to love you, dear,
But I must be leaving.

O it's broken the lock and splintered the door,
O, it's the gate where they're turning, turning;
Their boots are heavy on the floor
And their eyes are burning.

Auden's "O What Is that Sound"

LAURENCE PERRINE AND JANE JOHNSTON

Critics have been reluctant to be precise about the situation in W. H. Auden's ballad "O What Is That Sound" (entitled "The Quarry" in the 1958 *Selected Poetry*), probably because they start (as does Monroe K. Spears in *The Poetry of W. H. Auden,* London, 1968, p. 109) with the understandable but, we think, mistaken assumption that the woman is the first speaker. This assumption makes it difficult to explain why the first speaker kneels in stanza 4, and why the second speaker remains so calm throughout. If we reverse this assumption, these difficulties are resolved in what can be seen as a tale of double betrayal.

The man (who speaks in lines 1–2 of each stanza except the last, which is spoken by the poet) is a traitor or rebel who is hiding out with his mistress in a house on a mountainside; he is the "quarry" wanted by the soldiers. Knowing himself wanted, he is alarmed at the sound of troops in the distance, and his terror mounts as they approach. When they leave the road (stanza 4), he kneels so as not to be visible through the window. (In stanzas 2–4 his questions concern what *he* sees through the window; in subsequent stanzas he is dependent on the woman to report what *she* sees.) Having no reason to think his hiding place known, the man tries to convince himself that the troops are headed elsewhere— the doctor's, the parson's, or the farmer's—but they are coming for him. They come directly; they do not have to search or make inquiries; obviously, they have been tipped off. Who has tipped them off? Clearly the woman, whose vows have indeed been "deceiving," and who *may* be a secret agent. At any rate, she has betrayed him, just as he has previously betrayed, or plotted against, the government of his country. Her knowledge of the situation accounts for her coolness, so markedly in contrast to the hysteria of the man, and her purpose has been, by minimizing the import of the situation, to hold the man in the house until the soldiers can get there. (The drumming sound, she tells him, is "only" the soldiers, and they are "only" performing "their usual manoeuvres.") When it is too late for him to make a break, she leaves, so as not to witness any violence.

Reprinted from *The Explicator,* January 1972.

Auden's poem concerns terror, menace, and betrayal in a world where politics rule, not love. The initial obscurity of the situation increases the terror, and is appropriate to a world in which real purposes and motivations are kept concealed.

"This Is What Five Pounds Overweight Looks Like"

This is what five pounds overweight looks like.

If we looked at it this way—wearing our fat where everyone could see it—we'd surely all be thinner.

Right now there are 15 million overweight people in America. Many are plump candidates for coronary attacks, strokes or diabetes. Fattening themselves up for the kill, without knowing it.

You become overweight by eating too much and exercising too little. It's that simple.

So you've got to monitor what you eat or drink, as well as how much. And a more balanced diet is extremely important in controlling cholesterol and triglycerides, the fatty substances in blood that can manufacture heart attacks.

What about exercise? Too much sitting and reclining and no walking or activity causes obesity at least as much as too much eating. If you're overweight, a physical examination will tell you if your health is in danger. And how much exercise you can take.

Five pounds doesn't sound alarming. But that's what it is. An alarm. Because five can get you ten. Ten can get you twenty, and on and on.

Imagine what that would look like.

And what it would do to you.

LIBERTY NATIONAL
LIFE INSURANCE COMPANY
HOME OFFICE: BIRMINGHAM, ALABAMA

Reprinted from a Liberty National Life Insurance advertisement.

"Too Bad He Can't Be Released . . ."

THE CRIME VICTIM

Cartoon by Don Hesse, Distributed by *Los Angeles Times* Syndicate. Printed in the *Mobile Register & Press,* September 21, 1974, p. 4A.

Some Thoughts on Professor Shockley

S. L. VARNADO

I don't know anything about Science but I know what I like. And what I like is for Science to leave me alone. My attitude toward Science is the same as my attitude toward Rock Music, and might best be described as benign neglect. Let Science (and Rock Music, for that matter) go its way; I will go mine.

I know nothing, for instance, of DNA. I don't know what Boyle's Law is all about and I don't much care. I am not curious about Black Holes—in fact, I am not sure that I believe in them. Dr. B. F. Skinner grew old and famous before I even knew who he was. And when I found out, I labored for some time under the impression that *Beyond Freedom and Dignity* was some sort of study of marriage.

Enough, you say. The man is obviously an untutored lunatic, or at best an amateur obscurantist whose views need scarcely detain a denizen of the twentieth century. I admit this. There are scientists and pseudoscientists enow, and to them I leave the field. Once in a while, however, a scientist comes along with a theory that sets my ganglia on edge, and one such man is the eminent Professor William Shockley. I take a keen—even an unhealthy—interest in him. I see his theories as jeopardizing not only The Races of Man (a problem The Races of Man can worry about) but my own hitherto happy marriage. Of course, when something like this happens, I drop all pose of amateur obscurantist. Gathering my charts, my graphs, my proliferating data, and my Gatorade about me, I attack without quarter.

Professor William Shockley, as I suppose everybody knew before I did, is the genius who helped invent the conjunction transistor, for which feat he was awarded part of the Nobel Prize (and for which feat he must bear part of the guilt for Rock Music). Then, having no new solid states to conquer, and not content to rest upon his components, he turned a roving eye upon the science of genetics. This, I take it, is a dangerous thing to do, especially when you are approaching middle age, as Shockley was. It is the

Abridged from *National Review*, August 30, 1974, pp. 975, 993–994.

scientific equivalent of philandering, and if Shockley wasn't aware of the signs, his wife should have been. She should have put him to beating rugs and working crossword puzzles. But she didn't. The wife is always the last to know.

From Shockley's affair with Genes and Permutations came a number of conclusions (all of them disputable), which I shall attempt to summarize. First, Shockley has collected statistics which tend to show that the median IQ scores of the Black Race are 10 to 20 points lower than the median IQ scores of members of the White Race. Shockley, I have noticed, always says "10 to 20 points"—never "10 points" or "20 points." This gives his statistics a casual air that offends even such an obscurantist as I. (It is the way my wife talks.) Second, he has statistics indicating that the poorer members of both the Black and White Races—and especially those with low IQ scores—are outbreeding the rest of the population. This, he feels, is lowering the general IQ score of the nation, a condition that causes him great pain.

All this sort of thing (racial IQ disparity, overpopulation by low IQ scorers, etc.) Shockley calls by the name Dysgenics. Now *Dysgenics* is an interesting word. It means "the retrogressive evolution through the disproportionate reproduction of the genetically disadvantaged." Shockley apparently loves both the word and its fantastic definition. It has the sort of sesquipedalian hue that colors most of his statements. One imagines him going around the house muttering this sort of thing.`

At any rate, having analyzed the evils of Dysgenics, Shockley goes on to propose solutions. (By "evil," I mean evil to Shockley. To me, Dysgenics is an appealing process. Imagine people "evolving" backwards! I know several ladies I would much prefer as horses.) Shockley's solutions to this problem all turn, in one way or another, on sterilization. He wants to sterilize Poor Blacks and Poor Whites. He proposes to sterilize those who pay no income tax. And especially he hopes to offer monetary inducements to people below 80 IQ to get themselves voluntarily sterilized. That's his program.

It is solutions of this kind that have me stirred up. I am worried about the effects of this sort of thing on my marriage. Let me explain briefly.

I am married to a woman whose IQ score is 10 to 20 points higher than mine. (Count 'em: 10 to 20.) We have established this unhappy condition many times by taking *Reader's Digest* IQ tests. No matter how vigorously I concentrate, no matter how much extra time my wife allows me, the results are always the same. She comes out 10 to 20 points ahead. (Needless to say, my wife revels in this condition. She goes around the house complaining "I wish they would establish a chapter of Mensa in this hick town.")

Now in addition to my low IQ score, our marriage shows a tendency toward what Shockley calls "disproportionate reproduction." We have six children. Finally, while we are not statistically "poor" we are rapidly becoming so. My salary rises a bit every year but not so fast as to outpace that constantly rising mark which the government sets each year as its "poverty level." Some day it will undoubtedly overtake it, and when it does our marriage will have all the notes of classic Dysgenicism: a questionable IQ gradient (in at least one partner), a mass of progeny, and some degree of statistical destitution. My bitterness toward the Shockley theories should now be understandable. I am threatened.

But this is not the whole story.

Dysgenics is a two way street, and there is another side to the matter which Shockley ought to hear. There are factors in my marriage which work to ameliorate this seemingly hopeless situation, and I am going to tell them not only to refute Shockley, but to console other Dysgenics.

Despite her superior IQ score, my wife is the victim of a hereditary flaw. She has had from childhood what can only be described as a Bad Driveway Gene. She must have got it from her mother, since her father did not know how to drive. The Gene in question is, I am inclined to think, Recessive.

(I suppose I should stop, right about now, and explain for the lay reader the meaning of the terms *Recessive* and *Dominant*. Briefly, there are two kinds of Genes: Dominant and Recessive. A Dominant Gene is simply a gregarious, extroverted Gene—the sort that tries to "Take over." This Gene is much like the person who, when he goes to a party, drinks and talks too much and ends up forcing everybody to play charades. On the other hand, a Recessive Gene is an introvert—shy, sensitive, refined. It prefers a book or a quiet chat with a friend, it is easily exploited by a Dominant Gene, and its life is probably not too happy.)

My wife's Bad Driveway Gene, as I said, is of this Recessive type. It belongs to a group known as the Automobile Driving Complex, and the other Genes in this group (evidently Dominant) keep it under control on freeways and streets. But when it gets in a driveway—on home ground, so to speak—it feels more relaxed and begins to assert itself. It is this Bad Driveway Gene that causes my wife to run into things in driveways: garbage cans, mail boxes, you name it.

I discovered this particular Gene in my wife before we were married. After some sad experiences, she confessed she had driven through the garage doors twice. She had struck her mother's Lincoln several times. She had raked a visitor's Mercury, parted a caladium bed, and so forth. I married her anyway. I was not one to let Genetics impede the marriage of true minds. Besides, I knew my Driveway Gene was good, and being a male chauvinist, I figured it was Dominant. My children, I reasoned, would inherit from me—and as a matter of fact, they have. It is reassuring to watch the careful way in which they wheel their bicycles and velocipedes in and out of the driveway. (Our girl shows a tendency to follow in her mother's tire tracks, but I imagine it's psychological imitation.)

Now here is the point of my argument.

Suppose my wife, knowing my weak IQ score, had sacrificed herself to the Higher Genetics and married somebody more intelligent. She might have gotten some stuffy little prodigy who, unknown to her had a Driveway Gene as bad as her own. They would have then proceeded to unleash upon society a whole brood of Bad Driveway Factors. But as things stand now, we have bred out the bad strain.

A small victory, perhaps, but I often think of it when I read of Shockley, or observe the dents in our station wagon.

Pot: A Rational Approach

JOEL FORT, M.D.

There are an estimated 10,000,000 Americans who smoke marijuana either regularly or occasionally, and they have very obvious reasons for wishing that pot were treated more sensibly by the law. As one of the 190,000,000 who have never smoked marijuana, I also favor the removal of grass from the criminal laws, but for less personal reasons. It is my considered opinion, after studying drug use and drug laws in 30 nations and dealing with drug-abuse problems professionally for 15 years, that the present marijuana statutes in America not only are bad laws for the offending minority but are bad for the vast majority of us who never have lit a marijuana cigarette and never will.

That some changes in these laws are coming in the near future is virtually certain, but it is not at all sure that the changes will be improvements.

On May 19, 1969, the U. S. Supreme Court, in an 8–0 vote, declared that the Marijuana Tax Act of 1937 was unconstitutional. This decision delighted the defendant, Timothy Leary, and was no surprise at all to lawyers who specialize in the fine points of constitutional law. It had long been recognized that the Marijuana Tax Act was "vulnerable"—a polite term meaning that the law had been hastily drawn, rashly considered and railroaded through Congress in a mood of old-maidish terror that spent no time on the niceties of the Bill of Rights, scientific fact or common sense.

Celebrations by marijuanaphiles and lamentations by marijuanaphobes, however, are both premature. The Court, while throwing out this one inept piece of legislation, specifically declared that Congress has the right to pass laws governing the use, sale and possession of this drug (provided these laws stay within the perimeter of the Constitution). And, of course, state laws against pot, which are often far harsher than the Federal law, still remain in effect.

There were two defects found by the Supreme Court in the Federal anti-marijuana law—a section that requires the suspect to pay a tax on the drug, thus incriminating himself, in violation of the Fifth Amendment; and a section that assumes (rather than requir-

---

Abridged from *Playboy*, October 1969, pp. 131, 154, 216–218.

ing proof) that a person with foreign-grown marijuana in his possession knows it is smuggled. These provisions were perversions of
traditional American jurisprudence, no less than the remaining
parts of the law that are bound to fall when challenged before the
Supreme Court. These forthcoming decisions will, inevitably, affect the anti-marijuana laws of the individual states as well. However, the striking down of the old laws does not guarantee that the
new ones will be more enlightened; it merely invites more carefully drawn statutes that are less vulnerable to judicial review. In
fact, in a message to Congress, President Nixon specifically demanded harsher penalties for marijuana convictions. But every
sane and fair-minded person must be seriously concerned that the
new laws are more just and more in harmony with known fact
than the old ones. In my opinion, such new laws must treat marijuana no more harshly than alcohol is presently treated.

It is ironic that our present pot laws are upheld chiefly by the
older generation, and flouted and condemned by the young; for it
is the senior generation that should understand the issue most
clearly, having lived through the era of alcohol prohibition. They
saw with their own eyes that the entire nation—not just the
drinkers and sellers of liquor—suffered violent moral and mental
harm from that particular outbreak of armed and rampant puri-
tanism. They should certainly remember that attempts to legislate
morality result only in widespread disrespect for law, new markets
and new profits for gangsters, increased violence and such wholesale bribery and corruption that the Government itself becomes a
greater object of contempt than the criminal class. Above all, they
should be able to see the parallel between the lawless Twenties
and the anarchic Sixties and realize that both were produced by
bad laws—laws that had no right to exist in the first place.

"Bad law," it has been said, "is the worst form of tyranny." An
open tyranny breeds open rebellion, and the issues are clear-cut;
bad law, in an otherwise democratic nation, provokes a kind of cultural nihilism in which good and evil become hopelessly confused
and the rebel, instead of formulating a single precise program,
takes a perverse delight in anything and everything that will
shock, startle, perplex, anger, baffle and offend the establishment.
Thus it was during alcohol prohibition and thus it is under marijuana prohibition. The parallel is not obvious only because there
were already millions of whiskey drinkers when the Volstead Act
became law in 1919, leading to immediate flouting of "law and
order" by vast hordes—whereas the use of marijuana did not be-

come extensive until the early 1950s, more than 13 years after the Government banned pot in 1937. But the results, despite the delay, are the same: We have bred a generation of psychological rebels.

Banning marijuana not only perpetuates the rebelliousness of the young but it also establishes a frightening precedent, under which puritanical bias is more important to our legislators than experimentally determined fact—something every scientist must dread. Dr. Philip Handler, board chairman of the National Science Foundation, bluntly told a House subcommittee investigating drug laws, "It is our puritan ethics . . . rather than science" that say we should not smoke marijuana.

Consider the most recent study of the effects of marijuana, conducted under careful laboratory conditions and reported in *Science*. This is the research performed by Dr. Norman E. Zinberg and Andrew T. Weil at Boston University in 1968. This study was "double-blind": that is, neither the subjects nor the researchers knew, during a given session, whether the product being smoked was real marijuana (from the female Cannabis plant) or an inactive placebo (from the male Cannabis plant). Thus, both suggestibility by the subjects and bias by the experimenters were kept to the scientific minimum. The results were:

1. Marijuana causes a moderate increase in heartbeat rate, some redness of the eyes and virtually no other physical effects. Contrary to the belief of both users and policemen, pot does not dilate the pupils—this myth apparently derives from the tradition of smoking Cannabis in a darkened room; it is the darkness that dilates the pupils.

2. Pot does not affect the blood-sugar level, as alcohol does, nor cause abnormal reactions of the involuntary muscles, as LSD often does, nor produce any effects likely to be somatically damaging. In the words of Zinberg and Weil, "The significance of this near absence of physical effects is twofold. First, it demonstrates once again the uniqueness of hemp among psychoactive drugs, most of which strongly affect the body as well as the mind. . . . Second, it makes it unlikely that marijuana has any seriously detrimental physical effects in either short-term or long-term usage."

3. As sociologist Howard Becker pointed out long ago, on the basis of interviews with users, the marijuana "high" is a learned experience. Subjects who had never had Cannabis before simply did not get a "buzz" and reported very minimal subjective reactions, even while physically "loaded" with very high doses, while experienced users were easily turned on.

4. The hypothesis about "set and setting" strongly influencing drug reactions was confirmed. The pharmacological properties of a psychoactive drug are only one factor in a subject's response: equally important—perhaps more important—are the set (his expectations and personality type) and the setting (the total emotional mood of the environment and persons in it).

5. Both inexperienced subjects and longtime users did equally well on some tests for concentration and mental stability, even while they were on very high doses. On tests requiring a higher ability to focus attention, the inexperienced users did show some temporary mental impairment, but the veterans sailed right on, as if they were not high at all. In short, experienced potheads do not have even a *temporary* lowering of the intelligence while they are high, much less a permanent mental impairment.

6. On some tests, the experienced users scored even higher while stoned than they did when tested without any drug.

7. Not only alcohol but even tobacco has more adverse effects on the body than marijuana does.

As Zinberg and Weil noted sardonically in a later article in *The New York Times Magazine,* there is a vicious circle operating in relation to marijuana: "Administrators of scientific and Government institutions feel that marijuana is dangerous. Because it is dangerous, they are reluctant to allow [research] to be done on it. Because no work is done, people continue to think of it as dangerous. We hope that our own study has significantly weakened this trend."

One slight sign that the trend may have been weakened was the appearance last June of a study by the Bureau of Motor Vehicles in the state of Washington concerning the effects of Cannabis on driving ability. Using driving-traffic simulators, not only did the study find that marijuana has less adverse effect on driving ability than alcohol—which many investigators have long suspected—but also, as in the Boston study, the evidence indicated that the only detrimental effect is on inexperienced users. Veteran potheads behave behind the wheel as if they were not drugged at all.

In short, we seem to have a drug here that makes many users very euphoric and happy—high—without doing any of the damage done by alcohol, narcotics, barbiturates, amphetamines or even tobacco.

But we didn't have to wait until 1968 to learn that pot is relatively harmless. Some research has been done in the past, in spite of the vicious circle mentioned by Zinberg and Weil. As far back as

1942, the mayor of New York City, Fiorello La Guardia, alarmed by sensational press stories about "the killer drug, marijuana" that was allegedly driving people to rape and murder, appointed a commission to investigate the pot problem in his city. The commission was made up of 31 eminent physicians, psychiatrists, psychologists, etc., and six officers from the city's narcotics bureau. If there was any bias in that study, it must have been directed against marijuana, considering the presence of the narcotics officers, not to mention psychiatrists and M.D.s, who were then, as now, rather conservative groups. Nevertheless, after two years of hard study, including psychological and medical examinations of users, electroencephalograms to examine for brain damage, sociological digging into the behavior patterns associated with marijuana use and intelligence tests on confirmed potheads, the commission concluded:

Those who have been smoking marijuana for a period of years showed no mental or physical deterioration which may be attributed to the drug. . . . Marijuana is not a drug of addiction, comparable to morphine. . . . Marijuana does not lead to morphine or heroin or cocaine addiction. . . . Marijuana is not the determining factor in the commission of major crimes. . . . The publicity concerning the catastrophic effects of marijuana smoking in New York City is unfounded.

Even earlier, a study of marijuana use in the Panama Canal Zone was undertaken by a notably conservative body, the United States Army. Published in 1925, the study concluded, "There is no evidence that marijuana as grown here is a habit-forming drug" and that "Delinquencies due to marijuana smoking which result in trial by military court are negligible in number when compared with delinquencies resulting from the use of alcoholic drinks which also may be classed as stimulants or intoxicants."

What may be the classic study in the whole field goes back further: to the 1893 – 1894 report of the seven-member Indian Hemp Drug Commission that received evidence from 1193 witnesses from all regions of the country (then including Burma and Pakistan), professionals and laymen, Indians and British, most of whom were required to answer in writing seven comprehensive questions covering most aspects of the subject. The commission found that there was no connection between the use of marijuana and "social and moral evils" such as crime, violence or bad character. It also concluded that occasional and moderate use may be beneficial; that moderate use is attended by no injurious physical, mental or other effects; and that moderate use is the rule: "It has been the most striking feature of this inquiry to find how little the effects of hemp drugs have intruded themselves on observation. The large numbers of witnesses of all classes who profess never to have seen them, the very few witnesses who could so recall a case to give any definite account of it and the manner in which a large proportion of these cases broke down on the first attempt to examine them are facts which combine to show most clearly how little injury society has hitherto sustained from hemp drugs." This conclusion is all the more remarkable when one realizes that the pattern of use in India included far more potent forms and doses of Cannabis than are presently used in the United States. The commission, in its conclusion, stated:

Total prohibition of the hemp drugs is neither necessary nor expedient in consideration of their ascertained effects, of the prevalence of the habit of using them, of the social or religious feelings on the subject and of the possibility of its driving the consumers to have recourse to other stimulants [alcohol] or narcotics may be more deleterious.

Ever since there have been attempts to study marijuana scientifically, every major investigation has arrived at, substantially, the same conclusions, and these directly contradict the mythology of the Federal Bureau of Narcotics. In contrast with the above facts, consider the following advertisement, circulated before the passage of the 1937 Federal anti-marijuana law:

Beware! Young and Old—People in All Walks of Life! This [picture of a marijuana cigarette] may be handed you by the friendly stranger. It contains the Killer Drug "Marijuana"—a powerful narcotic in which lurks Murder! Insanity! Death!

Such propaganda was widely disseminated in the mid-1930s, and it was responsible for stampeding Congress into the passage of a law unique in all American history in the extent to which it is based on sheer ignorance and misinformation.

Few people realize how recent anti-marijuana legislation is. Pot was widely used as a folk medicine in the 19th Century. Its recreational use in this country began in the early 1900s with Mexican laborers in the Southwest, spread to Mexican Americans and Negroes in the South and then the North, and then moved from rural to urban areas. In terms of public reaction and social policy, little attention was paid to pot until the mid-1930s (although some generally unenforced state laws existed before then). At that time, a group of former alcohol-prohibition agents headed by Harry J. Anslinger, who became head of the Federal Bureau of Narcotics, began issuing statements to the public (via a cooperative press) claiming that marijuana caused crime, violence, assassination, insanity, release of anti-social inhibitions, mental deterioration and numerous other onerous activities.

In what became a model for future Federal and state legislative action on marijuana, Congressional hearings were held in 1937 on the Marijuana Tax Act. No medical, scientific or sociological evidence was sought or heard; no alternatives to criminalizing users and sellers were considered; and the major attention was given to the oilseed, birdseed and paint industries' need for unrestrained access to the hemp plant from which marijuana comes. A U. S. Treasury Department witness began his testimony by stating flatly that "Marijuana is being used extensively by high school children in cigarettes with deadly effect," and went on to introduce as further "evidence" an editorial from a Washington newspaper supposedly quoting the American Medical Association as having stated in its journal that marijuana use was one of the problems of greatest menace in the United States. Fortunately for historical analysis, a Dr. Woodward, serving as legislative counsel for the American Medical Association, was present to point out that the statement in question was by Anslinger and had only been reported in the AMA journal.

Dr. Woodward deserves a posthumous accolade for his single-handed heroic efforts to introduce reason and sanity to the hearing. Most importantly, the doctor (who was also a lawyer) criticized the Congressmen for proposing a law that would interfere with future medical uses of Cannabis and pointed out that no one from the Bureau of Prisons had been produced to show the number of prisoners "addicted" to marijuana, no one from the Children's Bureau or Office of Education to show the nature and extent of the "habit" among children and no one from the Division of Mental Hygiene or the Division of Pharmacology of the Public Health Service to give "direct and primary evidence rather than indirect and hearsay evidence." Saying that he assumed it was true that a certain amount of "narcotic addiction" existed, since "the newspapers have called attention to it so prominently that there must be some grounds for their statements," he concluded that the particular type of statute under consideration was neither necessary nor desirable. The Congressmen totally ignored the content of Dr. Woodward's testimony and attacked his character, qualifications, experience and relationship to the American Medical Association, all of which were impeccable. He was then forced to admit that he could not say with certainty that no problem existed. Finally, his testimony was brought to a halt with the warning, "You are not cooperative in this. If you want to advise us on legislation, you ought to come here with some constructive proposals rather than criticism, rather than trying to throw obstacles in the way of something that the Federal Government is trying to do."

A similar but shorter hearing was held in the Senate, where Anslinger presented anecdotal "evidence" that marijuana caused murder, rape and insanity.

Thus, the Marijuana Tax Act of 1937 was passed—and out of it grew a welter of state laws that were, in many cases, even more hastily ill conceived.

"Are We Blind to the Real Energy Crisis?"

Are we blind
to the real energy crisis?

The sad answer to that question could be yes. Unless we are aware of these facts:

By mid 1975 all industry in America, including electric utilities, must comply with the standards of the Clean Air Act. There is a possibility of a permissable extension to mid '76.

But whether it be '75 or '76, for many utilities there is no way on God's green earth that the present sulfur-dioxide emission standards can be met.

The "stack gas scrubber" that some say is the answer to removing sulfur-dioxide, doesn't exist in a practical working sense.

If such scrubbers did exist they couldn't be installed in time.

If they did exist and could be installed, the resulting ground pollution would be worse than any potential air pollution.

It is absolutely imperative that the Clean Air Act be amended. There is no other way.

The courts have already made it impossible for any government agency — including the Environmental Protection Agency — to grant a last minute reprieve.

Unless the Clean Air Act is amended we will have a *real* energy crisis.

And unless some responsible corporation brings these facts to light, this country of ours could be headed into chaos.

And shedding light is the sole purpose of this advertisement.

America has more coal than the Middle East has oil. Let's dig it!

American Electric Power System

Appalachian Power Co., Indiana & Michigan Electric Co., Kentucky Power Co., Kingsport Power Co., Michigan Power Co., Ohio Power Co., Wheeling Electric Co.

Advertisement appearing in *U.S. News & World Report* and other publications.

"And Senator McGovern Wants . . ."

Reprinted from *Choice:* 1972, published by Liberty Lobby, n.d., p. 3.

Criminals Can Be Brainwashed—Now

JAMES V. McCONNELL [1]

The purpose of a law is to regulate human behavior—to get people to do what we want them to do. If it doesn't, it's a failure, and we might as well admit it and try something else. Laws should be goal-oriented; they must be judged by their results, or we're just kidding ourselves. Any time we pass a law that more than a handful of people violate, the law is probably a bad one. Man is the only animal capable of shaping his own society, of changing his own destiny. We must use this capability to build a society in which laws become guidelines rather than threats, guidelines so strong that no one would want to do anything other than follow them.

Liberal doctrine assumes that crime is society's fault, not the fault of the individual who happens to commit the crime.[2] So you shouldn't punish the individual, you should try to change the sick society that spawned the crime in the first place.

The conservative tends to see mankind as basically evil, born with genetically determined instincts that force man to behave wickedly whenever possible. The only way to stop this innate immorality is to stamp it out. Stomp on it. Catch the criminal and

---

Reprinted from *Psychology Today*, April 1970, pp. 14–18, 74.

[1] The author is professor of psychology at the University of Michigan. Granting permission to reprint this article, he explained it derived from a speech given to a group of lawyers: "Back in 1969, many lawyers were not willing to accept behavioral data as being compelling, so I tried to write a compelling talk about what behavioral scientists *could* do and tried to enlist the audience in coming to some decisions about what we *should* do. However, the fact that we can 'brainwash' people doesn't mean that we have the right to do so, or that 'brainwashing' is the most effective way to turn most people into happy, productive law-abiding citizens. For my part, I am opposed to the use of any kind of punishment except in extreme cases, and I doubt that drugs, sensory deprivation, psychosurgery or 'brainwashing' would be of value in one case in a thousand. Rewarding convicts (or anyone else) for good behavior is demonstrably a better way to rehabilitate them than is punishing them for inappropriate behaviors. Unfortunately, when *Psychology Today* revised the speech for publication, they made it much more 'spectacular' and apparently punishment-oriented than I had intended it to be. For all these reasons, I don't believe that the 'Criminals' article is an accurate representation of my present views."

[2] But the doctrine is changing, as *Psychology Today* readers indicated by their responses [November] to our Law and Society opinion study.

245

beat the living hell out of him; that will make him a much better person. We've molly-coddled the bastards long enough.

Both positions are terribly, terribly naive and ineffective. Somehow we've got to learn how to *force* people to love one another, to *force* them to want to behave properly. I speak of psychological *force.* Punishment must be used as precisely and as dispassionately as a surgeon's scalpel if it is to be effective.

I've spent a good many years training flatworms in my laboratory, which is why I'm so knowledgeable about human behavior, of course. We can train flatworms to do a great many things because we've learned the proper techniques and because we follow instructions exactly. For example, suppose we want to train a worm to run through a maze, the worm must learn that the white alley is always safe, but the black alley will lead to punishment—painful electric shock. There is our worm wandering contentedly when it comes to a choice point. The worm heads into the black alley, for worms tend to prefer black before they're trained. So we give the beast a bit of a shock, just to teach it a lesson. It took us years to learn that we have to control the polarity of the shock very carefully, otherwise the shock itself will propel the animal into the wrong alley. The next thing we had to learn was *when* to give the shock. If you shock the worm too soon, it never learns to connect the punishment with the black alley. If you delay the shock even a couple of seconds after it has stuck its head in the black alley, the worm doesn't come to associate *entering* the black alley with the punishment, so it goes right on entering the black alley time after time after time.

The amount of punishment you give is important, too. We learned that if we gave our worms more than one or two very quick shocks when they entered the wrong alley, they became so disturbed that they would stop and refuse to move at all.

It took years, but we now know enough that we can train the animals very quickly. We have no trouble training worms, but we have one hell of a time trying to train new laboratory assistants. We explain our findings to them, and they nod their heads, but they don't really believe us and they don't really understand.

I have a friend, a distinguished scientist, who visited my lab one day. He was so fascinated by the worms that he wanted to train one himself. I explained everything to him and he nodded his head and insisted that he understood—after all, he had raised three kids, hadn't he, and he had taught several thousand medical students over the years. Reluctantly I put a fresh worm in the maze and handed this man the apparatus controlling the shock.

The flatworm crawled along the maze quite nicely, came to the first choice point, and headed into the black alley. Of course, my friend pressed on the wrong button, gave shock of the wrong polarity and propelled the poor worm into the black alley. "Silly animal," the man muttered; he pressed the wrong button again. The worm went further into the wrong alley. "Get out of there, you idiot," he shouted at the worm, and held the shock button down for several seconds.

The worm, I regret to say, went into convulsions about this time and simply lay on its back writhing. My friend thrust the control apparatus back into my hands, advised me that the damned worm was obviously too stupid to learn even the simplest task, and stalked out of the lab.

The more that I think about it, the more convinced I am that the mistake was all mine. Why should I let him try to train a worm . . . or a rat . . . or a human being . . . unless he had been given the proper education first?

Of course you see the trouble here. Each of us considers himself an unqualified expert on behavior, particularly on human behavior. It's utter nonsense, of course. We won't let a lawyer plead a case or a physician remove an appendix or a teacher conduct a class unless he's had extensive training and passed tests to prove his qualifications. Yet the only test a prospective parent has to pass is the Wasserman, and the only license he needs to practice the upbringing of children is obtainable for five dollars or so at the local marriage bureau.

But I digress. When you're training animals—be they humans or flatworms—there are times when you absolutely have to use punishment, for there are situations in which no other form of behavioral control works. But we use pain only when we wish to remove one very specific type of behavior from an organism's response-repertoire, and we use it very, very carefully.

In contrast to this scientific approach, the conservative insists that punishment be used not to control behavior—that is, to prevent crime—but rather as a kind of divine retribution to be enacted on those poor, miserable sinners who break the law. If the worm doesn't behave properly, shock the hell out of him. That'll learn 'im. Worms ought to be bright enough to know better. The conservative's viewpoint is utterly predictable to anyone who understands the relationship between frustration and aggression. It's very easy for a psychologist to devise a situation in which a laboratory animal is intensely frustrated. Under such conditions, the frustrated beast quite predictably turns on and attacks any scapegoat that happens to be handy. When humans are frustrated, they typically become aggressive. That's a natural law, not just an opinion of mine. When lawmakers don't understand some aspect of the world around them, and when they are frustrated by something the people do or the President does or the Supreme Court rules, the lawmakers typically respond by passing a highly punitive and aggressive law. Yet these are the very situations in which punishment has little or no effect on the behavior of the people the lawmakers want to influence or control. And so bad laws get written, not because they're effective but because they make the lawmakers feel good.

In effect, we have but two means of educating people or rats or flatworms—we can either reward them for doing the right thing or punish them for doing the wrong thing. Most people believe it's more humane to use reward. Surely we would all agree that rewards are usually more pleasant than punishments, and that love seems a nicer way of influencing people than hate. But blind love is even more dangerous than blind hate, for we can all identify hate and reject it, but love is something we've been told is good, good, good.

In Los Angeles there's a psychologist named Ivar Lovaas who is helping revolutionize the fields of clinical psychology and psychiatry. Dr. Lovaas works chiefly with autistic children, so socially retarded that they are little more than animals. They do not speak any known language, they seem to refuse all contact with other human beings. Until very recently they were considered almost hopeless; none of the usual forms of psychotherapy seemed to help them at all. And then along came behavioral psychologists like Ivar Lovaas who took a startling new viewpoint toward helping these kids.

The usual autistic child is lost in passivity, but a few of these very disturbed children go beyond passivity into self-destruction. The self-mutilating autistic child will tear at his flesh with both hands, bite off his own fingers, chew off his own shoulder. As you might guess, it's terrifying to watch these children.

Lovaas believes that autistic children cannot be brought back into the fold of humanity unless they can be taught to speak English or some other language. But how can you go about teaching a child to speak when he prefers to use his mouth to bite his own flesh rather than to speak words? Obviously, the first thing you have to do is to stamp out the self-destructive behavior and then worry about teaching the child how to talk.

Greg was about 11 years old when he was first brought to Dr. Lovaas' laboratory at UCLA. Greg had spent seven of his 11 years in a children's mental hospital. He was violently self-destructive; the nurses at the hospital were convinced that he would kill himself unless he were physically restrained 24 hours a day. None of the usual psychotherapy had worked with Greg. So, for seven years, Greg had been tied to a hospital bed, so tightly that he could barely move. When Greg first came to Lovaas' laboratory, his little body was so twisted from this confinement that he could barely walk.

It took Dr. Lovaas about 30 seconds to stamp out Greg's self-destructive behavior. Lovaas got a cattle prod—a long stick with electrodes at one end that deliver a very painful shock when they touch bovine—or human—flesh. He then turned Greg loose. As soon as Greg made his first self-destructive movement, Lovaas reached over and gave him a good jolt of electricity. Greg stopped moving and what might have been a puzzled look flashed across his face. He seemed to decide that the shock was a mistake, an accident, for a few seconds later he began to tear at his flesh again. Immediately Lovaas reached out with the cattle prod again and shocked the boy. Greg didn't like that at all, not one little bit. He looked up at Lovaas in disbelief and sat there for a few seconds more, then made one last attempt to hurt himself. One more jolt of electricity did the trick. Greg almost never again tried to harm himself when Lovaas was around. What standard therapy had been unable to do in seven years Lovaas did in 30 seconds. And then, once the self-destructiveness was gone, Lovaas could put the cattle prod aside and go on to the more important and difficult task of teaching Greg to speak by rewarding him whenever he made the proper sounds.

The behavior of children like Greg had been a great puzzle until people like Lovaas began analyzing it. Why would kids want to mutilate themselves? It didn't seem that any sensible goal could be achieved by such behavior, so the psychiatric world decided that these kids were hopelessly insane and they were locked up in hospitals and strapped down to beds all their short, miserable lives. But when Lovaas went to watch these kids in a hospital he noticed something rather strange. As soon as a child began self-destructive behavior, one of the nurses would run to his bed, wrap her arms around him and fuss gently that he mustn't do that sort of thing. Of course, the child couldn't understand much English, so the words were probably wasted on him. But the love and affection weren't. As soon as the nurse turned loose, the child began hurting himself again, and the nurse would return with more hugs and kisses, and the cycle repeated itself. The nurses genuinely loved the kids and wanted to help them. When Lovaas pointed out that they were killing the children with the wrong kind of love administered at the wrong times they refused to believe him. And they undoubtedly thought Lovaas was a terrible, cold-hearted and cruel scientist because he used punishment on kids when everybody knew that kids ought to be loved.

If you take an autistic child out of that hospital and bring him to Lovaas' laboratory, the chances are very good that he can be helped enormously. Leave him in the hospital with the loving nurses and he will probably stay sick the rest of his brief, unhappy life.

When you look at prisons you find much the same situation, I fear. Very few criminals are cured of antisocial behavior while they're in prison, just as very few patients are cured of sick behavior in today's mental hospitals. And in both cases, most of the blame can be placed squarely on staff. A psychologist at an Eastern university told me a most interesting story about a project that the university had undertaken at a large Federal penitentiary. It seems that someone had a great idea that group therapy with a mixed population of guards and prisoners might be productive. So a few therapy groups were formed and the guards and the prisoners had at each other—verbally, that is. After a few weeks, the project collapsed like a punctured balloon—the *guards* couldn't take it any longer. It seems that the therapy was working too well—for the first time the guards began to gain some insight into their own behavior patterns, and they just couldn't face up to what they were really like inside.

As far as most behavioral psychologists are concerned, sick behavior has to be learned. Autistic kids have to learn self-mutilating behavior—it doesn't come built into their genes. We help autistic kids get well by reeducating them, by retraining them, by undoing the bad things they learned so early in life and by teaching them healthy behavior instead. And most behavioral psychologists would insist that criminal behavior has to be learned too, and that whatever is learned can be unlearned.

Back in the early 1950s, the Canadian and U. S. Governments set up the Distant Early Warning (DEW) line of radar stations dotted in the ice and snow far above the Arctic Circle. There's not much up there for entertainment—those rumors about hospitality prostitution among the Eskimos are somewhat exaggerated. So the soldiers listened to radio; Radio Moscow came in much more clearly than most Canadian and American stations and beamed English-language broadcasts at DEW-line personnel. So the Canadian government called in Canada's greatest psychologist, Donald Hebb of McGill University, to determine whether soldiers isolated in boring environments are more than ordinarily susceptible to propaganda. And thus began a set of studies called experiments in sensory deprivation.

Hebb hired college students at $20 a day to do absolutely nothing. Each was confined to a tiny cubicle. An air conditioner obscured all outside noises. A mask over his eyes blocked out all visual stimulation. His arms were encased in long cardboard mailing tubes to prevent touching. He was fed and watered as necessary, but otherwise he was required to lie on a comfortable bed as quietly as he could.

Hebb expected the students to last at least six weeks. None of them lasted more than a few days. During the first 24 hours they caught up on their sleep, but after that the experience became progressively more painful for all of them. They reported long stretches in which they seemed to be awake, but their minds were turned off entirely—they simply didn't "think" at all. They were tested while they were in the cubicles, and most of them showed marked deterioration in intellectual functioning. Many experienced vivid hallucinations—one student in particular insisted that a tiny space ship had got into the chamber and was buzzing around shooting pellets at him. Most of all, though, the students were bored. They tried to trick the experimenter into talking with them. In a subsequent experiment, Hebb let them listen to dull recorded speeches which they could start by pressing a button. The experimenters, who had to listen too, almost went out of their minds, but the students seemed to enjoy thoroughly hearing the same stock-market report a hundred or more times a day. And when Hebb provided propaganda messages instead of stock-market reports, he found that whatever the message was, no matter how poorly it was presented or how illogical it sounded, the propaganda had a marked effect on the students' attitudes—an effect that lasted for at least a year after the students came out of the deprivation chambers.

Hebb's findings led many other investigators to begin work on sensory deprivation.

It is axiomatic in the behavioral sciences that the more you con-

trol an organism's environment, the more you can control its behavior. It goes without saying that the only way you can gain
complete control over a person's behavior is to gain complete control over his environment. The sensory-deprivation experiments
suggest that we should be able to do exactly that.

I believe that the day has come when we can combine sensory
deprivation with drugs, hypnosis and astute manipulation of reward and punishment to gain almost absolute control over an individual's behavior. It should be possible then to achieve a very rapid
and highly effective type of positive brainwashing that would allow
us to make dramatic changes in a person's behavior and personality. I foresee the day when we could convert the worst criminal
into a decent, respectable citizen in a matter of a few months—or
perhaps even less time than that. The danger is, of course, that we
could also do the opposite: we could change any decent, respectable citizen into a criminal.

We must begin by drafting new laws that will be as consonant
as possible with all the human-behavior data that scientists have
gathered. We should try to regulate human conduct by offering
rewards for good behavior whenever possible instead of threaten-
ing punishment for breaches of the law. We should reshape our
society so that we all would be trained from birth to want to do
what society wants us to do. We have the techniques now to do it.
Only by using them can we hope to maximize human potentiality.
Of course, we cannot give up punishment entirely, but we can use
it sparingly, intelligently, as a means of shaping people's behavior
rather than as a means of releasing our own aggressive tendencies.
For misdemeanors or minor offenses we would administer brief,
painless punishment, sufficient to stamp out the antisocial behavior. We'd assume that a felony was clear evidence that the criminal
had somehow acquired full-blown social neurosis and needed to be
cured, not punished. We'd send him to a rehabilitation center
where he'd undergo positive brainwashing until we were quite
sure he had become a law-abiding citizen who would not again
commit an antisocial act. We'd probably have to restructure his entire personality. The legal and moral issues raised by such procedures are frighteningly complex, of course, but surely we know by
now that there are no simple solutions.

Many cling to the old-fashioned belief that each of us builds up
his personality logically and by free will. This is as patently incorrect as the belief that the world is flat. No one owns his own personality. Your ego, or individuality, was forced on you by your

genetic constitution and by the society into which you were born. You had no say about what kind of personality you acquired, and there's no reason to believe you should have the right to refuse to acquire a new personality if your old one is antisocial. I don't believe the Constitution of the United States gives you the *right* to commit a crime if you want to; therefore, the Constitution does not guarantee you the right to maintain inviolable the personality it forced on you in the first place—if and when the personality manifests strongly antisocial behavior.

The techniques of behavioral control make even the hydrogen bomb look like a child's toy, and, of course, they can be used for good or evil. But we can no more prevent the development of this new psychological methodology than we could have prevented the development of atomic energy. By knowing what is scientifically possible and by taking a revolutionary viewpoint toward society and its problems, we can surely shape the future more sanely than we can if we hide our collective heads in the sand and pretend that it can't happen here. Today's behavioral psychologists are the architects and engineers of the Brave New World.

Amnesty: Transcending the Debate

MAX A. COOTS [1]

The hostile debates of a few years back seem but an angry echo
. . . the hawks and doves have flown the coop, and the era of
confrontation has ended with a whimper, but the question of amnesty persists. It has raised intense feelings about duty, conscience
and national interest—the very things that made Vietnam a nightmare.

Amnesty meant "salvaging the natural resources of our nation—
our lost youth" to Senator Taft, but he also asked that men repay
the nation for their evasion or desertion by a stint in the Peace
Corps, VISTA or some similar humanitarian service. Senator
McGovern suggested granting amnesty on a case-by-case basis,
while Rep. F. Edward Hebert (D., La.) said: "I would send them
out on a ship like the man without a country."

The amnesty controversy applies to draft dodgers, deserters and
imprisoned conscientious objectors, all of whom some regard as
traitors, some as victims of an ethical dilemma and some as heroes
whose conscience alerted the rest of the country. The numbers
and variety of men to whom amnesty might apply indicate that the
controversy involves more than armchair philosophy and political
popularity and the rhetoric these engender. Just since 1964, over
5000 men have been convicted of draft violations; 3200 were imprisoned; some still are. Draft dodgers at home and abroad number
over 70,000. Just since 1967, over 350,000 troops deserted, and
over 35,000 are still at large. If amnesty becomes a reality, it will
have to apply also to the 5000 troops being held in military stock-
ades for offenses committed in Vietnam.

Those who favor amnesty, with or without strings attached, appeal to history for precedent. There have been 37 instances of amnesty in American history. In 1795, Washington proclaimed a full
pardon to all who had taken part in the Pennsylvania Whiskey
Rebellion. In the early 1800s, there were a number of instances of
amnesty and mass pardons granted to rebels, deserters and pirates.
The Civil War saw 18 acts of amnesty, which began with the

Reprinted from *America*, June 15, 1974.

[1] Max A. Coots, minister of the Unitarian-Universalist Church in Canton, N. Y.,
is also an author and an adjunct professor of sociology at Clarkson College.

paroling of political prisoners in 1862 and ended 30 years after the war was over, when Congress approved the Universal Amnesty Act of 1898, which removed all disabilities against former rebels. The pardons granted by Lincoln during the Civil War were for deserters who returned to their posts, and to Confederates, as an obvious bid for support of the Union cause. Though there was no amnesty after World War I, Truman pardoned 1523 men out of 15,000 draft evaders who had been imprisoned in World War II. Korea saw no such action.

These precedents for amnesty are not as clear-cut as the unconditional-amnesty advocates today pretend. They came only after a war had ended and applied to rebellion and civil war, not foreign conflict. Vietnam is almost unprecedented in American history, and the scope of draft dodging, war crimes and desertion is the widest ever.

The resisters themselves do not appeal so much to history as to morality. Many of them will not accept anything but an unconditional amnesty, and some favor no amnesty at all on the grounds that it was the country, not they, who committed the wrong by participating in an immoral and illegal war. To some amnesty advocates, the proper reaction of the government would be nothing less than public penance for its sins in Vietnam. One commentator sees amnesty as a corrective judgment on future wars. He sees the men in question as a lever by which to move government in responsible directions.

Others argue that deserters and dodgers merely concluded early what most Americans concluded later—that Vietnam was wrong. Still others see them as victims forced in youth to wrestle with moral questions that old veterans and overaged patriots could comfortably avoid because they did not have to face the draft. Conscience, they say, is above all else, and there should be no penalty imposed on those who follow conscience. As does Senator Taft, they see amnesty as a restoration of a divided country. Russell Baker wrote confidently: "Of course there must be an amnesty. Not because it is essential to the spiritual recovery of the country . . . but because the irrepressible generosity of the American character will insist upon it."

Opponents of amnesty are not yet caught up in this mood of generosity. They feel like John Geiser, of the American Legion, when he said: "It may be laid down as a primary position . . . that every citizen who enjoys the protection of free government owes not only a portion of his property, but even his personal service to the defense of it." Loyalty is at the very heart of the controversy for many Americans, who believe that whether one likes it or not, everyone has a basic duty to his country, and that if he violates that duty, he must accept the label "outlaw."

Opponents of amnesty argue that it would pave the way to selective conscientious objection in which each person could select which war was "just," rather than objecting on the grounds that all war is unjustified.

William Buckley said: "By fleeing their obligation, they passed the buck to another American somewhere to serve in their stead, and, in many instances, the one who did his duty came back in a casket. . . ." Mr. Buckley sees an immorality in one man allowing another to assume his risks. We should also be careful, others suggest, in encouraging, by amnesty, the thought that individuals can be laws unto themselves, and that law can be easily broken or evaded with impunity.

But the greatest anger against amnesty and the deepest pain heard in the words of amnesty's opponents is found in questions like these: What of the 50,000 Americans who died in Vietnam and the hundreds of thousands who served there? Would unconditional amnesty say to them that they were suckers? How can amnesty be explained to parents, wives, children, who lost a son, husband or father in their country's service? How can we excuse ourselves, in the case of the remaining prisoners of war, the missing in action, or to their suffering families? "Amnesty," said one newspaper, "seems a bit like changing the rules after the game has begun. It doesn't seem quite fair to the people who didn't want to serve, but somehow did."

The patriotic argument against amnesty comes down to one of equity. It asks, how do you justify unconditional amnesty when other young men in the same situation have, usually against their wishes, gone to war?

It seems that the amnesty controversy is ultimately irreconcilable. It is not a simple conflict between right thinking and wrong, good people and bad, justice and injustice, morality and immorality. To settle every question embodied in the debate would be as endless as to review every one of the hundreds of thousands of individual cases. The questions to be answered are too many, and too often unanswerable. For one thing, this was not a civil war in which a Lincoln needed to reunite a nation in open military rebellion. America can do without its deserters, evaders, war criminals and prisoners, but this nation cannot make heroes of those men without making fools of others. Those who fought, right or wrong, and those families that lost their young men to death or wounds, cannot afford to have their wounds rubbed with the salt of moralization. Neither could we determine which deserters and evaders were moved by pure conscience and which were motivated by fear, by refusal to be inconvenienced or by emotional instability. Our exiles are not all saints untainted by unworthy motives, but neither should they be punished for conscience. For we claimed at Nuremburg that each man must act on conscience and not merely follow orders. Nor can we penalize them for stands most of us came to later in the war. Yet they broke the law, evaded governmental edict, allowed others to take their risks for them.

However you see the argument, there is hurt that no decree can soothe; there is injustice that no law can right; there is inequity no act can resolve. For any act that diminishes the inequity on one side enlarges it on the other. Surely a society has to define rules, laws and patterns of behavior for its operation and its practical self-preservation, and cannot allow individualism to take precedence over the general good. No moral person, however, can rely solely on custom, circumstance or law to resolve every moral dilemma. Conscience must be a reach that exceeds the social grasp. How can we then penalize, even by asking for service in humanitarian works, those who followed a higher law, even if we could determine who followed conscience and who followed selfishness?

It seems to me that the arguments for compassion are stalemated between compassion for those who served and those who fled. To resolve it by law would be endless and, from the point of view of psychology and philosophy, we are underequipped to resolve each of the thousands of cases. I do not find a solution in any of the arguments, pro or con. I find only compassion for a divided and wounded people. I find myself saying with Lincoln that we must transcend the debate to the level where we have "malice toward none . . . charity for all . . . [and] we strive on to finish the work we are in, to bind up the nation's wounds, to care for him who shall have borne the battle and his widow and his orphan, to do all which may achieve and cherish a just and lasting peace among ourselves. . . ."

To do that, I would have us grant an unconditional amnesty for all evaders, whether they are moral heroes, selfish cowards or egocentric rebels. I would suggest we review every one of the cases of war crimes such as those at My Lai, and where there is any slightest indication that the setting and situation of war prompted the crimes, however repulsive, we pardon them as well. I would also suggest that every deserter be received back to his military unit to be processed for voluntary release; that we pardon and release all imprisoned draft violators, drop all prosecutions now in progress against Vietnam veterans and evaders alike, stop the federal search for evaders and deserters, and compensate all Vietnam veterans and their families to the fullest level attained after World War II.

I say this, not because I am convinced of the pro-amnesty arguments nor because I am repelled by the anger of the amnesty opponents, but because we do not have the psychological insight, the legal apparatus, the moral rectitude or the political certainty to restore equitably the contents of the Pandora's box opened in Southeast Asia. Because we do not, we must go to a higher law than any thus far evoked. I refer to the law of love the Greeks called "agape," the love greater than that between a man and woman, greater than that between the members of a family—the love of God which is given not because the recipient is right or wrong, deserving or not, but simply because he exists.

No one would be happy with this answer, because it does not define right and wrong, duty and morality, loyalty and conscience. Evaders and deserters would not be justified under the law of love, veterans would not be heroes, widows and orphans would not be comforted, law would not be upheld or undermined and, in short, reward and punishment would not be given. But it would, instead, leave the moral judgment to the conscience of each person on both sides of the debate, and move us on to the future with the hope that time may heal our wounds.

Advertisement for *Hitler's Daughter* by Gary Goss

A novel about a normal American girl unfortunate enough to be closely related to Adolph Hitler.

Hitler's Daughter
GARY GOSS

"A brilliant academic satire....."
Dennis Renault
Sacramento Bee

"A hilarious time....."
Harry Cargas
Buffalo Spree

"Raunchy and unfair....."
Otto Tumiel
The Reading Intelligencer

Lyle Stuart, Inc. **$7.95**

Lyle Stuart advertisement appearing in *The New York Times Book Review,* April 21, 1974, p. 41.

Pamphlet of the American Cancer Society.

Part III

HOW TO WRITE
ARGUMENT

I have painted, and written music, and
I find that the art of constructing a mosaic of persuasion is no less stimulating and affords an unlimited opportunity for creative expression.

Louis Nizer, *My Life in Court* (1961)

How to Write Argument

Writing argument is not significantly different from writing letters, reports, term papers, and other kinds of expository prose. You locate your facts and put them on paper in an organized form that clarifies the ideas and makes someone else want to read them.

You can write persuasive essays by following six basic rules. And the first is the most important.

RULE 1: GET YOUR FACTS

Unless you have conducted a series of tests yourself, you will build your argument on testimony you can quote and on facts you can bring forward. You get such material from a number of sources.

Start at a good library. Large stores of information can be unearthed by using the card catalog (which lists author, title, and subject for every book in the library) and by checking the *Reader's Guide to Periodical Literature* (which, under subject headings, lists magazine articles printed over the years). Other general and specialized resources include:

Facts on File Yearbook
The New York Times Index
Encyclopedia Britannica (and annuals)
World Almanac
Bartlett's Quotations
The FBI's *Crime in the United States*
Who's Who
Fishbein's *Popular Medical Encyclopedia*
McGraw-Hill Encyclopedia of Science and Technology
Black's Law Dictionary

Congressional Directory
Menke's *Encyclopedia of Sport*
Yearbook of the United Nations
Oxford Companion to Music
Vital Statistics of the United States

The library has reference books covering a range of areas. You will need them to build your argument.

For specific facts, use your telephone. Libraries employ reference people who spend a good part of each day answering questions over the phone. (A question on page 104 asks about Bobby Bolin's pitching record with San Francisco in 1969. For this, you can either find the answer in a baseball almanac or phone your local reference librarian who will look up the information and call you back.) If you have a brief legal question, call a lawyer or law professor. If you need to know the current price of waste paper, phone a local junk yard. For specific information, don't hesitate to call your priest or banker or insurance agent or sheriff. Most of these people are willing to help you, and many will be happy to do so.

Write for facts that you need. United States government agencies will send you documents on a vast range of subjects. The television networks will mail you the script of any of their news specials. Organizations with a message will send you stacks of literature. (Both the American Cancer Society and the American Tobacco Company have pamphlets on smoking and health.) You can base your argument on material from Liberty Lobby, Common Cause, the Confraternity of Christian Doctrine, Ralph Nadar, the Teamsters, The American Medical Association, the U. S. Chamber of Commerce, and many comparable sources.

If you make the effort, you will find plenty of information to support your argument.

A warning: Get your facts right, but do not use the exact language of your sources. If an adversary can show errors of fact in your argument (even irrelevant errors) or if he can prove you have offered someone else's language as your own, he can hurt the credibility of your case.

RULE 2: NARROW YOUR TOPIC TO MANAGEABLE SIZE

Most arguments are subject to space and time limitations. You are writing a magazine advertisement or a campaign poster (one page). You are preparing an editorial or a letter to the editor (under 1000 words). You are writing a sermon or an after-dinner speech (20 minutes). Rarely does one have the opportunity which would permit, or the audience that would tolerate, an argument covering all aspects of a large issue.

Therefore, you must limit your subject. You cannot write simply of "Dieting." Even "Crash-dieting" is too general a topic. But you can argue that "Crash-dieting Is Dangerous." Similarly, do not speculate about "America's Unjust Drug Laws"; write "Alabama's Marijuana Laws Violate the Fifth Amendment."

A broad subject lends itself to vague generalizations. A limited topic calls for specific facts. You will need facts to build a persuasive argument.

RULE 3: ORGANIZE YOUR MATERIAL

Most essays—and indeed most letters and reports—are made up of an *introduction,* a *body,* and a *conclusion.* The introduction says "I am going to write about X." The body discusses X. And the conclusion says "That's what I have to say about X." A good writer will keep the pattern from being too obvious, but this is the pattern he will use.

The Introduction

Most topics contain a kind of natural division. An essay praising Johnny Bench might discuss his catching, his base-running, and his hitting. An argument against abortion might follow the growth of a fetus month by month. A case involving a physical (or social) disorder might describe the effect, then indicate probable cause.

The introduction—the first paragraph—announces the subject and the division that subject will take. Here are effective examples:

There can be no doubt that extrasensory perception exists. How else can one explain the results of the Spranches-Odom experiments conducted at UCLA in 1971? [The theme will describe the experiments.]

Legal abortion is necessary. Otherwise we will be back with vast numbers of women getting amateur surgery at bloody abortion mills. [The theme will discuss earlier years: (1) vast numbers of women, and (2) bloody surgery.]

The only way to stop inflation is to raise taxes and impose wage and price controls; but I don't think the president has the courage to urge these measures. [The theme will cover (1) anti-inflation measures: (a) a tax raise and (b) wage-price controls; and (2) presidential courage.]

A witty introduction can be used to win the reader's interest, but in most cases it should not be necessary. In argument, cleverness can be a liability. A political essay beginning "President Ford is moving to Canada" will need two or three sentences of explanation and transition before it gets to its point. A straightforward introduction probably would be more effective.

Keep your introduction short.

The Body

The introduction and conclusion are little more than a frame surrounding what you have to say. The paragraphs of the body of the essay *are* your argument.

Each paragraph presents a unit of that argument. This does not mean that each division of your topic—as announced in the introduction—must be covered in one paragraph. In the anti-inflation theme just introduced, the section on wage-price controls might take two, three, or six paragraphs.

Just as the introduction has a statement announcing what the whole essay is about, each paragraph has a topic sentence telling what it will cover. In argument, this is almost invariably the first sentence. Because they show exactly what the paragraphs will be about, these are effective topic sentences:

> Consider what the fetus can do in the third month of its growth.
>
> Why did the price of electricity go up?
>
> These gun laws haven't reduced the level of crime in Cleveland.
>
> Dr. Kissinger was equally successful in getting concessions from the Syrians.

A paragraph should not take up material beyond the scope of the topic sentence. The paragraph about gun laws in Cleveland, for example, should not discuss other crime-fighting measures in Cleveland; it should not mention crime in Detroit.

Topic sentences are effective in linking paragraphs. In the examples given, the reference to "*These* gun laws" and to Dr. Kissinger's being "*equally* successful" show a relation to previous paragraphs. Words like "therefore," "however," "such," "second," and "similarly" are useful in achieving this effect.

Within a paragraph, try to give the sentences the same grammatical subject. In the paragraph on Dr. Kissinger, for example, the subject of most of the sentences should be "he" (or "Kissinger" or "the secretary"). If you vary the kinds of sentences, as in the following example, the practice will not seem repetitive:

I learned more in speech classes than in those on literature. In speech, *I* learned to talk in front of a group. *I* learned to think on my feet. After a few dull efforts, *I* learn to make a talk interesting by referring to the audience or adding humor. And most important, *I* learned to say things directly—without all the cute ornament of poetry.

In some paragraphs, keeping the same grammatical subject will prevent you from saying what you want to say. Or it will make your writing stilted and artificial. In such cases, don't do it.

The Conclusion

The last paragraph of an essay echoes the introduction. It restates what you have been trying to prove.

Keep your conclusion short.

RULE 4: MAKE YOUR WRITING INTERESTING

Remember that no one has to read or hear your argument. Or, if they do have to face it, they do not have to pay attention. The burden is on you to make your material interesting.

This is not an arduous burden. If you have a case that you think is important and if you present it with clarity and detail, your reader will be interested.

In general, you maintain that interest by avoiding certain practices which deaden language.

Avoid Truisms

Don't say what everyone knows. Your reader will not be thrilled to hear that third-degree burns are painful or that the president of the United States bears great responsibilities. Don't write "Every great man has moments of profound sorrow, but Thomas Eaton's life was genuinely tragic." Write "Thomas Eaton's life was tragic."

Avoid Clichés

Don't use stale language. Your argument loses its punch if expressed in tired phrases like these:

first and foremost
on the other hand
fact of the matter is
in the final analysis
in a real sense
ad infinitum
burden of proof
considered opinion
the last straw
inevitable consequence
not a leg to stand on
beyond the shadow of a doubt
other things being equal
last but not least

As persuasive language, an "incontrovertible fact" is no better than a "gross exaggeration"; a "palpable lie," no worse than "the unvarnished truth."

Avoid Generalized Language

Write of real things. Use specific names, numbers, places, dates, and quotations. You can describe the same entity in a number of ways—for example:

an athlete
a ballplayer
a baseball player
a pitcher
an Oakland pitcher
Vida Blue

From such a selection, always choose the most specific word that serves the purpose of your essay. An effective argument uses proper names.

Your argument will be more interesting if you avoid the words "good," "bad," and "said." Substituted words are almost always more meaningful. Instead of "good," write "even-tempered," "inexpensive," "compassionate," or "crisp." Instead of "bad," write "pretentious," "degenerate," "bland," or "pushy." The word "said" is always acceptable, but you can add richness to your prose by substituting "whispered," "suggested," "boasted," "conceded," "protested," or "gasped."

Similarly, try to avoid forms of the verb "to be"—i.e., the words "is," "are," "was," "were," and phrases with "been." Very often, of course, you have to use these words, but substitutions are invariably more detailed and effective. For example, "Bob Huntley was injured" becomes "Bob Huntley broke his left wrist." And "The weather was horrible" becomes "Eight inches of snow fell on Mobile yesterday."

The next time you hear a dull speech or sermon, don't tune it out. Ask yourself why it is dull. Probably it is a collection of truisms, clichés, and generalities. Learn from examples of ineffective argument.

Rule 5: Make Your Writing Clear

If you are making a case and the evidence is all against you, you might need to resort to obscure phrases and high-sounding words. But generally, you want your argument to be clear. These recommendations should help.

Use Simple, Direct Language

The level of diction you choose for your argument depends on the subject you treat and the audience for which you write. But, almost invariably, simple, direct language is best. If you confuse your reader, you have little chance to persuade him. Therefore, try to avoid the following:

Foreign words—"bête noir," "vis-à-vis," "coup d'état," "ne plus ultra"

Learned words—"peruse," "penultimate," "datum," "quintessential"

Technical words—"manic," "upwardly mobile," "deep structure," "aleph-null"

Literary allusions—"protean," "Charon," "Lot's wife," "the sword of Damocles"

Current in-words—"parameter," "viable," "nitty-gritty," "ambience"

Avoid awkward or confusing references. Don't write "in view of the above" or "for the above reasons"; write "consequently" or "for these reasons." Try not to write "the addressee," "the executrix," "the former," or "the latter"; write "Freda Clary" (or "she" or "her"). Don't refer to yourself as "the writer" (or "we"); say "I."

Avoid Ambiguity

Confused meaning can come from several causes. You may have faulty pronoun reference ("He drove his Ford at 70 mph down Price Hill, which is always dangerous"). You may be relying on information the reader does not have ("Chicago is a great sports town. I lived in South Bend for three years and never missed a Bears game"). Or you may have a modifier in the wrong place ("When six years old, his grandmother came to live with him" or "I knew the plot well before seeing the movie").

It is not easy to avoid ambiguity, because you rarely know you are being ambiguous. For you, the meaning of the sentence is clear. Consequently, it is a good idea to have a friend or spouse or colleague or teacher look over your writing before you publish or deliver it.

RULE 6: MAKE YOUR WRITING EMPHATIC

Sometimes, unnecessary words or particular word forms detract from the point you want to make. These recommendations should help you emphasize the important features of your argument.

Avoid Wordiness

Unnecessary words may confuse, bore, or antagonize your reader. Say what you have to say as briefly as possible. Too often a series of words exists where one will do:

"due to the fact that" = "because"
"the man with the dark complexion" = "the dark man"
"people who are concerned only with themselves" = "selfish people"
"I do not agree with the conclusions offered by Professor Hamner" = "I disagree with Professor Hamner"
"this book concerns itself with language intended to deceive" = "this book is about lies"

And commonly one or more words appear where none is necessary:

"Molly ~~really~~ is a ~~very~~ beautiful girl."
"~~Personally,~~ I agree with him."
"~~There were~~ several people at the party ~~who~~ saw the fight."
"I was born in ~~the city of~~ Chicago."

Don't worry about wordiness when you are putting together the first draft of your argument. Just get down what you want to say. Direct, succinct prose usually comes with rewriting.

Write in the Active Voice

In active-voice sentences, the grammatical subject is the acting agent ("The Brezinsky Commission has attacked public apathy"). In passive-voice constructions, the subject receives the action of the verb ("Public apathy has been attacked by the Brezinsky Commission"). In sentences where the acting agent is obvious or irrelevant, you need passive-voice constructions. But use active voice whenever possible. This makes for a simpler, more straightforward style.

Make Your Most Important Feature the Subject-verb of Your Sentence

Express your main point in the subject-verb of your sentence and put lesser information in modifying phrases and clauses. Don't present your key feature as a modifier ("When Wilson shot himself, he was standing in line at the Roxy Theater"). Give it subjective-verb emphasis ("While standing in line at the Roxy Theater, Wilson shot himself").

Don't Waste the Ends of Your Sentences

Because the end of your sentence is a position of emphasis, don't use it for minor ideas or casual information. Don't write "Both candidates expect to speak here, if we can believe the reports." (This is correct only if you want to stress the doubtfulness of the reports.) Don't write "Kaempfer was a charlatan, however"; write "Kaempfer, however, was a charlatan."

Because the beginning of a sentence also gives a degree of emphasis, it is good practice to put minor modifiers like "however," "therefore," "on the other hand" (if you have to use it), and "nevertheless" in the middle of sentences.

Keep Your Sentences Relatively Short

To avoid a monotonous style, you should build your essay with sentences of different kinds and lengths. But using short sentences will help you avoid difficulties. When sentences go beyond fifteen or twenty words, punctuation—which can be a problem—becomes complicated; meaning gets diffuse; their pronouns get separated from the words they refer to; and the reader or listener finds it difficult to see the continuity and may lose interest. Short sentences are better.

Avoid Language Which Calls Attention to Itself

You want your reader to follow your meaning, the ideas in your developing argument. Do not distract him by using words or phrases that catch his eye. Try to avoid the following types of language.

Repetition. Repeating a word for emphasis can be effective ("government of the people, by the people, and for the people"); but usually it distracts attention. Avoid repetition of sentence form ("I went to see the accident. Fifteen people were there. Each told a different story"); of particular words ("Going to school is not going to be easy. If the going get tough . . ."); and even of sounds ("Bob Benson was badly beaten").

Elaborate figures of speech. A mixed metaphor always produces irrelevant laughter ("Into this forest the hand of man had never set foot"). But even a meaningful figure can be distracting. You could write "Nixon steered the ship of state over treacherous seas; he was a star-crossed president." But such a sentence stops the reader. Instead of following the rest of your argument, he pauses to interpret the figure of speech.

Abrupt changes in tone. An article on the United Nations Charter calls for formal diction; an essay on local fraternity experience can use colloquial (or even coarse) language. In either case, you should keep a consistent tone. Don't jar the reader by describing a U.N. charter provision as "a crap-headed experiment." And don't call the fraternity dining room "a haven of calculated insouciance."

Any time your reader is more impressed by your writing than by your meaning, you have erred. No one can improve on the valuable advice Samuel Johnson gave in the eighteenth century: "Read over your compositions, and where ever you meet with a passage which you think is particularly fine, strike it out."

FINAL COUNSEL

Don't Use Footnotes

Except in scholarly writing or in cases where you want to fool someone, don't use footnotes. In general, people do not read them. If you have information you want to get to your audience, put it in the text.

Similarly, give information about your sources in the text. Any of these forms is acceptable:

According to Susan Panzram (*Naked Stones,* 1968), man has existed . . .

In *Naked Stones* (1968), Susan Panzram argues . . .

In an article "Busy Creatures" (*Reader's Digest,* September 1972), Jim Hartman describes . . .

According to *Time* (November 13, 1971), President Johnson carried . . .

A good general rule is to give the reader enough information so he can check the source you used.

Use Your Speaking Voice

Try to get your speaking voice into your writing. In talking, you tend to use short sentences, plain words, the active voice, and so on. You won't worry about beginning a sentence with "and" or "but." You don't say "peruse" or "shall" or "secondly" or "the speaker" (meaning "I"). You don't intone, "Quiet was the night."

Trust your ear. What sounds like good spoken language—at a level suited to the subject and audience—will be good writing. In this book, you've been advised to keep the same grammatical subject through a paragraph and to tuck words like "however" and "therefore" in the middle of sentences. Anytime you think this advice would make your writing sound peculiar, don't follow it.

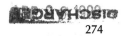

Get Help from Friends

In all likelihood, you will never be asked to write an essay that someone else will read and judge immediately. Impromptu themes may be assigned in college, but in the outer world, you will always have time for thought and revision. As part of your revision, have a friend or spouse or neighbor or teacher read your argument for clarity and correctness.

Correctness in matters of punctuation, italics, numbers, case, idiom, and spelling is important. A misspelled "their" or "its" makes a well-argued case seem illiterate. An omitted comma can make an important sentence almost unreadable. A "not" that is typed as "now" can be crippling.

Of course, you should resort to a dictionary or an English handbook when you have problems. But a serious error may exist where you don't recognize a problem. Ask a reliable friend to help you with your argument.

Remember Your Purpose

Remember that the point of your writing is to persuade someone of something. You want him to see that marijuana should be legalized, that gas rationing is essential, or that Sacco and Vanzetti were guilty. You want him to buy your product or to settle that insurance claim in your favor.

Anything that impairs the persuasiveness of your argument (misspelling, wordiness, errors of fact, etc.) should be avoided. And anything that contributes to making your particular case persuasive to your particular audience (even such features as profanity, an impressive letterhead, threats, neat typing, or footnotes) should probably be employed.

In general, you will find it easier to make a persuasive case if you are right.

DISCHARGED

MAY 18 1981

DECHAR 6 1990